Perfidy and Passion

Publication of this volume has been made possible, in part, through the generous support and enduring vision of WARREN G. MOON.

Perfidy and Passion

Reintroducing the *Iliad*

Mark Buchan

THE UNIVERSITY OF WISCONSIN PRESS

The University of Wisconsin Press
1930 Monroe Street, 3rd Floor
Madison, Wisconsin 53711-2059
uwpress.wisc.edu

3 Henrietta Street
London WC2E 8LU, England
eurospanbookstore.com

Printed in the United States of America

Library of Congress Cataloging-in-Publication Data

Buchan, Mark, 1966–
  Perfidy and passion : reintroducing the Iliad / Mark Buchan.
      p.   cm. — (Wisconsin studies in classics)
  Includes bibliographical references and index.
  ISBN 978-0-299-28634-7 (pbk. : alk. paper) — ISBN 978-0-299-28633-0 (e-book)
  1. Homer. Iliad. 2. Epic poetry, Greek—History and criticism. I. Title. II. Series:
Wisconsin studies in classics.
  PA4037.B785   2012
  883'.01—dc23

2011047343

For my students
If you become a teacher, by your pupils you'll be taught.

What we catch, we leave behind.
What we don't catch, we carry with us.

Contents

Preface

In a review of one of the many scholarly "Companions" to Homer, Richard Janko noted that in over eight hundred pages of scholarly analysis there was almost no effort "to appreciate the greatness of Homer's poetry and of his vision of humanity."[1] Janko echoes the frustration toward scholarship felt by the great New Critic F. R. Leavis nearly fifty years earlier. In *The Common Pursuit* Leavis noted that scholars are able to talk about an author (Milton, in the test case Leavis pursues) for a very long time without ever suggesting why the author is worth reading. But to find the reasons for such frustration we can go back further, to a provocative, almost off-hand remark by Karl Marx on the relationship of art to social production in the opening of the *Grundrisse*.

From another side: is Achilles possible with powder and lead? Or the *Iliad* with the printing press, not to mention the printing machine? Do not the song and the saga and the muse necessarily come to an end with the printer's bar, hence do not the necessary conditions of epic poetry vanish?

But the difficulty lies not in understanding that the Greek arts and epic are bound up with certain forms of social development. The difficulty is that they still afford us artistic pleasure and that in a certain respect they count as a norm and as an unattainable model.[2]

As if to prove Marx right, much of contemporary writing on Homer has focused on the conditions of production of the poetry, whether economic, historical, or artistic. But few attempt to grapple with the inexplicable surplus pleasure we gain from reading the poems. Research programs still take precedence over literary appreciation. So, in the spirit of Leavis and Marx, this book is a critical and literary introduction to Homer, not a scholarly one. As such, it looks back to several ambitious predecessors who have dared to offer a vision of the entire poem.³ Scholarship has its place only when it points us to the artistic pleasure Homer affords us.

Moreover, much of the theoretical debt underpinning the discussions is to literary formalism and New Criticism. The *Iliad* is great, at least in part, because its language is opaque and condensed, because it alienates us from the ordinary language we are accustomed to use as we try to make sense of the world, and this allows us in turn to reappraise our world. It is great because of the artful construction of its poetry, its attention to detail, and its self-consciousness as a work of art. I am, of course, uttering little more than formalist commonplaces. But the strategy is to put formalism to work in order to understand the themes of The *Iliad*. This is not to ignore the text's conditions of production. Indeed, as I try to show, part of the poem's artistry involves reflecting on the oral culture that it is a part of. The rhythm of Homeric poetry involves a to and fro between apparent narrative and verbal transparency and moments of challenge to this transparency. There are recurring twists in the story, cryptic turns of phrase, language that sticks out as strange and demands our attention. The *Iliad* is both a product of an oral tradition *and* great literature, and for largely conventional reasons. This does not, as a common critique of formalist approaches would have it, sever the poem from its culture because it is a self-contained work of art. If poetic language alienates and provokes, it must alienate and provoke from some set of cultural coordinates. We will pay attention to these, too.

After giving a talk on wordplay in the *Iliad*, I was immediately confronted with two questions. First, I was asked if there was any way of proving the presence of the punning wordplay I had tried to uncover. The second question was in many ways a comment on the first: why do puns make so many people uneasy? To that question, this book offers a formalist answer: for much the same reason that poetry itself makes us uneasy. It shakes up what we take for granted about language and the world it represents. Much like the puns Freud was so interested in, linguistic "slips" of the tongue that hint at other meanings lurking in the shared language we take for granted, puns can point us outside an overly narrow understanding of ourselves.

Consider the most discussed book by a classicist in recent decades, Victor Davis Hanson's *Who Killed Homer?* (1998). For Hanson, Homer stands for all the commonsense wisdom of Greco-Roman civilization; his blunt straightforwardness is used as a battering ram against the cultural relativism of postmodernity. But perhaps because of this emphasis on clarity, the book has nothing new to say about Homer's poetry. There is something self-defeating about criticism that can only restate the obvious. I hope a more difficult and challenging version of the *Iliad* can aid the noble project of coming to terms with our debts to Greco-Roman antiquity. If the Greeks are to be "foundational," with Homer as foundation for the Greeks, the poem can be a provocative and challenging foundation, not a two-dimensional blueprint for how to live.

Hanson attacks the obscurantism of literary deconstruction, and certain deconstructive practices of the past few decades are also to blame for the uneasiness scholars feel about wordplay. If deconstruction did much to make us aware of the instability of language, it did so by skirting an obvious danger. If language, by its very nature, can never quite mean what it seems to say, then any specificity of literary language may be swallowed up in this general instability. Without diminishing the exhilarating sense of freedom produced by early deconstructive efforts, the theoretical underpinning of this book is not deconstructive. Deconstructive criticism may persistently show us how the play of language undermines any illusion of meaning, and Homeric language is no more, or less, available for such a critical process than any other. But I am more interested in the internal dynamic between the language of transparency and opacity within the *Iliad*.

Adam Parry once argued that Achilles was a prisoner of traditional language. It has become fashionable to see this as a quaint, outdated notion of how language operates. But though it is far from the whole story, Parry registered an important aspect of how language works. It may not be entirely a prison house, but "traditional" language is surely in part experienced as such. The motivations of many of the characters of the *Iliad* can best be explained if we grant them an awareness of a cultural world that is not quite their own, and see them resisting it. Parry suggests that Achilles's inarticulate questions do this, since they gesture beyond any answers the culture can provide. But we can chart other ways. We will see characters fight over their fame, their self-presentation in words a battle against the representations of others; we will see them offering different possible stories of themselves as a way of escaping clichés that imprison them. We will also see characters lose control of the language they use to talk of themselves and others. Because their words never quite belong to them, because they are debased and abused by others, suffused with the desire of others, no story of the self can be simple. Hence I offer a "reintroduction" rather than an introduction to

Homer and his characters, and try to open up different ways of understanding them.

As for "proving" wordplay, our relative ignorance about the poem's conditions of production means that we have two recourses. We can turn to comparative work on oral poetics and try to find forms of sophistication comparable to Homer's techniques. We also have the richness of the literary and critical traditions that engage with the *Iliad*, beginning with the *Odyssey*. I make free use of this second course, in particular passages from the *Odyssey* that offer elliptical commentary on the *Iliad*. But in lieu of any systematic comparative effort to analyze oral poetry as such, I offer an anecdote from my own experience of oral poetic culture.

Visiting a New York City piano bar where Broadway show tunes are communally sung, I told the piano player that I loved a song I had recently requested, and that he kindly played for me. He immediately responded that I did not really love the song. When I was obviously perplexed by this riddle, he put me out of my misery. Having heard me fumble through the lyrics, he suggested that if I *loved* the song, I would know the words by heart. In the culture of New York's piano bars, the gap between audience and performer is blurred, not just because audience members are often potential performers, but also because appreciation of songs in this culture means *knowing* them. When one knows thousands of songs, one can see connections between them, common motifs, allusions. But one can also creatively play with both music and lyrics. I think it highly likely that a similar kind of song culture lies behind the Homeric poems. One critical job should be to try to uncover some of the sophistication such a culture produced. An overlooked truth of oral poetry is that at least part of the audience must always already know not just the plot of the epic, but the poetry itself, committed to memory through repeated performances. This means, among other things, that a striking phrase from, say, the last book of an epic poem can and should be remembered by an audience listening to something similar at the beginning.

We should make the effort to think of the Homeric poems as the product of a shared culture of sophistication, where audience and performer alike can create as well as enjoy the linguistic cleverness of whatever is on show. This might point to another reason why puns make people uneasy. To fail to understand, say, the wit of a Cole Porter lyric that hovers around obscenity can be to feel excluded from the club of insiders who take such wit for granted. But if cultures of sophistication

are worth their salt, they can also find ways to open up such sophistication to others, to teach it and help the "in-group" itself to grow. We can
imagine the "Homeric *tradition*" as the creation of this kind of cultural
group, passing on not only stories, but the tricks of verbal sophistication
that play a part in creating those stories.

But we should also resist the idea of finding "proof" of a pun, or
any subtle use of language. True, as the ancient cliché goes, what can
be asserted without reason can be denied without reason. But, thank-
fully, many literary readings cannot be categorized neatly into "true" or
"false." Rather than proof, it is a matter for argument, a "common pursuit" that tries to work through literary meaning in a way that can never
be reduced to a research program. An argument does not simply consist
of noticing linguistic irregularities or possible subtleties, but requires a
demonstration of how they might contribute to a more interesting reading of the poem, however controversial or counterintuitive such a reading might prove. In what follows I do not expect, or even desire, instant
agreement to all of my readings. I do hope to encourage efforts to make
sense of the *Iliad*'s greatness as a shared, and pleasurable, task. Accordingly the book is closer to the essay form than a conventional scholarly
monologue. The chapters are calculated literary gambles, attempts to
open up the poem, provocations that invite both active agreement and
disagreement. They are offered in the spirit of the kind of literary debate
that enlivens the classroom. Knowledge, especially literary knowledge,
is not something that can be poured like water from a full glass to an
empty one, to make use of an analogy of Socrates. It flourishes best in
an atmosphere of creative experimentation with the nuts and bolts of
poetry.

Though literary in its aims, this book introduces the *Iliad* by focus-
ing on issues that have been extensively debated. Each chapter focuses
on a theme, but the chapters also follow the rough chronological order
of major episodes within the poem. I discuss the subtlety of Homer's
characterization in the introduction. Chapter 1 considers both Achilles's
language and the literary dynamics of a tragedy that centers on a series
of betrayals. Chapter 2 considers Homeric laughter: its representation
within the poem and also Homer's own jokes. Chapters 3 and 4 discuss
the shield of Achilles, described in Book 18, and the funeral games of
Book 23. I suggest that we can tease out an aesthetic manifesto from
Homer's reflection on the creative process, and then use this to complicate the social and political questions that are under the spotlight in
the conflicts of the funeral games. The final two chapters deal with love

and desire. The *Iliad* in many ways is a series of failed love stories, in which couples come together only to be parted violently. I look closely at the language of love and sexuality and see how it resonates in the language of warfare, and the strange intimacy between men on show there. I conclude by considering the well-known biographical tale of Homer's death. Not merely an amusing curiosity, the story is, rather, a way of summarizing the *Iliad* itself, as well as suggesting ways to read it.

The conditions of production that have influenced this book *are* straightforward. Most of what I say has been culled from teaching Homer's *Iliad* over the last decade. It is impossible to say how much of what I write here is mine, how much a creative borrowing from a steady stream of graduate and, especially, undergraduate insights and originality. So although I dedicate this book to my students, it is as much by them as for them, a product of the living common pursuit of the classroom to which Leavis was so dedicated.

I would like briefly to acknowledge the nonstudents who have actively helped my thinking on the *Iliad*. Alex Purves, Deborah Steiner, and Patricia Rosenmeyer have all offered invaluable and detailed written criticism on earlier versions of the book. I have discussed the work more informally with Joy Connolly, Joshua Katz, Larry Kim, Sara Lindheim, Jim Porter, and Sira Schulz. One of the joys of writing a book is incurring a debt to intellectual friends such as these, and I look forward to repaying it. I am also grateful for the indulgence of scholarly audiences at New York University, Columbia, and Princeton.

Thanks also to J. Naomi Linzer for producing the index, and to Joseph O'Neill for the author photo that appears in the catalog and on the website. Finally, I owe much to the careful and generous editing skills of Jane Barry.

The University of Chicago Press kindly granted permission to use Richard Lattimore's translation of the *Iliad* (© 1961 by The University of Chicago). For the Greek, I make use of the Monro and Allen Oxford Classical Text (3rd ed., 1920).

Perfidy and Passion

Introduction
Riddles of Identity in the *Iliad*

Critics take for granted Homer's skill in portraying memorable characters. The opening book offers vignettes giving access to the protagonists' flaws and desires: the arrogant king who rejects a suppliant, the impetuous warrior who angrily challenges authority.[1] But in what follows I look at the question of character awry. Rather than the differences between Homer's characters, the individual desires and qualities that make them unique, I concentrate on the ways in which the desires of separate characters infiltrate the desires of others. Instead of asking *what* a character wants, we will ask *from where* he or she wants it. For the *Iliad* shows how these desires came to inhabit the characters' psyches. It traces the fluidity of human desires, the messiness of our motivations, the way human needs and wants are constructed in and through the needs and wants of others.

One consequence is that any definitive statements about identity, whether of an individual or a group—say, "Achilles is prone to anger," or "the Trojans are peace-lovers who are defending their families"—will turn out to be oversimplified, the beginning rather than the end of the inquiry. For what we can say about almost any character in the poem can be traced to the desires of others. Individual selves become less discrete, just as what is inside and outside of any character becomes much harder to gauge. Character is an ongoing interpretative challenge for us because it is already a problem for those within the poem. To "know thyself" is rarely easy.

To see identity as a problem to be contested is to venture into critical terrain more commonly associated with the *Odyssey*. Indeed, we can usefully transfer some of the central questions that have dominated critical approaches to Homer's *Odyssey* onto the *Iliad*. So at the risk of indirection, let us take a brief look at the well-known enigma that opens the *Odyssey*, before encountering a disguised enigma at the beginning of the *Iliad*.

Tell me, Muse, of the man of many ways, who was driven
far journeys, after he had sacked Troy's sacred citadel.
Many were they whose cities he saw, whose minds he learned of . . .

(*Od.* 1.1–3)

Ἄνδρα μοι ἔννεπε, Μοῦσα, πολύτροπον, ὃς μάλα πολλὰ
πλάγχθη, ἐπεὶ Τροίης ἱερὸν πτολίεθρον ἔπερσε·
πολλῶν δ' ἀνθρώπων ἴδεν ἄστεα καὶ νόον ἔγνω . . .

The name of the poem's hero is withheld, and this gives the poem the form of a typical Greek riddle. A riddle begins with an unnamed thing or person—"There is a thing which"—follows it with a series of puzzling and seemingly contradictory identifying descriptions, and provokes us into finding a solution. This riddling structure opens up as many questions as we will allow it to.[2] For example, it not only pauses over the identity of this unnamed man, but also asks what it means to be a man. How can one determine the identity of a single man when his essence seems to be in tension with the many *tropoi* (masks, turns, linguistic games) that he wears? Or, to use a later psychoanalytic vocabulary, what is a "man" beyond the sum total of ego-identifications, of roles that he takes up that are always socially defined and therefore created for him by others—and thus not so clearly his after all? Finally, though the temptation to find a referent is hard to resist, we should also notice that the question of who will hold power on Ithaca, be *the* man, is up in the air at the poem's beginning. This zero-sum struggle for power soon takes center stage, with pretenders to the title, including the suitors and Telemachus, as well as Odysseus himself. The question mark hovering over the identity of the man points toward social conflict alongside the problems of self-discovery.[3]

Now, this seems to contrast with the proem of the *Iliad*, where the subject matter, "anger," is explicitly attached to a name, "Achilles." Characteristics routinely attributed to each of these heroes—Achilles as truth-teller, Odysseus as trickster—would therefore find a correlative in the form of representation at work in each poem: the *Odyssey* as deceptive, the *Iliad* as clear. But before letting the certainty of this critical commonplace take over, let us move forward to the first appearance in the *Iliad* of the *Odyssey*'s riddling word *andra*. It comes in the speech of Calchas. Achilles has made a general request for an explanation of the plague that besets the Achaeans, and the prophet steps forth to make his answer.

'You have bidden me, Achilleus beloved of Zeus, to explain to you this anger of Apollo the lord who strikes from afar. Then I will speak; yet make me a promise and swear before me readily by word and work of your hands to defend me, since I *believe I shall make a man angry who holds great kingship over the men of Argos, and all the Achaians obey him.* For a king when he is angry with a man beneath him is too strong, and suppose even for the day itself he swallow down his anger, he still keeps bitterness that remains until its fulfillment deep in his chest. Speak forth then, tell me if you will protect me.'

(*Il.* 1.74–83; emphasis added)

"ὦ Ἀχιλεῦ, κέλεαί με, Διῒ φίλε, μυθήσασθαι
μῆνιν Ἀπόλλωνος ἑκατηβελέταο ἄνακτος·
τοιγὰρ ἐγὼν ἐρέω· σὺ δὲ σύνθεο καί μοι ὄμοσσον
ἦ μέν μοι πρόφρων ἔπεσιν καὶ χερσὶν ἀρήξειν·
ἦ γὰρ ὀΐομαι ἄνδρα χολωσέμεν, ὃς μέγα πάντων
Ἀργείων κρατέει καί οἱ πείθονται Ἀχαιοί·
κρείσσων γὰρ βασιλεὺς ὅτε χώσεται ἀνδρὶ χέρηϊ·
εἴ περ γάρ τε χόλον γε καὶ αὐτῆμαρ καταπέψῃ,
ἀλλά τε καὶ μετόπισθεν ἔχει κότον, ὄφρα τελέσσῃ,
ἐν στήθεσσιν ἑοῖσι· σὺ δὲ φράσαι εἴ με σαώσεις."

These lines seem a perfect example of the straightforwardness and rapidity of the Homeric narrative. The prophet establishes the simplicity of cause and effect. Agamemnon angers Chryses, Chryses appeals to Apollo, who punishes Agamemnon, and Achilles reacts to the punishment. Calchas, a stand-in for a reliable narrator, then gives us access to the logic of this causal chain. But we should allow his words to be more puzzling. Calchas, a prophet, is introduced as an expert "who knew all things that were, the things to come and the things past" (*Il.* 1.70). Later, when he has been guaranteed the protection of Achilles and offers an analysis of the plague, it is a routine, non-vatic, analysis of what he says has happened, and there is no apparent prophecy there at all, at least insofar as we expect prophets to speak in veiled terms of the future. There is only an analysis of the past ("it is not for the sake of some vow or hecatomb he blames us, / but for the sake of his priest whom Agamemnon dishonored," *Il.* 1.92–93), even though he does seem to have supernatural access to the workings of the god.

But now contrast this with his first speech: "I think I will anger a man." Here, in words that seem not to be those of a prophecy, we have the form of a prophecy and a prediction of what he believes will happen. There is a second contrast. When he later speaks of the plague, his language is as clear as can be. Apollo has caused the plague. He is angry because of Agamemnon's treatment of Chryses. We now have a second prophecy, but this comes in appropriately enigmatic terms, with the riddle word that opens the *Odyssey*, *andra*, at the very center of the phrase.

As with the opening line of the *Odyssey*, there is a huge temptation to fill in the blank, to assume that this man is Agamemnon. And there are certainly reasons to do this. The poem depicts an atmosphere of tension and fear, where to utter any complaint against the chieftain is to risk death. To name names, to speak in anything other than riddles, is to court danger, and one can pay for one's words with one's life. To name the name of Agamemnon, as Achilles will soon do, is a dangerous breach of social tact. Those in the know must not reveal that the king has no clothes, or insult him in public, but must play the game of recognizing his power even in its emptiness. Calchas's speech is a provocation, and Achilles's answer takes up the challenge. To insult Agamemnon is to give oneself the authority to say what one likes against the king, and therefore automatically to question his power. These readings are all available to us, if we think Achilles is right in his reading of Calchas's *andra*.

But need we identify this man as Agamemnon? In doing so, we identify with Achilles's identification of him. But what does this tell us about Achilles? For Achilles, only Agamemnon is quick to anger and overzealous in his use of power. But to complicate this we have the simplicity of the proem to fall back on. For Achilles's anger, not Agamemnon's anger, is our subject. And what has just happened? Achilles has acted as king, bringing together an assembly, trying to find out the source of the plague among the Greeks. The Greeks have obeyed him, and he has accordingly exercised his power over them. On this reading Calchas's words offer up an eerie premonition of the plot itself. Calchas will indeed make a man angry, but Achilles's anger will have far greater repercussions. He will swallow it down for a while, even as he is angry with "a lesser man," but it eventually comes to painful fulfillment. Provoking us to pinpoint the anger's source is part of the poem's opening strategy. For after the proem announces its theme, the *menis* of Achilles, we are given a series of examples of anger before we reach the anger of Achilles, as if the poem is both teasing us as to its proper beginning (the anger of Achilles begins with the anger of Apollo, Agamemnon . . .), but also showing us that anger itself is irreducibly relational and social.

In Achilles's reading of words that seem not to be a prophecy but function as one, we can read him, and already make out some of the blind spots that will generate much of the drama. Compare his reaction to Calchas's prophecy with the well-known Delphic riddle given to Croesus in the first book of Herodotus. Croesus asks the oracle if he should invade Persia, and it replies that, if he does so, he will destroy a great empire. Croesus, in interpreting the oracle as about the objective world, forgets that he is a part of that world, and acts as if it cannot apply to him; he marches to war and destroys an empire: his own (Hdt. 1.91–92). With hindsight, the oracle offers him a reading less of his hesitation to go to war, more of his hasty desire to believe in his own invulnerability. His apparent doubt, which led to his overture to Delphi, masked a pseudo-doubt that wanted only confirmation of his own certainty. He finds out "objectively" what he already believes, and this corrupts the search. In the case of Achilles, he can never see himself as victim of anger, or as pretender to power. Anger, for Achilles, is the anger of others, just as power belongs to others, while he sees himself as sealed off from those others. So Achilles protects a priest from the anger of another, and sets in motion a process by which his own anger will destroy him.

Calchas's association of an unnamed man with anger has thematic weight. But so too does the *form* of Calchas's words, the vagueness of the expression that seems to withhold as much information as it gives away: "I think I will anger a man." Compare the words of Agamemnon to Nestor, which are in part a parody of the words of the prophet.

'Yes, old sir, all this you have said is fair and orderly.
Yet here is a man who wishes to be above all others,
who wishes to hold power over all, and to be lord of
all, and give them their orders, yet I think one will not obey him.[']

(*Il.* 1.286–89)

"ναὶ δὴ ταῦτά γε πάντα, γέρον, κατὰ μοῖραν ἔειπες·
ἀλλ' ὅδ' ἀνὴρ ἐθέλει περὶ πάντων ἔμμεναι ἄλλων,
πάντων μὲν κρατέειν ἐθέλει, πάντεσσι δ' ἀνάσσειν,
πᾶσι δὲ σημαίνειν, ἅ τιν' οὐ πείσεσθαι ὀΐω . . ."

The discourse of the prophet is treated contemptuously, but by a man who believes his own power can bring about the future. Agamemnon parodies Calchas's fearful euphemisms. For Agamemnon's caustic irony to work, the demonstrative ὅδ' must refer to Achilles, and the pseudo-uncertainty of the third person indefinite pronoun τιν' to Agamemnon, as he blasts apart the impotence of prophecy. With no need for prediction, Agamemnon offers more straightforward access to the future. But even here the mockery of any science of prediction harbors its own complexity. For the situation, rather than Agamemnon's intent, complicates matters. If we read Agamemnon's words in reverse, with "this man" referring to himself, "someone" to Achilles, we have a perfect description of the *present* situation. After all, Agamemnon's authority has been challenged, his response is a desire to restore power, and Achilles's ongoing refusal of his orders will be the central narrative dilemma of the poem. Here, Agamemnon's parody tries to state the obvious, to supersede the pretentious ambiguities of Calchas and replace enigma with the clarity of force. But the words themselves correctly register the ambiguity of the situation: they are an echo of the disobedience of Achilles, and betray Agamemnon's identification with Achilles, even as Agamemnon is trying to reassert his own authority and identity. Even his prediction of the future, "I think," returns us not simply to the speech of Calchas, but to the words of Achilles in the interim, who has formed his own habit of making predictions about the future: "I am returning to Phthia, *nor do I think* I will stay here dishonored" (*Il.* 1.170); "I tell you this, and *I think* it will be accomplished" (*Il.* 1.205; both my translation). In this appropriation of the language of prophecy in the words of the protagonists, the *Iliad* secularizes the concerns that are associated with prophecy, making them part of a human power struggle. But the resonances of the language itself mock their desires to control it.

This conflict over *andra* might help us notice an ambiguity in the naming at work in the proem of the *Iliad*: "Since that time when first there stood in division of conflict / Atreus' son the lord of men and brilliant Achilleus." We all know that the son of Atreus *means* Agamemnon, just as we know that the man of the opening line of the *Odyssey* is Odysseus. So to focus on the ambiguity of the patronymic might seem pedantic, did not the ensuing narrative of the poem draw attention to it. We find out that a priest loses his daughter and turns his attention to the people, but especially to *both* sons of Atreus, Agamemnon and Menelaus. If we identify with Chryses, we find that the question of which brother is more important for the expedition is left open until line 24. It is only then that Agamemnon appears, drowning out whatever desires Menelaus may have, who in turn becomes swallowed up in the "all" who support respect for the ransom.

This overwriting of one man's desires by another is a crucial thread of the poem. The *Iliad* expands the range of the conflict by replacing one expected protagonist, Menelaus, with Agamemnon, just as Hector replaces Paris as the leading figure in Troy. But the poem is interested not only in these replacements, but in examining their effects. The displacements are part of a process, a struggle, and residual resentments and worries are left in their wake. A strain is placed on the use of the dual form in line 7. We have a quarrel between two men; but one of them gains his position at the expense of the other half of the Atreid pair, Menelaus. The dual forms themselves cannot quite contain the conflict, and the mode of expression suggests a proliferation of rivalries. The tension between Agamemnon and Menelaus will come more and more to the surface throughout the poem. Indeed, the repeated use of the duals in episodes where two heroes act together (we can take the joint spying mission embarked upon by Odysseus and Diomedes in *Iliad* 10 as paradigmatic) suggests that this grammatical form gestures toward a wider Iliadic fantasy of male like-mindedness and solidarity that functions as a counterpart to the *Odyssey*'s fantasy of like-mindedness between husband and wife (*Od.* 6.180–85). The conceit of the *Odyssey* is that the shared worldview of Penelope and Odysseus, sundered by so many years of separation, and figured as the fundamental building block of the *oikos*, can be restored. The *Iliad* begins with the sundering of male trust, and will never stop trying to heal the wound that this opens up. When Agamemnon later dreams of a world where his thoughts matched those of Achilles ("If ever we can take one single counsel, then no longer / shall the Trojans' evil be put aside," *Il.* 2.379–80), his wild utopianism stands in stark contrast to the world of division and conflict constantly before us.

Determining the nature of the conflict in the poem is thus far from simple. Characters cannot be reduced to any ideologies they seem to represent: say, the clash between martial merit (Achilles) and social power (Agamemnon), the ability to kill men and the ability to control men. For characters come to inhabit these beliefs in a particular way. I believe in ideology x: say, that social worth should be determined by martial ability. But do I really? Do my words and actions reflect my apparent desires? And if not, do I really desire what I purport to desire? What if my beliefs about myself are full of curious blind spots and omissions, and these are potentially readable in everything I say and, more importantly, in what I do? And if my desires are not my own, whose are they, and where do they come from? Let me tease this out by a closer look at the discrepancy between the words and deeds of the protagonists, Achilles and Agamemnon. For, as in the case of the opening of the *Odyssey*, the desires of the protagonists are strangely hamstrung.

Agamemnon's Desire

There is something shocking about the actions of Agamemnon in the opening of the *Iliad* that his later certainty about the rightness of the struggle in some ways clouds, in others confirms. It is obvious, with hindsight, that he is unsure about both the continuation of the mission to Troy and his own actions. Think only of his ongoing vacillations over whether to return to Greece. But what these vacillations leave in place is an overall presumption that what Agamemnon wants, but cannot be sure he can have, is to sack Troy. But consider what he actually does in *Iliad* 1. Here is the opening prayer of Chryses, as he makes his request for the return of his daughter.

'Sons of Atreus and you other strong-greaved Achaians,
to you may the gods grant who have their homes on Olympos
Priam's city to be plundered and a fair homecoming thereafter,
but may you give me back my own daughter and take the ransom,
giving honour to Zeus' son who strikes from afar, Apollo.'
   Then all the rest of the Achaians cried out in favour
that the priest be respected and the shining ransom be taken;
yet this pleased not the heart of Atreus' son Agamemnon . . .

                (*Il.* 1.17–24)

"Ἀτρεῖδαι τε καὶ ἄλλοι ἐϋκνήμιδες Ἀχαιοί,
ὑμῖν μὲν θεοὶ δοῖεν Ὀλύμπια δώματ' ἔχοντες
ἐκπέρσαι Πριάμοιο πόλιν, εὖ δ' οἴκαδ' ἱκέσθαι·
παῖδα δ' ἐμοὶ λύσαιτε φίλην, τὰ δ' ἄποινα δέχεσθαι,
ἁζόμενοι Διὸς υἱὸν ἑκηβόλον Ἀπόλλωνα."
 Ἔνθ' ἄλλοι μὲν πάντες ἐπευφήμησαν Ἀχαιοὶ
αἰδεῖσθαί θ' ἱερῆα καὶ ἀγλαὰ δέχθαι ἄποινα·
ἀλλ' οὐκ Ἀτρεΐδῃ Ἀγαμέμνονι ἥνδανε θυμῷ . . .

It is worth pausing over the different reactions of the men and Agamemnon, not to mention an interesting and often overlooked aspect of Chryses's speech, which can go some way to explain those reactions. For, as with his later prayer to Apollo to smite the Achaeans with a plague, there is here too an implied prayer, and, I think, an implied exchange: that the Greeks can sack the city of Troy in exchange for the return of Chryses's daughter. When the Achaeans react favorably to the speech, it is not only out of general respect for a priest, but also in reaction to the content of that speech: the hope that Troy will be sacked. Agamemnon's isolation is thus all the more shocking. When Troy's capture is hinted at, he is the only Greek who demurs. A similar scenario repeats itself later in the quarrel with Achilles. Achilles, when Agamemnon demands recompense for the loss of Chryseis, suggests that the Achaeans will pay him three- or fourfold should they sack Troy. Agamemnon responds that Achilles is trying to cheat him, that the offer of a future gift is a cunning way of denying him one in the present. This opens up the ongoing Iliadic discourse of what an object is worth for creatures of and in time. But perhaps we identify too closely with the quarrel, and forget what Agamemnon seems to have forgotten: the possibility of taking Troy. The unity of purpose between the other Greeks and Agamemnon is first shattered as he isolates himself from the desires of the other Greeks, and shattered a second time as he rejects a second chance from Achilles, the ability to identify with the shared mission of sacking Troy.

So what does Agamemnon want, and where does it come from? A possible answer lies in the manner in which he rejects Chryses. For Chryses not only offers the sack of Troy to the Greeks; he prays that they will have a safe homecoming. Agamemnon, in his response, seems to parody or mock this part of the prayer.

[']So go now, do not make me angry; so you will be safer.'

(*Il.* 1.32)

"ἀλλ᾽ ἴθι, μή μ᾽ ἐρέθιζε, σαώτερος ὥς κε νέηαι."

The sack of Troy and a safe *nostos*, a return home, for all the Greeks is replaced by the expulsion of the priest, but, paradoxically, an expulsion that results in Chryses's own safe return: if he avoids Agamemnon's anger, he can "go home" safer. And his safety will result in the exact opposite for the rest of the Greeks, many of whom will stay, but without safety, their *nostos* destroyed because of Agamemnon's desire. So later, when he claims, somewhat defensively, that he will give back the girl because he desires that the people be safe, not perish, the words are at best a qualification, at worst a retraction, of what he has previously said to Chryses. Yet these words have already escaped through his teeth.

One might find the source for Agamemnon's antipathy toward his people already at work in the words of Chryses. After all, in offering his hopes for the destruction of Troy in exchange for his daughter, he shows a striking lack of concern for the welfare of a nearby city. But Agamemnon's refusal of his offer sets in motion a series of exchanges that become increasingly complex. Consider Chryses's prayer.

[']Smintheus, if ever it pleased your heart that I built your temple,
if ever it pleased you that I burned all the rich thigh pieces
of bulls, of goats, then bring to pass this wish I pray for:
let your arrows make the Danaans pay for my tears shed.'

(*Il.* 1.39–42)

Notice first the reciprocity between the pain experienced by the priest, materialized in the tears he sheds, and the arrows cast. We imagine a one-to-one correspondence, a mathematical precision in the calculus of suffering that matches Danaan deaths to individual tears, mediated by Apollo's arrows. Soon after, when Apollo's arrows strike and keep striking, the deaths continue apace with the crying: tears falling, arrows falling. The equation will then be transferred onto Achilles, who in turn will suffer loss, and will also repeatedly cry: "But Achilleus / weeping went and sat in sorrow apart from his companions" (*Il.* 1.348–49; cf. 1.357). His tears too will produce a prayer, and a protracted attempt to cure a personal wound by the infliction of sufferings on others. The new equation will involve Greek deaths exchanged for Achilles's tears, and all to produce a psychological wound to bend the mind of the instigator of the quarrel. A similar economy of help and helplessness is traced out in the details of Chryses's request. Chryses reminds Apollo of the way he roofed over his temple, an act of protection to preserve the sanctity of the place of the god, and perhaps to remind us that these anthropomorphic Homeric gods have their vulnerabilities too. And in return for this creation of a safe space for the god, the god will fire weapons from a quiver that in turn happens to be roofed over (τόξ' ὤμοισιν ἔχων ἀμφηρεφέα τε φαρέτρην, *Il.* 1.45); violence is linked to perceived vulnerability.

This emotional economy is also at the center of the wider story of the war. Agamemnon fights the war in order to avenge the "longings and groans of Helen" (τίσασθαι δ᾽ Ἑλένης ὁρμήματά τε στοναχάς τε, *Il.* 2.355). Here, however, any simple equivalence is harder to compute: are these the groans of Helen herself, the finite pain she is imagined to suffer during the abduction? If so, the pain must be imagined, as the *Iliad* offers us no repetition of it in her sexual encounter with Paris in Book 3, despite her initial resistance. Or are these the groans suffered *for* Helen, the desires and urges men feel for her? If the latter, equivalence becomes almost impossible to work out, the payment required spiraling out of control with every passing battle scene. This exact phrase, uttered first by Agamemnon, is later repeated by Menelaus (*Il.* 2.590), offering us the possibility of different resonances of the same phrase in the mouths of the different brothers. One might see in the second statement the personal reaction of a cuckolded husband, and thus a greater concern with what he imagines to be Helen's subjective pain, whereas the groans of the soldiers seem to be more appropriate for the leader of the army. Unless, of course, Agamemnon identifies with the pain of the brother, and so voices his desires for him once more. In Book 6, as Menelaus is about to release the suppliant Adrastus, Agamemnon reminds him of his treatment at the hands of Paris, and in *Iliad* 3 part of Menelaus's desire for a duel with Paris derives from his embarrassment at the scale of Greek destruction for his sake. In this poem, people do not always feel things directly. They need to be reminded of what they feel, as if their identities require support from elsewhere.

There Is Much That Lies between Us

This intermingling of desires also traverses the *Iliad*'s major ethnic divide—the one between Greeks and Trojans. It is well known that the *Iliad* begins *in medias res*, not at the better-known mythical beginnings of the Trojan War, whether the judgment of Paris or the abduction of Helen from Sparta. It is also well known that this beginning of the story, where two men argue over a woman whose status is in question (Chryseis is a slave-girl, but one who seems on the verge of becoming a wife, a replacement for Clytemnestra; Briseis is a slave-girl whom, nevertheless, Achilles might marry) duplicates the general problem of this war fought over a woman. But given Agamemnon's actions in the opening book, can we not specify exactly where his desire originates? For in his willful and stubborn attachment to a woman, not only in opposition to his people, but also in such a way as to lead to the destruction of the Greeks, is he not replaying the desire of Paris for Helen? Little that is said of Paris throughout the *Iliad*, from his lack of concern for his people to his intrigues with women that produce disaster for his people, could not be uttered about the Agamemnon of the opening book.

This should perhaps cause us to question any easy separation between Greeks and Trojans. In the middle of the quarrel with Agamemnon, Achilles utters famous lines about the emptiness of his quarrel with the Trojans.

[']I for my part did not come here for the sake of the Trojan
spearmen to fight against them, since to me they have done nothing.
Never yet have they driven away my cattle or my horses,
never in Phthia where the soil is rich and men grow great did they
spoil my harvest, since indeed there is much that lies between us,
the shadowy mountains and the echoing sea . . .'

(*Il.* 1.152–57)

"οὐ γὰρ ἐγὼ Τρώων ἕνεκ' ἤλυθον αἰχμητάων
δεῦρο μαχησόμενος, ἐπεὶ οὔ τί μοι αἴτιοί εἰσιν·
οὐ γὰρ πώ ποτ' ἐμὰς βοῦς ἤλασαν οὐδὲ μὲν ἵππους,
οὐδέ ποτ' ἐν Φθίῃ ἐριβώλακι βωτιανείρῃ
καρπὸν ἐδηλήσαντ', ἐπεὶ ἦ μάλα πολλὰ μεταξὺ
οὔρεά τε σκιόεντα θάλασσά τε ἠχήεσσα . . ."

Achilles's speech tries to reassert boundaries, enforcing distinctions between public and private quarrels, Greeks and Trojans. But is this not hopelessly naive? After nine years of war, nine years of living in tents on the outskirts of Troy, it is hardly true that there is much between the Greeks and Trojans. If anything, the words are a perfect lie. There is too little between the Greeks and Trojans, shut up as they are in an interminable and claustrophobic conflict.

This will also become more and more geographically true in the course of the story. The Greeks will soon build a wall, and the safety it promises will be balanced by the way they will be hemmed in between walls and the shore. On the Trojan side, the escape from the city onto the plain produces, at least for Hector, a terror of returning to the confinement of the city itself. But Achilles also makes the first of many doomed attempts of Greeks and Trojans to extricate themselves from each other, to return to some kind of ethnic solidarity that the poem exposes as an impossible fiction, most famously in the strange encounter between those friends-enemies in *Iliad* 6, Glaucus and Diomedes. When Menelaus, in Book 3, eagerly accepts the offer of a duel from Paris, his hope is both for resolution and for a separation of the two sides.

'Listen now to me also; since beyond all others this sorrow
comes closest to my heart, and I think the Argives and Trojans
can go free of each other at last. You have suffered much evil
for the sake of this my quarrel since Alexandros began it.
As for that one of us two to whom death and doom are given,
let him die: the rest of you be made friends with each other.[']

(*Il.* 3.97–102)

"κέκλυτε νῦν καὶ ἐμεῖο· μάλιστα γὰρ ἄλγος ἱκάνει
θυμὸν ἐμόν, φρονέω δὲ διακρινθήμεναι ἤδη
Ἀργείους καὶ Τρῶας, ἐπεὶ κακὰ πολλὰ πέπασθε
εἵνεκ᾽ ἐμῆς ἔριδος καὶ Ἀλεξάνδρου ἕνεκ᾽ ἀρχῆς·
ἡμέων δ᾽ ὁπποτέρῳ θάνατος καὶ μοῖρα τέτυκται,
τεθναίη· ἄλλοι δὲ διακρινθεῖτε τάχιστα."

Menelaus's repetition of the verb διακρίνω itself mixes two meanings
lurking in the word, both "separation" and "decision." Lattimore offers "the rest of you be made friends with each other" for a phrase that
more literally means "may the rest of you be separated as fast as possible." Menelaus's hope, ultimately illusory, is that a decision in their
duel will allow a separation of Greeks and Trojans, an end not only to
their entanglements as peoples, but to the entanglement of the problems of his household with those of so many others. What for Achilles
is a statement, "there is much that lies between us," is, for Menelaus, a
desperate, utopian desire.

When the Greeks build the defensive-aggressive wall in Book 7 that
the Trojans will spend much of the poem attacking and finally breach-
ing, even the boundaries between attacker and aggressor will be blurred.
The wall is officially a defensive structure, but also a last-ditch attempt
to guarantee these boundaries between friend and enemy, Greek and
non-Greek. Perhaps this is why the discourse of separation returns.
Here is Nestor's speech that leads to the construction of the wall.

'Son of Atreus, and you other great men of all the Achaians:
seeing that many flowing-haired Achaians have died here,
whose dark blood has been scattered beside the fair waters of Skamandros
by the fierce war god, while their souls went down into the house of Hades;
therefore with the dawn we should set a pause to the fighting
of Achaians, and assembling them wheel back the bodies
with mules and oxen; then must we burn them a little apart from
the ships, so that each whose duty it is may carry the bones back
to a man's children, when we go home to the land of our fathers.

And let us gather and pile one single mound on the corpse-pyre
Indiscriminately from the plain, and build fast upon it
Towered ramparts, to be a defence of ourselves and our vessels.'

(Il. 7.327–38)

"Ἀτρεΐδη τε καὶ ἄλλοι ἀριστῆες Παναχαιῶν,
πολλοὶ γὰρ τεθνᾶσι κάρη κομόωντες Ἀχαιοί,
τῶν νῦν αἷμα κελαινὸν ἐΰρροον ἀμφὶ Σκάμανδρον
ἐσκέδασ' ὀξὺς Ἄρης, ψυχαὶ δ' Ἄϊδόσδε κατῆλθον·
τώ σε χρὴ πόλεμον μὲν ἅμ' ἠοῖ παῦσαι Ἀχαιῶν,
αὐτοὶ δ' ἀγρόμενοι κυκλήσομεν ἐνθάδε νεκροὺς
βουσὶ καὶ ἡμιόνοισιν· ἀτὰρ κατακήομεν αὐτοὺς
τυτθὸν ἀποπρὸ νεῶν, ὥς κ' ὀστέα παισὶν ἕκαστος
οἴκαδ' ἄγῃ, ὅτ' ἂν αὖτε νεώμεθα πατρίδα γαῖαν.
τύμβον δ' ἀμφὶ πυρὴν ἕνα χεύομεν ἐξαγαγόντες
ἄκριτον ἐκ πεδίου· ποτὶ δ' αὐτὸν δείμομεν ὦκα
πύργους ὑψηλούς, εἶλαρ νηῶν τε καὶ αὐτῶν."

The logic here should surprise us. At first, we expect him to urge that the war be ended, and with unusual immediacy. Many have died, and therefore it is necessary to stop the war to bury the dead. There is even mention of a return home, and the handing of the bones over to the dead man's children. But as he utters this, he immediately qualifies it. The burial, instead of a final separation, suggests to him the idea of a wall arising out of the mass tomb itself, a last-gasp bastion of defense and separation that will allow the war to continue. All the care involved in distinguishing individual warriors in the first act of cremation, "so that each may carry the bones back to his children," disappears in the collective tomb, where corpse will blend into ethnic identity without distinction, ἄκριτον, *akriton*.

But this word itself, "without distinction," is elaborated when Nestor's vision is finally realized. The sides separate, a truce for burial goes into operation, and the poet describes the troops as they look for corpses.

The Trojans assembled together. They found
it hard to recognize each individual dead man;
but with water they washed away the blood that was on them
and as they wept warm tears they lifted them on to the wagons.
But great Priam would not let them cry out; and in silence
they piled the bodies upon the pyre, with their hearts in sorrow,
and burned them upon the fire, and went back to sacred Ilion.

(Il. 7.423–29)

οἳ δ' ἥντεον ἀλλήλοισιν.
ἔνθα διαγνῶναι χαλεπῶς ἦν ἄνδρα ἕκαστον·
ἀλλ' ὕδατι νίζοντες ἄπο βρότον αἱματόεντα,
δάκρυα θερμὰ χέοντες ἀμαξάων ἐπάειραν.
οὐδ' εἴα κλαίειν Πρίαμος μέγας· οἳ δὲ σιωπῇ
νεκροὺς πυρκαϊῆς ἐπινήνεον ἀχνύμενοι κῆρ,
ἐν δὲ πυρὶ πρήσαντες ἔβαν προτὶ Ἴλιον ἱρήν.

The description of the burial begins with a brief sentence. Translated by Lattimore as "assembled together," it more literally means, "They met each other." It is commonly used of martial encounters, and specifically returns us to the encounter between Glaucus and Diomedes in the previous book, a meeting that promoted a different kind of confusion about identity. In talking to each other they find out that they too did not properly know who the other was, until they fortuitously exchanged stories about their grandfathers, who turned out to be guest-friends. Here, the language of meeting in battle, the arena where the certainty of the difference between friend and enemy is played out to the death, is dragged into a quite different context. The unmarked pronoun "they" is a prelude to the way their conception of the differences between them is in tension with the awful, material sameness of mangled corpses. Retroactively, Nestor's phrase ἄκριτον ἐκ πεδίου changes its meaning. It at first signifies ethnic solidarity, a human attempt to impose order on the mass of Greeks; regardless of their individual identity, they will be treated as Greek, one and all. But the phrase returns us to a prior moment, as putative Greeks and Trojans are confronted with corpses that cannot be identified as either Greek or Trojan. In building this collective tomb, Nestor erects a monument to ethnic difference at the time it has been most challenged. But even after they seem to have sorted out the corpses successfully, difficulties of distinction continue. The Trojans, earlier characterized by the loudness of their speech in contrast to the silence of the Greeks (*Il.* 3.1–9), are now silenced by Priam, as if they are learning to become Greek. As for the Greeks, in an unintended consequence of the building of the wall, they become defenders of a mini-city whose defense is equated with their very survival, a mirror of Troy itself.

Another puzzling word might give us some clue to the thinking of Nestor. For why, at the moment when his language seems to suggest a return home, does he come up with the idea of a defensive wall? He suggests, in a puzzling phrase, that they "circle the corpses," κυκλήσομεν ἐνθάδε νεκρούς. The verb is usually understood as referring to the wheels of the wagons as they drag the bodies away. This is unparalleled, but it at least makes some sense, and the addition of "wagons and mules," in the next line, seems to confirm it. But without rejecting this meaning, we can still ask what sort of connotations the word "circle" might have here. I offer as a possibility that Nestor has in mind the protection to the dead offered by circular tombs. So, as the logic of this signifying chain unfolds, the circling of corpses suggests the idea of a protective wall, a tomb that becomes a defense, itself an imperfect double of the circular walls that surround Troy. But the substitution works both ways. We can also see the uselessness of such protection in Troy itself—a walled city protecting its citizens, but already also a collective tomb, a city doomed to death. As such, it echoes the words of Hector from the previous book: "For I know this thing well in my heart, and my mind knows it: / there will come a day when sacred Ilion shall perish" (*Il.* 6.447–48).

The Greeks and Trojans are implicated in each other's desires, and these begin to have spatial effects on the way they organize their camps. Let us reflect on the tension opened up by beginning the poem *in medias res*. The poem's narrative constraints, which necessitate an introduction to both sides (and so the catalogue of ships, the *teichoskopia* in *Iliad* 3) are in tension with verisimilitude: why would Priam need to know who the Greeks are after nine years of war? But this kind of naiveté is not simply an effect of the narrator's decision; rather, it has internal implications for those within the poem. For we have an array of social actors who act and think about their situation as if the war had just begun, as if the social identities of Greek and Trojan, attacker and aggressor, were utterly discrete and therefore manageable. The problem of verisimilitude is not something external to the poem itself, but is reflected back onto the characters within it, and in turn is responsible for much of the tragedy of misrecognition that is at the poem's heart. The false certainty of feeling Greek and Trojan sustains the war itself. The poem offers us the possibility of interrogating the ongoing denial implicit in that deceptively simple phrase, "there is much that lies between us."

The Desire to Know

If the *Iliad* memorializes the dead and remembers their names, one could offer a competing critical account that focuses instead on the appearances of unnamed men, where the uncertainty of identification takes hold of the narrative, where the straightforward attachment of name to hero is suspended and the expectations set up by the endless naming at work in Homer's battle scenes are disrupted. We should not underestimate this desire to find a fixed identity, to be able to attach name to referent; it drives the poem's plot. But what the opening line of the *Iliad* takes for granted, the attachment of anger to a man first named, then given a patronymic, can be seen retroactively as a ruse, an over-easy demonstration of what the poem suggests is fraught with anxiety and tragedy. To give only two examples, Diomedes is painfully dependent on and sensitive to stories of a father he has never seen, whereas all of Achilles's reflections on Peleus, still alive, are colored by our knowledge that their seemingly temporary, contingent separation is all too permanent. So to begin this alternative account, I try to show how the identities of the protagonists—Achilles, Agamemnon, Hector—become less and less discrete, and then look at the crucial moment in the poem's plot when the desire for a named, stable identity takes over.

ACHILLES AND AGAMEMNON

In Book 2 a divine dream comes to Agamemnon, offering him the illusory hope of capturing Troy.

'Son of wise Atreus breaker of horses, are you sleeping?
He should not sleep night long who is a man burdened with counsels
and responsibility for a people and cares so numerous.[']

(*Il.* 2.23–25)

"εὕδεις, Ἀτρέος υἱὲ δαΐφρονος ἱπποδάμοιο·
οὐ χρὴ παννύχιον εὕδειν βουληφόρον ἄνδρα,
ᾧ λαοί τ᾽ ἐπιτετράφαται καὶ τόσσα μέμηλε . . ."

The dream's version of kingship is thoroughly performative. How do you define a king? He is the sort of person who does not sleep when cares befall his people. What if you are asleep when cares befall you? Then you are not a king. Of course Agamemnon *is* currently asleep, which would mean, somewhat strangely, that the dream might not be addressing a king at all. The encounter seems to pose a question: how long has Agamemnon been asleep, at least in terms of the relinquishing of the duties of a "man of responsibility"? The thought is picked up when Agamemnon begins to marshal his forces, after Pandaros violates the truce of Book 3, in an embarrassing narrative reminder of the narcoleptic tendencies of power: "Then you would not have seen brilliant Agamemnon asleep nor / skulking aside" (*Il.* 4.223–24). So the dream opens up a chasm between the social role of king and the person of Agamemnon.

But was Agamemnon not always aware of his own deficiencies, even if his knowledge of this could not be made public? There are problems in this intersection of a person with political authority that the *Iliad* invites us to examine, and that should help us to recognize how acute Agamemnon's dilemma is. For can a king, as king, doubt himself? A king who hesitates violates a crucial element in his own mastery, for those who obey must believe that he is infallible. The external figure of the dream sent by Zeus is simultaneously the voice of Agamemnon's deepest internal anxieties. But in order to be a proper figure of authority, a king needs to be able to silence any critical challenge to his power. A king who listened to reason, heard all the debates, and made decisions accordingly could never be sure he was exercising his own authority instead of rubber-stamping the beliefs of others. Monarchy floats into deliberative democracy. The *Iliad* opens with a perverse test case for political authority: how can a king be sure of his power, that all will obey him regardless of the content of his message? Only by exercising it in the face of the desires of all others. So the *Iliad* is not just about the inner conflict of a man "not up to the job," but also about the theoretical problem of a figure of authority whose identity consists, ultimately, in the arbitrariness of his power.

Let us return to his words in response to Nestor, who valiantly but uselessly tries to maintain a distinction between king and best warrior: "Yet here is a man who wishes to be above all others, / who wishes to hold power over all, and to be lord of / all, and give them their orders, yet I think one will not obey him" (*Il.* 1.287–89). The trouble is that these words are doubly true. First, if we identify the man who wishes to have power as Achilles, then Agamemnon is quite right. To obey Achilles would put Agamemnon on the wrong end of an order. Achilles has given *semata* to all by bringing together an assembly, and Agamemnon is not far off the mark in suggesting that the resultant recommendation that he give back the girl is a kind of order. But doubly correct because, since we are aware of a gap between the social role of king and Agamemnon himself, and he himself is aware of it, then the words equally well apply to him. For he is also a man who dreams of having power over all, and yet is constantly failing in this endeavor. To borrow the words of the dream, he has been asleep throughout the first book, a sleep that has allowed Achilles to usurp him. Power, in this poem, is not something that has a proper, established place. It is a peculiar force that exerts its anxieties on those it falls upon. Its presence is a kind of drug, producing a desire for sleep that transfers the power itself to others, and then the awareness of its absence brings back the desire for it. Anger, the theme of the poem, functions as a reaction, a subjective protest, against the awareness that elements of the social world are not in their established places, that the protagonists of the poem expect, but are unable to find, a status quo.

But the words of Achilles too will constantly rebound against the speaker, and not just in his attempt to understand Calchas's riddle. For Achilles and Agamemnon are less in control of their desires than they are constantly each other's dupes and puppets. Here is Achilles, as he asks his mother to punish the Greeks for the madness of Agamemnon.

[']Sit beside him and take his knees and remind him of these things
now, if perhaps he might be willing to help the Trojans,
and pin the Achaians back against the ships and the water,
dying, so that thus they may all have profit of their own king,
that Atreus' son wide-ruling Agamemnon may recognize
his madness, that he did no honour to the best of the Achaians.'

(Il. 1.407–12)

"τῶν νῦν μιν μνήσασα παρέζεο καὶ λαβὲ γούνων,
αἴ κέν πως ἐθέλῃσιν ἐπὶ Τρώεσσιν ἀρῆξαι,
τοὺς δὲ κατὰ πρύμνας τε καὶ ἀμφ' ἅλα ἔλσαι Ἀχαιοὺς
κτεινομένους, ἵνα πάντες ἐπαύρωνται βασιλῆος,
γνῷ δὲ καὶ Ἀτρεΐδης εὐρὺ κρείων Ἀγαμέμνων
ἣν ἄτην ὅ τ' ἄριστον Ἀχαιῶν οὐδὲν ἔτισεν."

"So that they may all have profit of their own *basileus*." Who might this *basileus* be? From now on, any recognition of the powers of Agamemnon will go hand in hand with the recognition of the absence of that other *basileus*, Achilles. Merely to look at Agamemnon will be to miss Achilles. Or, in this zero-sum game of power that Achilles both constructs and is victim of, popular recognition of Agamemnon as king will be recognition of Agamemnon's failure as a king, and the other, absent king constantly engineers his humiliation. Finally, in this triangular game of recognition and its costs played out between Agamemnon, Achilles, and the Greeks, it is never quite clear what is to be recognized. The phrase γνῷ δὲ καὶ betrays a hesitation: "that even he might know," or "that he might know in addition"? The latter suggests that Agamemnon's knowledge comes late, parasitic on the knowledge of all the others. But what exactly do they know now, and what will they come to know in the future, and by what means? Belatedly, as they die, they are to recognize Achilles as *aristos*, the best of the Achaeans. But what they will not know, as they die, as they reevaluate their present king, Agamemnon, against the absent one, Achilles, are these words themselves—Achilles's prayer for their deaths. As they experience their deaths, and blame Agamemnon, and contemplate the seeming passivity of the absent Achilles, his active insistence on their death remains unthinkable. Achilles tries to set up a neutral experiment that will measure Agamemnon's worth. How will he fare in battle on his own, without the help of the greatest warrior? But the experiment itself is not neutral; he has orchestrated Agamemnon's humiliation by means of his own destruction of the Greeks. His words open up, for us, a missing link: what the people will not, but should, experience of this other *basileus* is that he is not only the absent, best warrior, but the architect of their deaths. This betrayal of the people is perhaps the greatest taboo of the *Iliad*.

HECTOR AND ACHILLES

As Hector triumphs in Achilles's absence, the Trojan warrior Poulydamas has a series of interchanges with him. In Book 13 he addresses him and urges the Trojans to withdraw.

[']Draw back now, and call to this place all of our bravest,
and then we might work out together our general counsel,
whether we can fall upon their benched ships, if the god might
be willing to give such power to us, or whether thereafter
we can win away from the ships unhurt; since I fear
the Achaians might wreak on us requital for yesterday;
since beside their ships lurks a man insatiate of fighting
and I think we can no longer utterly hold him from the fighting.'

(*Il*. 13.740–47)

"ἀλλ᾽ ἀναχασσάμενος κάλει ἐνθάδε πάντας ἀρίστους·
ἔνθεν δ᾽ ἂν μάλα πᾶσαν ἐπιφρασσαίμεθα βουλήν,
ἤ κεν ἐνὶ νήεσσι πολυκλήϊσι πέσωμεν,
αἴ κ᾽ ἐθέλῃσι θεὸς δόμεναι κράτος, ἤ κεν ἔπειτα
πὰρ νηῶν ἔλθωμεν ἀπήμονες. ἤ γὰρ ἔγωγε
δείδω μὴ τὸ χθιζὸν ἀποστήσωνται Ἀχαιοὶ
χρεῖος, ἐπεὶ παρὰ νηυσὶν ἀνὴρ ἄτος πολέμοιο
μίμνει, ὃν οὐκέτι πάγχυ μάχης σχήσεσθαι ὀΐω."

Poulydamas's words strangely echo the problems we encountered in the words of Calchas to Achilles. Once again we have an unnamed man, and once again we have a temptation to fill in the blank with the obvious absentee, Achilles. Should we do so, the taboo felt by Calchas in even uttering Agamemnon's name in *Iliad* 1 recurs, but now the taboo centers on Achilles; to speak his name out loud might bring panic.

But once more, this interpretation is not enough. Poulydamas, in his previous attempt to give defensive advice to Hector, was violently rebuffed (*Il.* 12.231–50). Hector refused to return to Troy and instead pushed ahead to fight by the ships of the Achaeans. So in his closing description of this unnamed man, Poulydamas's words, potentially about Achilles, also double as the current situation of Hector. For his speech purports to drag back a man insatiate of fighting from the ships of the Greeks. Of course, the irony in this case is that Hector does listen to Poulydamas's advice, though whether he obliquely recognizes himself in the words of the counselor is impossible to know. More interesting, however, is the implied doubling of Hector and Achilles, as men "insatiate of fighting," and also the isolation of Hector from the rest of the Trojans. Is he one of the "best" who must gather together, or rather an isolated warrior, incapable of listening to collective reason? Does he listen to the implied threat at work here in Poulydamas's words? Once more, the prophetic discourse confounds attempts to draw easy boundaries between heroes. Can we distinguish so easily between Achilles as individualistic pursuer of glory in opposition to Hector as family man and social hero? Instead, we have a depiction of the heroic isolation of Hector that doubles that of his Greek counterpart and paves the way for their encounter in Book 22. Both are warriors on the fringes of their society, but both also are propelled by an ignorance of the self, and their actions are in marked discord with what they seem to believe about themselves. The *Iliad* encourages us to see similarities at the level of what people do that are in conflict with distinctions that they, or the poet, try to draw in words.

ACHILLES AND PATROCLUS

After he has rejected the gifts offered by the embassy in Book 9, what prompts Achilles's return to fight? The answer lies less in what he knows of the suffering of the Greeks than in what he does not know.

> So they fought on in the likeness of blazing fire. And meanwhile
> the horses of Neleus sweating carried Nestor away from
> the fighting and carried also the shepherd of the people, Machaon.
> Now swift-footed brilliant Achilleus saw him and watched him,
> for he was standing on the stern of his huge-hollowed vessel
> looking out over the sheer war work and the sorrowful onrush.

At once he spoke to his own companion in arms, Patroklos,
calling from the ship, and he heard it from inside the shelter, and came out
like the war god, and this was the beginning of his evil.
The strong son of Menoitios spoke first, and addressed him:
'What do you wish with me, Achilleus? Why do you call me?'
　　　　Then in answer again spoke Achilleus of the swift feet:
'Son of Menoitios, you who delight my heart, o great one,
now I think the Achaians will come to my knees and stay there
in supplication, for a need past endurance has come to them.
But go now, Patroklos beloved of Zeus, to Nestor
and ask him who is this wounded man he brings in from the fighting.
Indeed, seeing him from behind I thought he was like Machaon,
Asklepios' son, in all ways, but I got no sight of the man's face
since the horses were tearing forward and swept on by me.'

                                                        (*Il.* 11.595–614)

　Ὡς οἱ μὲν μάρναντο δέμας πυρὸς αἰθομένοιο·
Νέστορα δ' ἐκ πολέμοιο φέρον Νηλήϊαι ἵπποι
ἱδρῶσαι, ἦγον δὲ Μαχάονα ποιμένα λαῶν.
τὸν δὲ ἰδὼν ἐνόησε ποδάρκης δῖος Ἀχιλλεύς·
ἑστήκει γὰρ ἐπὶ πρύμνῃ μεγακήτεϊ νηΐ,
εἰσορόων πόνον αἰπὺν ἰῶκά τε δακρυόεσσαν.
αἶψα δ' ἑταῖρον ἑὸν Πατροκλῆα προσέειπε,
φθεγξάμενος παρὰ νηός· ὃ δὲ κλισίηθεν ἀκούσας
ἔκμολεν ἶσος Ἄρηϊ, κακοῦ δ' ἄρα οἱ πέλεν ἀρχή.
τὸν πρότερος προσέειπε Μενοιτίου ἄλκιμος υἱός·
"τίπτέ με κικλήσκεις Ἀχιλεῦ; τί δέ σε χρεὼ ἐμεῖο;"
　τὸν δ' ἀπαμειβόμενος προσέφη πόδας ὠκὺς Ἀχιλλεύς·
"δῖε Μενοιτιάδη, τῷ ἐμῷ κεχαρισμένε θυμῷ,
νῦν ὀΐω περὶ γούνατ' ἐμὰ στήσεσθαι Ἀχαιοὺς
λισσομένους· χρειὼ γὰρ ἱκάνεται οὐκέτ' ἀνεκτός.
ἀλλ' ἴθι νῦν, Πάτροκλε Διῒ φίλε, Νέστορ' ἔρειο
ὅν τινα τοῦτον ἄγει βεβλημένον ἐκ πολέμοιο·
ἤτοι μὲν τά γ' ὄπισθε Μαχάονι πάντα ἔοικε
τῷ Ἀσκληπιάδῃ, ἀτὰρ οὐκ ἴδον ὄμματα φωτός·
ἵπποι γάρ με παρήϊξαν πρόσσω μεμαυῖαι."

All the problems of the poem crystallize in this passage. Achilles finally
gets what he wants, the unendurable need of the Greeks, but this re-
port of the war's progress tells us just as much about the person who
reports it to us. As their need becomes unendurable, Achilles suffers his
own unendurable need to know about their need, a need that cannot be
openly admitted, but instead is relayed to the Greeks through the proxy

of Patroclus. There is the contrast between the emphatic descriptions of the identity of Patroclus, with patronymic and epithet (son of Menoitios, beloved of Zeus) and the anonymity of the man Achilles sees. He is not just nobody, a thing of no concern, but a potential someone who sustains Achilles's desire to find out more about himself and his own relative social worth. This unnamed man piques his curiosity. Achilles, the poet of *Iliad* 9, who sings the famous deeds of men, is in the anxious position of the Homeric narrator who is unable to name the heroes who die, whose fiction of omniscience comes crashing to a halt in the face of a single unknown soldier. There is also Achilles's pointed desire for a universal supplication; after the partial supplication of the embassy, an embassy that itself stands in for Agamemnon, already a false representative of the people as such, the desire for universal supplication is a retroactive reading of what the embassy lacked. The absence of the king was designed to preserve his dignity and power, the very things that Achilles wants to see undermined.

The opacity of the wounded warrior's identity is thus a threat to the control over the world that Achilles seeks to maintain. His absence undermines Achilles's efforts to measure his own self-worth via Greek suffering. In typical Homeric fashion, this brief narrative detail about Achilles, who has been absent from the poem since the end of Book 9, provides a surfeit of retroactive information. That all along he has been watching, listing, and mentally recording the suffering of the Greeks, counting names, compiling a roster of wounding and death that is the obverse of the catalogue of ships. The question mark over the identity of the wounded man disrupts this strategy, but also demonstrates its ultimate futility. For to what end can this game properly be played? Only the perverse scenario of the torture and death of everyone—though that would destroy the game itself.

Yet Achilles is not fascinated by the anonymity of just anyone. He already imagines an answer in the contours of Machaon. Why a healer? This surprises too. He left the embassy with the impression that he would return to the fighting when the fire had struck his own ships. But well before this, while classifying the wounds of Book 11, he becomes fascinated by a special kind of man, a healer who is "worth many men." For Machaon too is a double of Achilles. Not only is his own game one of implied quantification (how many men am I worth?), but he also seeks to control the degree of Achaean helplessness. It is one thing to suffer pain, as the parade of wounded Greeks in Book 11 shows, quite another to lose the socially established means for healing that pain in

the recourse to healers. In contemporary parlance, this is to lose even
the possibility of belief that, if one were to call an emergency number,
anyone would arrive. Physical pain is shadowed by psychic pain, the
thought of hopelessness in the face of that pain. Machaon, therefore,
reveals himself as both a threat to Achilles's status as ultimate healer-
destroyer of the Greeks and, simultaneously, a sign of a victory to come
when Achilles will entirely replace him. As Socrates would later put
it, the person who heals is simultaneously the person who can inflict
pain. This kind of knowledge necessarily works both ways, and Achilles seeks to live on the cusp: he cares and destroys.

But the presence of Machaon, whose name itself signifies this ability
to contrive against pain, to have a *mechos* against it and thus not be helpless, is also an answer to another of the riddles embedded in the poem.
For before he continued with his project of measuring Greek suffering,
Achilles was given a warning by Odysseus.

> Up, then! if you are minded, late though it be, to rescue
> the afflicted sons of the Achaians from the Trojan onslaught.
> It will be an affliction to you hereafter, there will be no remedy
> found to heal the evil thing when it has been done. No, beforehand
> take thought to beat the evil day aside from the Danaans.
>
> (*Il.* 9.247–51)

> ἀλλ' ἄνα, εἰ μέμονάς γε καὶ ὀψέ περ υἷας Ἀχαιῶν
> τειρομένους ἐρύεσθαι ὑπὸ Τρώων ὀρυμαγδοῦ.
> αὐτῷ τοι μετόπισθ' ἄχος ἔσσεται, οὐδέ τι μῆχος
> ῥεχθέντος κακοῦ ἔστ' ἄκος εὑρεῖν· ἀλλὰ πολὺ πρὶν
> φράζευ ὅπως Δαναοῖσιν ἀλεξήσεις κακὸν ἦμαρ.

It is easy to see Odysseus's words as prophetic, a foreshadowing of
the incurable loss that Achilles will indeed suffer, the loss of Patroclus.
There is also a linguistic parallel to the doubling of healer and sufferer
in the pun on the words for pain and cure, *akos* and *achos*. But perhaps,
in identifying the major strands of the story to come, we rush forward
too quickly, and miss out on the ways Odysseus's words will play themselves out in the immediately ensuing narrative. For Achilles, far from
being afraid of the moment when there is no means to cure the pain of
the Greeks, wants exactly this. In Book 11 he becomes most interested
in the events of battle at the very moment when there is no *mechos*,
made flesh in the person of Machaon the healer, to cure the aches of the
Greeks. The paradox of the *Iliad*, and Achilles, is that what Odysseus

believes he is afraid of, this moment of helplessness, is simultaneously the very thing that he desires.

Patroclus later picks up the link between pain and cure when he begs Achilles to return to battle.

'Son of Peleus, far greatest of the Achaians, Achilleus,
do not be angry; such grief has fallen upon the Achaians.
For all those who were before the bravest in battle
are lying up among the ships with arrow or spear wounds.
The son of Tydeus, strong Diomedes, was hit by an arrow,
and Odysseus has a pike wound, and Agamemnon the spear-famed,
and Eurypylos has been wounded in the thigh with an arrow.
And over these the healers skilled in medicine are working
to cure their wounds. But you, Achilleus; who can do anything
with you?[']

(*Il.* 16.21–30)

"ὦ Ἀχιλεῦ, Πηλῆος υἱὲ, μέγα φέρτατ' Ἀχαιῶν,
μὴ νεμέσα· τοῖον γὰρ ἄχος βεβίηκεν Ἀχαιούς.
οἳ μὲν γὰρ δὴ πάντες, ὅσοι πάρος ἦσαν ἄριστοι,
ἐν νηυσὶν κέαται βεβλημένοι οὐτάμενοί τε.
βέβληται μὲν ὁ Τυδεΐδης κρατερὸς Διομήδης,
οὔτασται δ' Ὀδυσεὺς δουρικλυτὸς ἠδ' Ἀγαμέμνων,
βέβληται δὲ καὶ Εὐρύπυλος κατὰ μηρὸν ὀϊστῷ.
τοὺς μέν τ' ἰητροὶ πολυφάρμακοι ἀμφιπένονται,
ἕλκε' ἀκειόμενοι· σὺ δ' ἀμήχανος ἔπλευ, Ἀχιλλεῦ."

After the roll call of the wounded, Patroclus suggests that Achilles is *amechanos*. He is unmanageable, impossible to move to pity, inhuman, as he deliberately withholds his fighting skills. But he is also *not* a Machaon, at the very moment when he is given a narrative invitation to step into his shoes. Instead, the ruse of sending forth Patroclus as a replacement healer-destroyer allows Achilles to prolong his social experiment.

One might imagine that the *Iliad* is a tragedy of knowledge, that Achilles's problem is one of an imprecision over what he wants that becomes registered in his prayer to his mother. He says, "Harm the Greeks," but he does not mean Patroclus. But is there not something too neat here? To believe this necessitates believing that we always properly know what we want, but language improperly registers those desires, that we are transparent to ourselves, even if our desires are not transparent to others. This theory of psychic transparency thus forms a neat complement to the belief in the transparency of Homeric language. But in looking at the ways in which the central characters are plagued by their own blindness, I have tried to show that the poem offers us something more troubling. Rather than a tragedy of failed knowledge, it is one of the opacity of desire. Achilles does not know what he wants, and is able to recognize himself only in and through the desires of others, so that the contours of his desire are only available retroactively. On this reading, the tragedy of the *Iliad* is not simply that Achilles suffers the incurable loss of Patroclus, but that, in a more profound way, we find out that this is the very thing that he desired all along. The pain of the Greeks was always bound up in his pain, fixed in his own name, *Achos* and *laos*—the pain of the people.[4] Even as he becomes the architect of their unendurable need, he finds that he cannot endure watching this need, and that their pain melds with his own. So when he sends Patroclus to find out about Machaon, he already identifies himself, obliquely, as Greek, not as an asocial outcast, but as one of them, linked to them through the mediation of Patroclus, who, on his mission, will become reintegrated into the Greeks, and even play out Achilles's role as healer of them. The loss of Patroclus is perhaps the key that allows Achilles to find out what he was doing all along—the truth of his desire, not the falsity of others' misunderstanding of it.

1

The Tragedy of Achilles
The *Iliad* as a Poem of Betrayal

[Animals] manage to throw their pursuers off the scent by briefly going in one direction as a lure and then changing direction. This can go so far as to suggest on the part of game animals the nobility of honoring the parrying found in the hunt. But an animal does not feign feigning. It does not make tracks whose deceptiveness lies in getting them to be taken as false, when in fact they are true—that is, tracks that indicate the right trail.

Lacan 2004

[N]o fighter in the *Iliad* displays the inconstancy of a Helen or the treachery of a Clytemnestra.

Felson and Slatkin 2004

The belief that the *Iliad* is straightforward has been partially fuelled by identification with the poem's protagonist, Achilles. Though in this case, at least, even in antiquity there was some hesitation. Was Achilles really so truthful? When the embassy arrives to lure him back into the war in Book 9, and Odysseus lists the gifts Agamemnon is willing to offer by way of apology, Achilles's response is to condemn lying.

For as I detest the doorways of Death, I detest that man, who
hides one thing in the depths of his heart, and speaks forth another.

(*Il.* 9.312–13)

How we read the *Iliad* might ultimately depend on how we read these lines, perhaps the best known in the entire poem, and riddles lurk here too.

One possibility is to take him at his word. Achilles would then be a naive truth-teller, an innocent opposed to the social deceptions that are so much a part of social life. But this simplicity allows him to transcend the particular social life around him, to distance himself from his traditional culture and offer a critique of it. He is the child who says that the emperor is naked. His truth telling has a compelling nobility that rejects all pragmatism. This version of Achilles can take an existentialist turn, as in the magisterial interpretation of Cedric Whitman.[1] For Whitman, Achilles's active confrontation with the distortions and hypocrisy of the world around him launch him into a deeper journey into the meaning of the self. There is an overlap between his near inarticulateness and his profundity. As Adam Parry once famously argued, because Achilles is a creature of the traditional language that imprisons him, his only means of transcending it is to offer up unanswerable questions that cannot be answered in traditional terms. A question such as "Why fight?" within the heroic tradition is utterly nonsensical, and yet it is a productive nonsense. If half-intelligible to the heroic world, it also threatens to turn the world upside down and remake it. There is a fissure in the heart of heroic discourse, a gap between the actual world of the poem's protagonists and a utopian world where Achilles's blunt questions could perhaps be answered, where openness would replace hypocrisy. Pragmatism (say, the pragmatism of Odysseus) seeks to erase this gap in the name of the ongoing functioning of this actual social world.[2]

A second version of Achilles refuses to take him at face value and simultaneously rejects the romantic notions of the social world that lurk behind the existentialist story. On this reading Achilles is no child, but a sophisticated liar, a sort of super-sophist. This tradition begins at least as early as Plato's *Hippias Minor* but finds its current intellectual descendants in historicist readings of the poem. Let's start with Plato. In the *Hippias Minor* Socrates takes issue with a conventional dichotomy between the two major Homeric heroes made by Hippias. For Hippias, Achilles is the nobler hero because he tells the truth, whereas Odysseus is cunning, tricky, and a liar. To counter this, Socrates offers his own naive, literal reading of *Iliad* 9. Socrates points out that Achilles says mutually contradictory things throughout Book 9. He tells Odysseus that he is going home, later tells Phoenix that he will stay for at least a while and debate the return home with him later, and ends by telling Ajax that he will stay, but will only fight when the fire reaches his own ships. When Hippias defends his truthful Achilles by arguing that he does not mean to lie, for Socrates this makes him more of a sophist. Not only does he objectively lie; he has the uncanny ability to make everyone think he is telling the truth in the midst of his lies. It is not Odysseus but Achilles who is the figure of cunning. This kind of Achilles returns in recent portraits of him as a scheming calculator embedded in a competitive culture of gift giving, a view inspired by the anthropological studies of Pierre Bourdieu.[3] At the very moment when Achilles seems to be rejecting his world, threatening to abandon his comrades and the epic forever, and from this position of relative distance from his own cultural coordinates, we are invited to see this as a ruse, an attempt to gain more prestige within a historically specific game of gift exchange. The moment he seems to reject his culture is the moment he is most a part of his culture, as he plays a game to maximize his honor.

So must we choose between these interpretations of Achilles's remarks on lying, or are there alternatives? It is worth pausing over what they agree on: that Achilles's words make sense, and that he is in some way in control of them. Reasonable interpretative charity is at work here. Achilles's words and behavior in Book 9 obey a hidden logic; they are not simply mad or vicious, as Ajax later suggests when he calls Achilles *agrios*, bestial (*Il.* 9.629). Interpretations split only over the nature of that logic. For historicist readings, the sense is less in the words themselves than in the imagined cultural context that would explain them: they form part of an objective cultural truth, but one that takes some historical digging, and a suspension of our own time-bound prejudices, to recuperate. For romantic readings, even if Achilles's questions have no definite answers, the authenticity of the questions is absolute: they have a subjective truth.

But do not both these versions of Achilles miss the obvious: that the poem hangs on, and is obsessed with, the unreliability of language? This is not just the problem of whether a phrase is true or false. Rather, it is the deeper problem of the opacity of the intentions of social actors, to others and ultimately to themselves. If there is a strength in Socrates's position that the more recent, historicizing views of Achilles lack, it is that he forces us to puzzle over the difficulty, if not impossibility, of understanding what his words mean in *Iliad* 9. To offer a counter-theory to go along with this insight, I suggest that in the *Iliad* there is no integrity in either the social world or the subjects within it, and that the poem takes place at their point of intersection. For Homeric society is inconsistent, irrational, shot through with hypocrisy, and the central figure not only recognizes the hypocrisy but mirrors it, without ever fully understanding what he is doing. For to talk of the sophistication of Achilles's deception overlooks something obvious; we have a poem of betrayal, and all based upon a much more blunt lie than the historicists or the existential camps want to acknowledge. The Achilles whose attachment to the social world is fractured by the hypocrisy of Agamemnon, and the later Achilles who, consciously or unconsciously, is acting out that hatred in order to renegotiate his position within the world, both forget this betrayal. For Achilles does not simply desire to be desired by the Greeks at Troy, in whatever material form. He also desires to destroy them. So when a pair of critics make the extraordinary statement that "no fighter in the *Iliad* displays the inconstancy of a Helen or the treachery of a Clytemnestra," both these interpretative traditions—the existentialist and the historicist one—support them. This particular whitewashing of the actions of the poem's central hero, the critical disavowal of Achilles's betrayal, resurfaces in the identification of women as treacherous.[4]

"I detest as the gates of Death." What Achilles fails to tell the embassy, and indeed fails to tell Patroclus, is that he is not just passively allowing the deaths of the Greeks; rather, he is actively responsible for them. The Greeks die because he asked his mother to kill them. And is this not the obvious, crucial thing that Achilles himself "hides in his heart," while he says other things? But even as he hides it, his words reveal it. For the mention of death is more than an implied threat to those around him—"Lie to me, and I will kill you!"—it is also a betrayal of what is already happening: "Agamemnon lied to me, and I currently am killing you." His secret is that he causes his comrades' deaths. And the poem itself sets up this lie by the secrecy of the encounter with Thetis.

> But Achilleus
> weeping went and sat in sorrow apart from his companions
> beside the beach of the grey sea looking out on the infinite water.
> Many times stretching forth his hands he called on his mother . . .
>
> (*Il.* 1.348–51)

> αὐτὰρ Ἀχιλλεὺς
> δακρύσας ἑτάρων ἄφαρ ἕζετο νόσφι λιασθείς,
> θῖν’ ἔφ’ ἁλὸς πολιῆς, ὁρόων ἐπ’ ἀπείρονα πόντον·
> πολλὰ δὲ μητρὶ φίλῃ ἠρήσατο χεῖρας ὀρεγνύς . . .

He goes to the sea to call her on his own. The point is not only that his isolation mirrors his existential crisis, though this is not to reject readings that have emphasized this loneliness. Nor is it his liminal status between human and god, mirrored in the boundary between land and sea; since his mother is a sea-goddess, he himself lives between the worlds of land and sea. This may well be true. But identification with Achilles's feelings must not blind us to the way the plot itself sets up a secret, and it is this secret that reminds us of what Achilles does not say to the embassy, his great speech's most striking lie of omission.

More specifically, Achilles's words recall his prior exchange of words in the poem, as his mother asks him to reveal what has brought about the quarrel with Agamemnon.

[']Tell me, do not hide it in your mind, and thus we shall both know.'
Sighing heavily Achilleus of the swift feet answered her:
'You know; since you know why must I tell you all this?[']

(Il. 1.363–65)

"ἐξαύδα, μὴ κεῦθε νόῳ, ἵνα εἴδομεν ἄμφω."
Τὴν δὲ βαρὺ στενάχων προσέφη πόδας ὠκὺς Ἀχιλλεύς·
"οἶσθα· τίη τοι ταῦτα ἰδυίῃ πάντ' ἀγορεύω;"

Achilles goes on to give a long, partial, and selective account of the quarrel with Agamemnon. He claims his account is superfluous, but at the very least it offers us the chance to see what is different between Achilles's account and the narrator's. For example, he broadens the scope of the story to include his capture of Briseis, and gives a context for his affective ties to her. But he somehow forgets that he was the one responsible for summoning Calchas, unable to see himself as a candidate for power, an agent in the quarrel rather than a victim. Achilles also reverses the cause and effect with regard to Calchas's prophecy.

[T]ill the seer,
knowing well the truth interpreted the designs of the archer.
It was I first of all urged then the god's appeasement . . .

(Il. 1.384–86)

ἄμμι δὲ μάντις
εὖ εἰδὼς ἀγόρευε θεοπροπίας ἑκάτοιο.
αὐτίκ' ἐγὼ πρῶτος κελόμην θεὸν ἱλάσκεσθαι . . .

In Achilles's version, a prophet comes from nowhere to blame Agamemnon, and then urges appeasement of the god. In the narrator's account, the prophet is summoned by Achilles, and then Agamemnon, for all his anger, immediately acquiesces to the request that he return the girl. His response to the challenge to his authority is not just to speak abusively to Achilles, but to act, to issue orders for the return of the daughter to the priest, and to cement himself as the one who is a giver of orders to others, as he once accused Achilles of doing as a way of replacing him (*Il.* 1.289). But Achilles describes things in reverse. He forgets his political act (the summoning of the assembly), but remembers it instead as a pious one (the appeasement of the priest, which actually is performed by Agamemnon), only to end his speech with the most powerful words of all: a prayer to his mother for Greek deaths. Here, in our examination of the language of Achilles, we could ask: What kind of speech act does Achilles use here? He moves starkly from language that he believes to be purely descriptive to the final, performative request of the speech.

[']Sit beside him and take his knees and remind him of these things
now, if perhaps he might be willing to help the Trojans,
and pin the Achaians back against the ships and the water,
dying, so that thus they may all have profit of their own king,
that Atreus' son wide-ruling Agamemnon may recognize
his madness, that he did no honour to the best of the Achaians.'

(Il. 1.407–12)

"τῶν νῦν μιν μνήσασα παρέζεο καὶ λαβὲ γούνων,
αἴ κέν πως ἐθέλησιν ἐπὶ Τρώεσσιν ἀρῆξαι,
τοὺς δὲ κατὰ πρύμνας τε καὶ ἀμφ' ἅλα ἔλσαι Ἀχαιοὺς
κτεινομένους, ἵνα πάντες ἐπαύρωνται βασιλῆος,
γνῷ δὲ καὶ Ἀτρεΐδης εὐρὺ κρείων Ἀγαμέμνων
ἣν ἄτην, ὅ τ' ἄριστον Ἀχαιῶν οὐδὲν ἔτεισε."

This is the part of the speech that will not be publicly available, and it is his ultimate answer to Agamemnon. If he cannot kill the leader directly, he will kill the leader's people indirectly, deceptively. It is what "they both will know," what will not be hidden in Achilles's heart from Thetis, but will be hidden from everyone else. Even the poetic conceit of the omniscience of the gods, their knowledge of all affairs without any dependence on interpreting the language of others, is made use of to highlight the depth of the secret. For when Thetis visits Zeus alone, Hera immediately perceives her, and this threatens to cause a rift between the king and queen of the gods. But what Hera suspects but remains powerless to change is for the Greeks a more profound and complicated ignorance. The poem's protagonist, the figure of action and not of words, is at his most active through words, when he is physically doing nothing.[5] And in a further twist, much of Homeric criticism has taken his nonparticipation at face value, identifying with the ignorance of the Greeks, acting as if the request to Thetis does not happen.[6]

But if the Greeks do not know, at the very least the text remembers this scene, in the words of both Achilles and the Greeks around him, whose dependence on Achilles and innocence of his plan is so often in the spotlight. The narrative repeatedly reminds us of his absence from the fighting; for example, the Myrmidons play an anomalous role in the catalogue of ships, idle because their leader remains angry, even though the poet foreshadows his future return, and, we might add, their own return to proper membership of the Greek force (*Il.* 2.681–94). It also remembers via the obvious errors the Greeks make as they remember Achilles. Ajax conceives of Achilles as skulking in his tent in anger at Agamemnon, but he cannot conceive that his anger has widened to include a death wish for the Greeks (*Il.* 7.229–32). Were he to do so, the working premise of the embassy, the attempt to use Achilles's love for the other Greeks to bring him closer to the entire expedition led by Agamemnon, would be impossible. We also witness the emergence of this forgetfulness. It begins in the way Achilles's request for the death of his comrades is relayed back to Zeus from Thetis. Achilles begins his speech euphemistically, asking merely for the Greeks to be pinned against the ships, only to supplant this, at last, with one extra word: "dying," κτεινομένους. When Thetis later relays the message to Zeus, we have no hint of deaths, simply a request for "strength" for the Trojans until her son is honored. She buries the request in the discourse of reciprocity between her and Zeus, and this softens our perception of the content of the request: kill Greeks.

'Father Zeus, if ever before in word or action
I did you favour among the immortals, now grant what I ask for.
Now give honour to my son short-lived beyond all other
mortals. Since even now the lord of men Agamemnon
dishonours him, who has taken away his prize and keeps it.
Zeus of the counsels, lord of Olympos, now do him honour.
So long put strength into the Trojans, until the Achaians
give my son his rights, and his honour is increased among them.'

(*Il.* 1.503–10)

Thetis turns to the past and deflects attention from what is soon to come: the murder of Achilles's own ethnic group. When she emphasizes that her son is the most "short-lived," we can perhaps catch a glimpse of the unspoken other lives that will be foreshortened because of Achilles's desire. In a final irony, this simultaneous forgetting and remembering of his own request will rebound on Achilles himself, setting up the central tragedy of the *Iliad*. For he forgets that Patroclus is a Greek, partially embedded, or at least unable to shake the belief that he is embedded, in that particular ethnic identity.

Consider another example, directly from the language of Achilles in *Iliad* 9, and often presumed to be the protagonist at his most sublime. In his verbal response to the vastness of material wealth offered him by Agamemnon, with all the social strings attached, Achilles seems to offer a view of life as a unique source of value.

> For not
> worth the value of my life are all the possessions they fable
> were won for Ilion, that strong-founded citadel, in the old days
> when there was peace, before the coming of the sons of the Achaians . . .
>
> (*Il.* 9.400–403)

οὐ γὰρ ἐμοὶ ψυχῆς ἀντάξιον οὐδ' ὅσα φασὶν
Ἴλιον ἐκτῆσθαι εὖ ναιόμενον πτολίεθρον,
τὸ πρὶν ἐπ' εἰρήνης, πρὶν ἐλθεῖν υἷας Ἀχαιῶν.

Historicist readings have been reluctant to take this at face value, instead translating his stark statement into the terms of the calculating Achilles they conjure up. Roughly, Achilles means that the gifts are not worth his life *in this instance*, because of the peculiar insult to his honor that Agamemnon has instigated. There is no general condemnation of the process of gift giving, no universal claim being made of the value of life. Even the statement itself is part of the game, an attempt to procure more prestige. For romantics, the reference to life suggests an absolute, incommensurable value.

But what both miss is an inverted message lurking in Achilles's words. Let us broaden our view beyond the encounter with the embassy, and out into the events that frame it. When Achilles says "not worth my life," is not the hidden message that this fight for value *is* worth everyone else's life, or at least the value of the lives of the Greeks who are dying because of his request? The position from which he speaks, as he enunciates this breathtaking comment about the value of human life, is paid for in the currency of Greek lives: without their deaths, no great antiwar speech of *Iliad* 9. So when later, after the death of Patroclus, he actively seeks to kill Trojans, retroactively valuing their lives as nothing in comparison with the value of Patroclus's life, this inverts an evaluation of life he performs already in Book 9: active killing of another ethnic group replacing the passive killing of his own.

The Doloneia as a Memorial of Betrayal

The Greeks do not officially know about the encounter between Achilles and Thetis. And yet, do they not seem to know? Before the embassy begins, there is tension between Agamemnon and Diomedes. Agamemnon, in despair, suggests that the Greeks should return home. Diomedes responds by saying that he will stay and fight with Sthenelus until the bitter end, if need be. At this point, Nestor intervenes, ostensibly to put an end to this intra-Greek conflict.

Out of all brotherhood, outlawed, homeless shall be that man
who longs for all the horror of fighting among his own people.
(*Il.* 9.63–64)

If this intervention succeeds in healing the quarrel between Diomedes and Agamemnon, it hits upon the much more significant truth of what Achilles is doing. Nestor's words hint not only at his desire, but his situation, as he lingers on the edge of the law, in a home on the fringes of society, and replaces a general brotherhood, the companionship of his comrades, with the friendship of a single man, Patroclus. The embassy to Achilles is a symptom of Achilles's indecision about what he wants; his desire to be desired, his need to be needed, orchestrates the movements of the whole Achaean army. But the Greeks also seem caught up in disavowal, since their logic in sending the embassy is not just "Let us get Achilles back because we need him to fight," but also, "Let us get him back to our side, so we can continue in our belief that *no one is so mad as to long for the horror of fighting among his own people.*" The plea for help is also a plea to keep a certain ideal of the world, a test to see how much they can stand to know about the human propensity to betray. They know very well that people do betray, and yet cannot quite place Achilles in that category.

It is this motif of betrayal that continues to haunt the following book. For after Achilles's rejection of the embassy, there follows a puzzling and seemingly inorganic interlude. The Greeks react by going on a nighttime spying mission, sending Diomedes and Odysseus into the no-man's-land between Greeks and Trojans to find out future attack plans. While there, they coincidentally meet a Trojan spy, Dolon, sent forth for the same purpose. After they pretend to offer him his life for information, he tells them about the Thracian troops led by Rhesus who have recently arrived. They willingly take the information but go back on their promise and kill Dolon as he supplicates them. They then go on a grisly spree, killing sleeping Thracians, and return home in triumph. Many critics either ignore this episode or excise it, seeing no relevance to the immediate plot. But if critics seem to find this book hard to stomach, it is surely not just because it seems out of place in the narrative. The events show, in an unusually vivid and disturbing way, an ugly, non-heroic side of the war. Far from heroic etiquette and *noblesse oblige*, the hand-to-hand combat of the day, we have a mass of corpses, slaughter of the defenseless, deceit, and a callous disregard for the rights of a suppliant. But here is the rub. A need to detach these motifs from *Iliad* 9 depends upon a curiously idealized reading of *Iliad* 9. But what if the Doloneia is, at least in part, the darkest of comedies, a farcical parody of the preceding book?

Dolon himself is described physically as a second-rate double of Achilles. He too is swift of foot, though ugly to look at, not beautiful (*Il.* 10.315–16). He is also rich, and yet wants something beyond wealth, the immortal horses of Achilles. Within the book these seem to represent the impossible desire for immortality.[7] So too we have just left Achilles rejecting material wealth with the claim that he does not need it, and yet still wanting something beyond any material form of prestige. But there is a far more perturbing similarity. For when he is captured alive, Dolon chooses not only to betray his Trojan comrades but, more importantly, does so *because of the value he places on his own life*. It is as if, after the heady romance of Achilles's speech on the unique value of life, its irretrievability once it has passed through the "barrier of the teeth," we have a figure who takes that calculation quite literally and simply, without any high rhetoric: his companions' lives are not worth his, so he trades Thracian lives for his own. Achilles claims that nothing is exchangeable for life, and yet orchestrates a situation in which the deaths of Greeks are the key that allows him to try to evaluate his own life. Dolon betrays his people far more openly. But his exchange of life for lives is not allowed to stand because of his own betrayal by Odysseus.

Let us linger over the logic of supplication within the poem. In supplication, we find not simply that finite goods are exchanged for one life; instead, there is a fiction of limitless goods that need to be exchanged because of the immeasurable value of life. Dolon offers a perversion of this ritual, which embodies much of what Achilles says in Book 9: "not worth my life." Here, once more, one could square the circle between the competing accounts of historicism and existentialism. Historicists demand that we remember that what Achilles says is not somehow free from the world around him, but is entirely prompted by the culture of that world: hence, his vision of the "absolute" is historically contingent. But heroic culture already has a place for the "absolute" within its own social logic: believing in the unique value of life beyond any cultural exchange is what heroes used to do (or what the logic of supplication did to heroes) every day, until the pressure of war itself began to strain the ritual. Cedric Whitman's insistence that Achilles stands up for the absolute value of life, incommensurable with goods, is the lurking logic of the historically specific ritual of supplication. Homer's Greeks did not know that they were practical believers in the absolute value of life, but they were doing it in their daily, ritualized lives. Achilles, in Book 9, becomes the first theorist of the significance of that ritual. The truth is "out there" in what the Greeks and Trojans do, not in what they think they do.

What of the Greeks, and their motivation for the spying trip? Part of the interest in this poem lies in the way that the major characters seem to blur into each other and defy the usual easy separation that character-based criticism has been quick to offer up. Books 9 and 10 of the *Iliad* stage a disturbing, politicized version of this problematic, one often associated with the essence of the political itself: is it possible, with any certainty, to tell an enemy from a friend? The problem of lying, announced by Achilles in the opening of his great speech, is transformed in the Doloneia into the question of political betrayal. Indeed, far from ignoring the dilemmas produced by Achilles' rejection of Agamemnon's gifts in the preceding book, the actions of the Greeks in *Iliad* 10 can't stop remembering them. Let me give some examples.

Consider this exchange between Agamemnon and Nestor, which jump-starts the spying operation.

[']There are men who hate us sitting nearby, nor do we know
that they might not be pondering an attack on us in the darkness.'
Thereupon the Gerenian horseman Nestor answered him:
'Son of Atreus, most lordly and king of men, Agamemnon,
Zeus of the counsels, I think, will not accomplish for Hektor
all his designs and all he hopes for now; I think rather
he will have still more hardships to wrestle, if ever Achilleus
turns again the heart within him from its wearisome anger.[']

(*Il.* 10.100–107)

Agamemnon seems to refer to the Trojans. But after *Iliad* 9, is not Achilles the more obvious referent? He too sits nearby, on the fringes of the

Greek army, nearly but not quite breaking the spatial divide that separates Greeks from Trojans, and already having executed a secret plan for Greek destruction. As such, Agamemnon's words can be read either as revealing unconscious knowledge of the truth of Achilles's rejection or as a cruel textual joke on him by Homer. Nestor's reply that Zeus will not accomplish all his designs for Hector is just as far from the mark. Ironically, Zeus is currently accomplishing all his designs for Hector, but on behalf of Achilles.

Later, Nestor's request for a spy also can be read as another obsessive remembering of the failed trip to Achilles's tent.

'O my friends, is there no man who, trusting in the daring
of his own heart, would go among the high-hearted Trojans?
So he might catch some enemy, who straggled behind them,
or he might overhear some thing that the Trojans are saying,
what they deliberate among themselves, and whether they purpose
to stay where they are, close to the ships, or else to withdraw back
into their city, now that they have beaten the Achaians.
Could a man learn this, and then come back again to us
unhurt, why huge and heaven-high would rise up his glory
among all people, and an excellent gift would befall him . . .[']

(*Il.* 10.204–13)

We have had no spying missions to the Trojan camp as yet in the poem. But we have had two missions to the tent of Achilles, both shrouded in an atmosphere of uncertainty, first by the heralds in Book 1, in order to retrieve Briseis, and most recently in the embassy of Book 9. In the first case, at least, the heralds followed Agamemnon's orders in going but were terrified at the moment they confronted him (*Il.* 1.331–33); for this man, on the outskirts of the Greeks, might consider them enemies because of their status as representatives of Agamemnon. So the request for a daring spy to find a lingering enemy in the Doloneia doubles the trip to Achilles himself, the figure whose status is most in question. Even the content of their spying mission, to find out the Trojan movements, mirrors the confused response to the embassy offered by Achilles: will the Trojans stay by their ships (or will Achilles) or go back to their city (or will Achilles go home)? The Doloneia is a symptom of the failure of the far more significant mission of the previous book.

But there is one more distorted remembering of *Iliad* 9 in Nestor's speech, which can also allow us to consider one of the oldest scholarly controversies from *Iliad* 9. Achilles ends his second speech to Phoenix with a refusal of his plea, but also a statement that puts the very question of who is a friend, who an enemy, under the spotlight.

[']Stop confusing my heart with lamentation and sorrow
for the favour of great Atreides. It does not become you
to love this man, for fear you turn hateful to me, who love you.
It should be your pride with me to hurt whoever shall hurt me.
Be king equally with me; take half of my honour.
These men will carry back the message; you stay here and sleep here
in a soft bed, and we shall decide tomorrow, as dawn shows,
whether to go back home again or else to remain here.'

(*Il.* 9.612–19)

Achilles stands for a zero-sum game of friendship and enmity. Phoenix must choose sides, in line with the ancient ethical principle that friends help friends and harm enemies.[8] This simplicity contrasts with his own problematic status, somewhere in between Trojans and Greeks. Still, if Achilles's purposefulness masks a more profound indecision, the luxury of indecision will not be available to those around him, who must choose. Phoenix does stay behind, and disappears from the epic until Book 23. But Nestor's speech, and the reference to an enemy "straggling behind," might make us pause to think over what happened during the embassy. If five men set out, only four returned, with Phoenix himself the straggler. As a simple math problem, the embassy was a failure. It not only fails to convert Achilles; it produces a convert to him.

Now, much scholarly ink has been spilt over a similar math problem in *Iliad* 9, but one that occurs at the beginning of the embassy, not the end. The embassy to Achilles consists at first of three named members (*Il.* 9.168–69), then of two (182–200), and then again of the original three (222). This inconsistency is routinely explained away as a symptom of the oral nature of Homeric poetry, a slip of editing from an oral tradition that is inevitable in a poem of this scale. More ambitiously, others have tried to see the embassy to Achilles as a conflation of different stories that changed over time. Some, for example, see Phoenix's participation as a later addition to the original tale, but with the conflicting numbers never properly edited out. But what should be given more attention is the way our text, far from burying it, lingers over the difficulty of number in all the Greek dealings with Achilles, reevaluating who is a friend, who an enemy. Not only does the status of Phoenix retroactively change their number, but the first description of the embassy, using the Greek "dual" form signifying two members, should alert us to the problem of counting the first embassy to Achilles in *Iliad* 1.

> So these two walked along the strand of the sea deep-thundering
>
> . . .
>
> (Il. 9.182)

> 'Go now
> to the shelter of Peleus' son Achilleus, to bring back
> Briseis of the fair cheeks leading her by the hand. And if he
> will not give her, I must come in person to take her
> with many men behind me, and it will be the worse for him.'
>   He spoke and sent them forth with this strong order upon them.
> They went against their will beside the beach of the barren
> salt sea . . .
>
> (Il. 1.321–28)

Here also there is a strange inconsistency over numbers. Two go to the tent of Achilles, but surely Achilles would not have expected this. For Agamemnon had been quite clear that he would go to Achilles's tent to retrieve Briseis in person and on his own (*Il.* 1.137 and 1.184–85). When the heralds themselves go, though the actual number of those going is greater, the absence of Agamemnon is striking. The poem sets up a future duel between Achilles and Agamemnon, only to frustrate it, just as Hera frustrated Achilles's attempt to kill him in the quarrel. The elaborate confusion the poem constructs over who will go to Achilles in *Iliad* 1 thus sets up the visitors who go in *Iliad* 9. However many they are, and they could be many more (as Agamemnon says), they always carry the implied threat of even greater numbers because they are only representatives of the masses of soldiers under Agamemnon's command, although the most important, Agamemnon himself, is absent. The *Iliad* lays bare the vexed problem of successful classification of men into friends and enemies, into who is for you and against you, and offers this up as a fickle and changing process.

Regardless of the origin of the problem of the duals, the text constantly remembers it—not only the *Iliad*, but also the *Odyssey*, which offers up its own oblique commentary on the embassy to Achilles. In Book 9 of the *Odyssey*, Odysseus tells of his encounter with the Lotus-Eaters, a tribe who almost, though not quite, lure his men away from the group.

> But after we had tasted of food and drink, then I sent
> some of my companions ahead, telling them to find out
> what men, eaters of bread, might live here in this country.

I chose two men, and sent a third with them, as a herald.
My men went on and presently met the Lotus-Eaters,
nor did these Lotus-Eaters have any thoughts of destroying
our companions, but they only gave them lotus to taste of.
But any of them who ate the honey-sweet fruit of lotus
was unwilling to take any message back, or to go
away, but they wanted to stay there with the lotus-eating
people, feeding on lotus, and forget the way home. I myself
took these men back weeping, by force, to where the ships were,
and put them aboard under the rowing benches and tied them
fast, then gave the order to the rest of my eager
companions to embark on the ships in haste, for fear
someone else might taste of the lotus and forget the way home . . .

(*Od.* 9.87–102)

Odysseus sends two men, making use of the dual (ἄνδρε δύω κρίνας), and picks a third to go as herald. Later, without ever quite explaining whether he was part of the original party or not, we find out that he himself is responsible for bringing them back. Is this an attempt of the *Odyssey* to clarify the problem set up by the duals of *Iliad* 9 (reading Odysseus and Ajax as the "two men," with Phoenix as herald), or does the possible allusion lie in the vagueness of the numbers? We can see this fantastic story as a mystical allegory of the embassy to Achilles. For what will keep the companions with the Lotus-Eaters is not force but food, the peculiar power of their hospitality. Can we not now try to imagine the surprise of what happens to the embassy? What they get is not a skulking, angry Achilles, but instead a perfect host, who immediately sets in motion the preparation of food and wine, transferring the competition between himself and Agamemnon out of the arena of war and into that of hospitality. When Odysseus opens his speech by pointing out the good food that is available both in Agamemnon's tent and in Achilles's (*Il.* 9.225–27), he registers Achilles's hospitality as a near threat, which will eventually be realized in the loss of Phoenix. For he will forget how to take a message back to Agamemnon, forget how to make his way home to the Greeks. More poignantly, what is promised by the loss of the return home to the Greek host, at least in *Iliad* 9, is the more utopian possibility of a return home, alive, to Greece and away from the war. So too in the *Odyssey* the promise of the Lotus-Eaters, of a kind of eternal, utopian peace, runs alongside our unpleasant knowledge of what actually happens to the companions, their ongoing, protracted deaths. Achilles's tent, on the edges of the Greek camp, is a space that offers the constant possibility of saying no to Agamemnon, or, from Agamemnon's perspective, of betraying him.

Achilles as Thing of Nothing

When we join Achilles's quest to find the value of the self to the problem of what is missing from the poem's elaborate lists, we can begin to understand the central tragedy of the poem, the death of Patroclus. Achilles may indeed be a super-sophist, utilizing strategies of exchange in order to evaluate himself. But the objects cast away in the hope of self-knowledge are other lives, not goods. Rather than seeking the kind of gift that would return him to the fold, we should ask if there is a particular life that would halt his anger, a life that Achilles may not even imagine to be part of the list.

The answer is first suggested in *Iliad* 16, after Patroclus asks him to return to the fighting.

[']Father Zeus, Athena and Apollo, if only
not one of all the Trojans could escape destruction, not one
of the Argives, but you and I could emerge from the slaughter
so that we two alone could break Troy's hallowed coronal.'

(Il. 16.97–100)

The possibility of the complete destruction of the heroic world, of Trojans and Greeks, seems to be Achilles's deepest desire, and this desire answers the dilemma of Book 9. Achilles's implied question is "how many Greek deaths are enough to give me what I want?" The answer is formally traced in his response to Agamemnon's gifts: not as many as the grains of sand. To translate into the more fundamental discourse of lost Greek lives: no amount would satisfy me. Or: I want them all to die.

But one death is different, the death of Patroclus. A joke from the 1960s describes an American man feigning madness in order to avoid the Vietnam War. When he goes to the draft office, he starts looking around for a piece of paper. When the military officials try to calm him down, he becomes all the more frantic, mumbling, "I must find this piece of paper, I must find it." After several minutes of this, the officials finally give up, sign the forms indicating his unfitness to serve, and hand them to him. "At last, I've found it," he replies. The very thing he wants removes him from the world he does not want to inhabit: the world of possible military service. The story of Achilles suggests a darker version of this joke. He seeks what? The very thing that will restore him to the social world that must be "worth his life," and therefore worth returning to battle to risk it. But if the draftee who fakes madness seeks his own life, Achilles seeks the exact opposite—the death of someone who is the answer to the implied question lurking in the rejection of gifts: "What is worth my life?" So even as he removes himself from battle, he looks less for an exit strategy from the war and more for something to die for, a life that could be measured against his own. The string of deaths he sees unroll before him are not enough. Until Patroclus. With hindsight, one can read riddling references to Patroclus in his own prophetic language.

> and yet I have said
> I would not give over my anger until that time came
> when the fighting with all its clamour came up to my own ships.
>
> (*Il.* 16.61–63)

What can the vague phrase "to my own ships" mean here? Its imprecision suggests an answer; he waits until the Trojan attack he orchestrates threatens his inner circle. But it is ultimately an inner circle of one. Then he will give over one form of his anger, only to see it metastasize into something appallingly different.

So as Achilles asks what his *psyche* is worth, he rejects any discourse of quantity (no number of goods or lives suffice), and replaces it with a discourse of quality (the answer to Achilles's quest comes in the person of Patroclus). But perhaps we even take unity of the self, the integrity of the individual bodies that Achilles counts, too much for granted. It is a commonplace of Homeric scholarship that there is no word for the living body in Homer, and the difficulties and vulnerabilities of the agent have often been linked to this philological fact.[9] But there can also be individual selves that exist but have no value. From the opening of the poem, Achilles granted the Greeks existence without worth because of their status as slaves of Agamemnon; he rules over "no-bodies," *out-idanoi*. In Book 18 the tables are fully turned. For this book stages a double shift in the complex story of Achilles's self-evaluation. He retroactively realizes the worth of Patroclus to him, but in doing so comes to terms with his own nothingness. But this does not happen all at once, but limb by limb, body part by body part.

The news of Patroclus's death is brought to Achilles in Book 18 by the "swift of foot" Antilochus ("Antilochos came, a swift-footed messenger, to Achilleus," *Il.* 18.2). The poet's transfer of Achilles's epithet to the person of another is striking; we see not the usual Achilles, but one deprived of his key symbolic quality. Three escalating kinds of passivity characterize Achilles. First, he fails to fight and rejects his essential nature, his love of battle, strife, and violence. Second, he fails to help his comrade who died during the fighting. But in Book 18 both failures are lived through a third kind. He is ignorant of Patroclus's death and must listen in helplessness as another tells him the truth. If Antilochus's entrance focuses our attention on Achilles's symbolic loss of his swiftness of foot, the next form of enforced passivity is more brutal, and turns attention from feet to hands. After releasing the news, Antilochus binds Achilles's hands, in fear lest he "might slit some throat."

On the other side Antilochos mourned with him, letting the tears fall,
and held the hands of Achilleus as he grieved in his proud heart,
fearing Achilleus might cut his throat with the iron . . .

(*Il.* 18.32–34)

He seems to fear suicide, though already in antiquity the vagueness of the phrase was noticed. What form will Achilles's anger take here? Will he kill himself? Find another throat to slit, perhaps that of the messenger? We have an unfocused anger that is turned away from possible action against his own person, only to be turned, later, against the killers of Patroclus. It is a moment of unpredictability, of a pure madness of grief when the hands could do anything, divorced from any central agency that might control them. With all four limbs, those engines of human activity, successively immobilized, the poem can put on display the perfection of the passivity he is now forced to endure. When he later calls himself "a useless burden," this can refer not only to his self-removal from the battle, but to his most recent experience as a motionless receptacle of Antilochus's words.

The episode suggests another—this time in the *Odyssey*—where passivity takes center stage. When Odysseus sails past the island of the Sirens, in order to hear them he has his crew bind his hands and his feet to the mast (*Od.* 12.177–80). Is this not the moment when Odysseus willingly turns himself into a "useless burden," depriving himself of the organs of action that constitute a heroic man? In the *Odyssey* the passivity was part of a strategy to enable the hero to receive a message of joy, however dangerous the experience of such a song might be. In *Iliad* 18, the removal of limbs is forced upon Achilles by Antilochus against his will. When Achilles does passively experience the news, it will be all pain. The Sirens offer up the deadly possibility of the knowledge of everything, the full repertoire of stories of heroes past and present. What Achilles is forced to hear is the one thing that will symbolically destroy him. But we can narrow the gap between the stories. The joy of the song of the Sirens masks deadliness, as the enjoyment of the listeners is linked to the piles of bones on the island. So too the horror of Achilles at the news of the death of Patroclus is complicated; he asked for and desired this death. If the Sirens' song is deadly because it offers the suffocating horror of granting everything that one would want to know, leaving no gap for any desire, the horror of Patroclus's death is increased because it is suffused with Achilles's desire for it. So might not the deadliness of the Sirens' song consist in the mythical possibility that, for each of us, they know the very thing that will untie the knot of our most troubling desire?

Patroclus's Death as Riddle

Let me end this discussion of Achilles by turning to two other riddles that structure the narrative of Patroclus's death. Consider Achilles's words at the beginning of the book, before he has heard of the death of his comrade. He remembers a prophecy from his mother about the death of the "best of the Myrmidons" (translated as "bravest" by Lattimore).

> May the gods not accomplish vile sorrows upon the heart in me
> in the way my mother once made it clear to me, when she told me
> how while I yet lived the bravest of the Myrmidons
> must leave the light of the sun beneath the hands of the Trojans.
>
> (*Il.* 18.8–11)

But how can the best of the Myrmidons leave the light of the sun when Achilles, supposedly the best of the Greeks, is still alive? One answer is a retroactive one, and offered by Achilles himself: at the time Patroclus fights, Achilles is not the best, but rather a "useless burden," a nothing. Because he is not active, and his social identity is based on heroic performance, he was not the best of the Myrmidons at the time of his friend's death. Once more, the inability to understand the riddle comes from a deep self-ignorance and is an inverted image of the blindness on show in his response to the words of Calchas. In *Iliad* 1, he was blind to his own activity in the world of words, the implicit threat against Agamemnon's power he makes by calling the assembly. This time, he is blind to the effects of his inactivity. If he was a nothing when Patroclus died, he did not know he was a nothing, trapped in the illusion that he was still the best warrior, as if the term *aristos* were a constant attribute or property of the self, rather than the temporary designator of a victor in a social struggle. The contrast is even more perfect, as Patroclus biologically dies at the very moment when he is most socially active, while Achilles is acting out a living death, a being biologically alive who might as well be dead.

The second puzzle is set up in Book 16 but finally answered in Book 18. Following an old problem from the *Oedipus Tyrannus*, we can call it the puzzle of the many murderers of Patroclus. For why is Hector not allowed to kill Patroclus directly, but instead is the "third killer," as Patroclus himself claims, after Apollo and Euphorbos?

> No, deadly destiny, with the son of Leto, has killed me,
> and of men it was Euphorbos; you are only my third slayer.
> (Il. 16.849–50)

The surfeit of surface partial killers hides the killer that matters, and as is the case with Oedipus, this killer will eventually self-convict.

> [']These things are brought to accomplishment
> through Zeus: in the way that you lifted your hands and prayed for,
> that all the sons of the Achaians be pinned on their grounded vessels
> by reason of your loss, and suffer things that are shameful.'
> Then sighing heavily Achilleus of the swift feet answered her:
> 'My mother, all these things the Olympian brought to accomplishment.
> But what pleasure is this to me, since my dear companion has perished,
> Patroklos, whom I loved beyond all other companions,
> as well as my own life. *I have killed him*, and Hektor, *having savaged* him,
> has stripped away that gigantic armour . . .[']
> (Il. 18.74–83; the phrases in italics are my own translation)

> "τὰ μὲν δή τοι τετέλεσται
> ἐκ Διός, ὡς ἄρα δὴ πρίν γ' εὔχεο χεῖρας ἀνασχών,
> πάντας ἐπὶ πρύμνῃσιν ἀλήμεναι υἷας Ἀχαιῶν
> σεῦ ἐπιδευομένους, παθέειν τ' ἀεκήλια ἔργα."
> Τὴν δὲ βαρὺ στενάχων προσέφη πόδας ὠκὺς Ἀχιλλεύς·
> "μῆτερ ἐμή, τὰ μὲν ἄρ μοι Ὀλύμπιος ἐξετέλεσσεν·
> ἀλλὰ τί μοι τῶν ἧδος, ἐπεὶ φίλος ὤλεθ' ἑταῖρος,
> Πάτροκλος, τὸν ἐγὼ περὶ πάντων τῖον ἑταίρων,
> ἶσον ἐμῇ κεφαλῇ· τὸν ἀπώλεσα, τεύχεα δ' Ἕκτωρ
> δῃώσας ἀπέδυσε πελώρια, θαῦμα ἰδέσθαι,
> καλά . . ."

The phrase I translated "I have killed" is ambiguous in the Greek, and the source of some debate. It can mean either "kill/destroy" or "lose," and the vast majority of scholars and translators have preferred the latter. There is a good reason for this, as they are following the path of Achilles, who will also be quick to forget the truth that is revealed in his own words.[10] But the entire narrative anticipates this verbal ambiguity. The many murderers of Patroclus are a series of red herrings, a preparation for Achilles's punch line: I killed him. The shock of the language comes once more from the contrast with the euphemisms of his mother, who speaks only of "shameful things" and Greeks "pinned to ships," but does not utter the word "death," or "dying," the crucial word in Achilles's first request. In part, the contrast comes with the rest of what Achilles will say, as his own self-blame is diverted onto Hector. But nevertheless in τὸν ἀπώλεσα, "I killed him," we have the one true thing that this hater of liars, this hero routinely identified with truthfulness, says in the entire poem, a truthfulness that coincides perfectly with his own self-conviction for the murder of the only Greek who matters to him, and by association, an awareness of his responsibility for the murder of the other Greeks. But it is *not* uttered directly. The possibility of "I lost him" suggests that even here Achilles utters the truth in a veiled form.

But does this mean that, after Book 18, we have a different Achilles, one who knows and understands at least partially what he is doing, and is free from the hesitation and disavowals that have characterized him throughout the poem? Or does he instead replace one kind of forgetfulness with another? Let us return to his reaction to Patroclus's death. Soon after the momentary insight of the phrase "I killed him/lost him," he tells his mother that he must kill Hector, and she replies that this will lead to his own death.

> Then deeply disturbed Achilleus of the swift feet answered her:
> 'I must die soon, then; since I was not to stand by my companion
> when he was killed. And now, far away from the land of his fathers,
> he has perished, and lacked my fighting strength to defend him.
> Now, since I am not going back to the beloved land of my fathers,
> since I was no light of safety to Patroklos, nor to my other
> companions, who in their numbers went down before glorious Hektor,
> but sit here beside my ships, a useless weight on the good land,
> I, who am such as no other of the bronze-armoured Achaians
> in battle . . .[']
>
> (*Il.* 18.97–106)

The speech allows us to see how pivotal Patroclus is to the poem's plot and how crucial to Achilles. Before Patroclus's death, Achilles sought the death of the Greeks ostensibly in order to gain prestige. But Patroclus too was a Greek. Indeed, Patroclus becomes more and more of a Greek, and less and less of a *philos* of Achilles, as he sees more Greek wounds and hears tales of their losses from the lips of Nestor in Book 11. But when Achilles remembers Patroclus after his death, it is not just as any *philos*. He is a Greek friend. Achilles transfers the hatred he once felt for the Greeks, itself transferred from the hatred he felt toward Agamemnon, onto those who murdered not just Patroclus, but all Greeks. From a perfect separation from Greeks, Achilles now becomes the representative of them all: "I was no light to Patroclus, or *any other Greek*." From a disavowed identification with Greeks, since the only way Achilles can find of measuring their care for him, as he cares for them, is through contriving their deaths, we have a hyper-identification with the Greek cause, an identification that will demand not only that he kill Trojans, but that he kill them in a way that ignores any of the rules and regulations, the etiquette of heroic warfare that he had hitherto obeyed (he kills suppliants, exults in human sacrifice, etc.). He lives out Patroclus's desire to help the Greeks to the fullest. The *Iliad* is routinely viewed as the first document of pan-Hellenism, a poem about the Greeks that simultaneously constructs the unity of the Greeks. And to be sure, we could see this as an alternative title of the story of Achilles himself—*The Iliad; or, How Achilles Becomes a Greek*. But it is a far more disturbing form of Greekness than is usually recognized.

There is, moreover, a more powerful form of forgetting at work. Achilles's choice to identify with the Greeks against Hector is a violent form of acting out in order to forget the truth he himself utters: that he killed Patroclus. The assumption of his own biological death, intertwined with his recaptured sense of Greek identity, replaces the social death that he constructs for himself and is aware of in Book 18. After the betrayal of his Greek comrades, his distancing from them, he finds out that he has also betrayed the friend he loves, the person with whom he shared that space of separation. With nowhere to go, he returns to the Greek fold as if Hector, and not himself, had killed Patroclus and the Greeks alike. But in the haste of this turnaround, in the urgency to get back to battle, much is overlooked. Achilles knows his own role in Patroclus's death and is far from curious about the other details. Antilochus, quite reasonably, does not even tell him that Hector was the killer. This might be because, in one way, Achilles already knows enough, and far more than Ajax, when he recognizes that he himself has indirectly killed Patroclus. But the death of Patroclus has also been elaborately prepared for within the narrative by a prophetic utterance of Achilles to Patroclus as he sends him into battle.

> you must not set your mind on fighting the Trojans, whose delight
> is in battle, without me. So you will diminish my honour.
> You must not, in the pride and fury of fighting, go on
> slaughtering the Trojans, and lead the way against Ilion,
> for fear some one of the everlasting gods on Olympos
> might crush you.
>
> (*Il.* 16.89–94)

One can imagine an *Iliad* without this warning, which would make Achilles's reaction to Patroclus's death less puzzling. For given that Achilles was sure of the dangers that Patroclus had to skirt in order to avoid death, why does he ask nothing about them? What is being elided here?

It is obvious that Patroclus himself, as he turns to battle in the place of Achilles, in the armor of Achilles, is close to a double of Achilles. But the doubling is not only of the body of Achilles, but of his dilemma. Specifically, it doubles the dilemma that afflicted Achilles in *Iliad* 9 as he rejected the series of gifts from Agamemnon. The gifts were rejected as the offer of a patron, with generosity masquerading as a show of power, an offer as a veiled command. So for Achilles to accept the offer was tantamount to becoming a no one, a slave. But compare this with Achilles's advice to Patroclus. He asks him not to fight too much, and the language is one of symmetry, of equality; he speaks of the diminishment of his own honor, and will try to replace that zero-sum game with the fantasy of the mass destruction of Greeks and Trojans. But Achilles envisions a fair, equal division of the heroic spoils—for them at least, if not for the corpses around them. But the problem, as with Agamemnon's offer of gifts, is how this discourse of symmetry is framed. To make use of a key question that Agamemnon once asked of Achilles: is Achilles *asking* Patroclus to do this or *telling* him? Does the command to share something equally with someone undermine the equality itself?

For Patroclus to be free, he cannot be Achilles's stooge. He must act in relative freedom from his commands, or his independence means nothing. But the moment of his actual freedom coincides with the necessity of his death, and with his betrayal of Achilles. So what Achilles elides in his speeches in Book 18, just as the narrative constantly elides

Achilles's betrayal of the Greeks, is Patroclus's betrayal of him. Not just of his command not to fight, but of his entire fantasy of their mutual carving up of Troy. Indeed, when the two will later meet in a dream, as Patroclus's shade comes to Achilles, what is most striking is the absence of truth, the illusions they cling to, what they don't tell each other.

No longer shall you and I, alive, sit apart from our other
beloved companions and make our plans, since the bitter destiny
that was given me when I was born has opened its jaws to take me.
And you, Achilleus like the gods, have your own destiny;
to be killed under the wall of the prospering Trojans.

(*Il.* 23.77–81)

Patroclus reminisces about the mutual talking and planning that they used to do, apart from other companions, and nostalgically returns to a time before the *Iliad* itself begins. He forgets his own choice of heroic death over his friendship with Achilles, and is still unaware of Achilles's secret betrayal of the Greeks, which caused his death.

I began this chapter by suggesting that neither a romantic, existentialist view of Achilles nor a historicist, culturalist one can do justice to the problems of the poem. So where does this leave us? Perhaps we might do better to see the poem as a critique of the impasses of both, as the efforts of Homeric heroes to avoid their own subjective impasses lead to ruin. So we can end this chapter with the author we started with, and Jacques Lacan's forceful, if enigmatic, critique of the enterprise of existentialism, and read it as a commentary on the dynamics of the *Iliad*.

At the end of society's historical enterprise to no longer recognize that it has any but a utilitarian function, and given the individual's anxiety faced with the concentration-camp form of the social link whose appearance seems to crown this effort, existentialism can be judged on the basis of the justifications it provides for the subjective impasses that do, indeed, result therefrom: a freedom that is never so authentically affirmed as when it is within the walls of a prison; a demand for commitment that expresses the inability of pure consciousness to overcome any situation; a voyeuristic-sadistic idealization of sexual relationships; a personality that achieves self-realization only in suicide; and a consciousness of the other that can only be satisfied by Hegelian murder.[11]

2

Comedy and Class Struggle

The *Iliad* begins with anger, but Book 1 ends with "Homeric laughter." As Zeus and Hera embark on a quarrel that mirrors the one between Achilles and Agamemnon, Hephaestus intervenes. He counsels his mother to yield to his father, and then busies himself serving wine to the gods. Presumably the clumsiness with which the lame Hephaestus performs this task makes it funny.

But among the blessed immortals uncontrollable laughter
went up as they saw Hephaistos bustling about the place.

(*Il.* 1.599–600)

ἄσβεστος δ' ἄρ' ἐνῶρτο γέλως μακάρεσσι θεοῖσιν,
ὡς ἴδον Ἥφαιστον διὰ δώματα ποιπνύοντα.

The contrast between the proliferating tears of the mortal world and the laughter of the gods is a critical commonplace. Mortals inhabit a tragic space, whereas the laughter of the gods suggests a frivolous and comic existence. The portrait of divine beings free from mortal concerns, mere spectators of the struggles of heroes, becomes a protracted, melancholy commentary on the human world and its constant backdrop of death. The gods seem to live in a world of a plenitude of pleasure, where laughter is in never-ending supply.

But there is something amiss here. For one thing, the gods are capable of far less pleasant emotions. Zeus accuses Hera of desiring to eat the Trojans raw, and her hatred is linked to the pettiest feelings of jealousy and *amour propre*. Zeus himself will make the sky rain down blood in response to the death of his son Sarpedon. Humans also laugh at crucial times in the poem. So we need to consider in more detail the kinds of laughter each world produces.

We can use as a guide the most influential modern tract on laughter, Freud's *Jokes and Their Relation to the Unconscious*. Freud's book is structured in the form of an anti-joke. Freud leads us through a discussion of the technique of jokes and the relationship of their technique to the mechanisms of the unconscious; he then offers a final attempt to relate jokes to the wider categories of the comic and the humorous. But nothing quite prepares us for the brutal brevity of the last paragraph.

For the euphoria we endeavour to reach by these means [jokes, the comic, humour] is nothing other than the mood of a period of life in which we were accustomed to deal with our psychical work in general with a small expenditure of energy—the mood of our childhood, when we were ignorant of the comic, when we were incapable of jokes, and when we had no need of humour to make us feel happy in our life.[1]

Jokes, for Freud, have a tragic context. The pleasures of the laughter only help us regain a small measure of a far greater source of pleasure that is lost forever. Humor provides just enough pleasure to give us something less than happiness and remind us of the pittance of pleasure that is our human, mortal lot. All humor becomes a form of gallows humor, as Freud drives a wedge between laughter and happiness. True happiness would have no need of laughter to prop it up. We can conjure up a lost utopian time when we simply were happy, effortlessly, whereas even humor is caught up in a process of effort, the day-to-day struggle of living up to cultural norms that exhaust us, the discontent of civilization itself. Laughter, for Freud, occurs when we unexpectedly get back a quota of mental energy that we normally expend, without knowing it, on this cultural work. In the case of jokes, wordplay releases us momentarily from the duty to make sense.

Now, one way of conceiving this utopia would be to exaggerate the pleasure of our laughter. We could think of laughter without pause, free from the kind of temporal constraints of human laughter, the temporary discharge of pleasurable energy that punctuates a more generalized sadness, before returning to silence and the absence of pleasure once more. And, as it happens, in the *Iliad* the major examples of human laughter are broken, as the momentary feeling of joy fails to overcome the poem's general feeling of doom, whereas the laughter of the gods is described as "unquenchable," with at least the suggestion of something unbroken and unending, an infinity of pleasure. The laughter of the gods goes on and on, whereas human laughter is troubled, self-conscious, necessarily attached to other experiences. Examples could include the pained laughter of the troops at the upstart Thersites as he is beaten by Odysseus in Book 2 (οἳ δὲ καὶ ἀχνύμενοί περ ἐπ' αὐτῷ ἡδὺ γέλασσαν—"even though they were troubled, they laughed at him," *Il.* 2.270; my translation) or the laughter of Hector and Andromache at the fear shown by their child, Astyanax, when he sees his father's blood-spattered helmet, before it quickly turns to tears (6.471–83).

This contrast between endless and broken laughter could be linked to another passage of the *Iliad* that explores the difference between humans and gods, as the poet contrasts his own skill with that of the Muses. For as he approaches the task of naming the ships of the Achaeans, he claims he could not do this, even if he had an unbroken voice (φωνὴ δ' ἄρρηκτος, χάλκεον δέ μοι ἦτορ ἐνείη, *Il.* 2.490). Unquenchable laughter finds its counterpart in a voice whose power is in stark contrast to the broken speech of mortals. Mortal language would thus be as necessarily fragmented and partial as mortal laughter.

The gods indulge in something actively avoided by Agamemnon and Achilles. There is little danger of laughter breaking through to release any tension there. But the contrast is thematically deeper, since a lurking motivation of Achilles, the poem suggests, is his horror of being laughed at. Let us return to Achilles in Book 1 and look in detail at the way he describes his relationship with Agamemnon.

> ['].. . and I am minded no longer
> to stay here dishonoured and pile up your wealth and your luxury.'
>
> (*Il.* 1.170–71)

> "οὐδέ σ' ὀΐω
> ἐνθάδ' ἄτιμος ἐὼν ἄφενος καὶ πλοῦτον ἀφύξειν."

Achilles refuses, literally, to "draw wealth" for Agamemnon, and makes use of a metaphor that resonates throughout the first two books. The metaphor is from drawing liquids, either water from a well or wine from a bowl for guests. In both cases, the act is a form of servile labor. His refusal of Agamemnon is embedded in the horror of becoming Agamemnon's slave, of the humiliation involved in working for another. Even more pointedly, the work is not just any kind of work but is linked to the other's immediate enjoyment—the pleasure of drinking wine, for example.

Now, the same word appears at the moment the crisis on Olympus is averted, but this time no longer as metaphor. Hera and Zeus argue, and their argument threatens to disrupt both the feast and the relationship of amity among the gods. But Hephaestus preserves the peace by doing

the very thing that Achilles refuses to do: he draws wine and serves all
the gods.

> He spoke, and the goddess of the white arms Hera smiled at him,
> and smiling she accepted the goblet out of her son's hand.
> Thereafter beginning from the left he poured drinks for the other
> gods, dipping up from the mixing bowl the sweet nectar.
>
> (*Il.* 1.595–98)

Ὣς φάτο, μείδησεν δὲ θεὰ λευκώλενος Ἥρη,
μειδήσασα δὲ παιδὸς ἐδέξατο χειρὶ κύπελλον·
αὐτὰρ ὃ τοῖς ἄλλοισι θεοῖς ἐνδέξια πᾶσιν
οἰνοχόει γλυκὺ νέκταρ ἀπὸ κρητῆρος ἀφύσσων . . .

Hephaestus's actions give retroactive meaning to Achilles's metaphor.
Whereas Achilles refuses to be a slave, and refuses to be laughed at,
Hephaestus acts as a voluntary slave, choosing to debase himself on
behalf of someone else and endure the laughter. The zero-sum game of
power so disastrously at work in the quarrel between Agamemnon and
Achilles is defused by comic theater. Hera and Zeus have their quarrel
resolved because the humiliation of giving in, eating humble pie, and
working for another is assumed by Hephaestus. Even his act of servitude is quickly generalized. He not only serves Zeus but moves on to
everyone in turn. The political implications of this are striking. Not only
is a conflict resolved, but the form of Hephaestus's actions reaffirms a
community of equals, a primitive symposium where each member is
both served in turn and also has someone to laugh at. In the case of
the human world, Achilles refuses to be placed in a comic relation to
Agamemnon, and no other mortal is willing to take his place. Nestor
comes close, but crucially chooses to hold on to his own dignity.

The final appearance of the verb *aphusso* offers one last narrative
twist. Achilles draws wine as he prays that Patroclus will first drive the
fire from the ships and then return home safely.

> Inside this lay a wrought goblet, nor did any other
> man drink the shining wine from it nor did Achilleus
> pour from it to any other god, but only Zeus father.
> He took this now out of the chest, and cleaned it with sulphur
> first, and afterwards washed it out in bright-running water,
> and washed his own hands, and poured shining wine into the goblet
> and stood in his middle forecourt and prayed, *and poured the wine*, looking
> into the sky, not unseen by Zeus who delights in the thunder . . .
>
> (*Il.* 16.225–32; italics added)

But at the moment the poem showcases Achilles's vulnerability in the depth of his feelings for Patroclus, Zeus exercises his own authority, separating his own counsel and desires from those of Achilles: he will allow Patroclus to push the Trojans back, but not to come back alive. The *peripeteia* is cruel and appropriate. Zeus, whose own will has been subordinated to the plot of Achilles and Thetis, shows his power at the moment when Achilles' manifests a desire for what will prove to be the most valuable thing of all to him: the life of Patroclus.

The emergence of laughter as the sign of a fragile peace on Olympus opens up other contrasts between the opening and closing of Book 1. The conflict in the human world is set in motion by sexual tension as a woman changes beds. On Olympus also sexual tension and infidelity threaten to spiral out of control, for the enmity of Hera toward Zeus is linked to her barely concealed jealousy of Thetis, and the favor she received from Hera's husband. But whereas on earth one woman in the wrong bed sets off a chain reaction (first Chryseis replaces Clytemnestra, then she is replaced by Briseis), in the case of Olympus the banquet ends with spouses going to bed with each other, even, and most significantly, Zeus and Hera.

> Afterwards when the light of the flaming sun went under
> they went away each one to sleep in his home where
> for each one the far-renowned strong-handed Hephaistos
> had built a house by means of his craftsmanship and cunning.
> Zeus the Olympian and lord of the lightning went to
> his own bed, where always he lay when sweet sleep came on him.
> Going up to the bed he slept and Hera of the gold throne beside him.
>
> (*Il.* 1.605–11)

> Αὐτὰρ ἐπεὶ κατέδυ λαμπρὸν φάος ἠελίοιο,
> οἳ μὲν κακκείοντες ἔβαν οἶκονδὲ ἕκαστος,
> ἧχι ἑκάστῳ δῶμα περικλυτὸς ἀμφιγυήεις
> Ἥφαιστος ποίησεν ἰδυίῃσι πραπίδεσσι·
> Ζεὺς δὲ πρὸς ὃν λέχος ἤϊ᾽ Ὀλύμπιος ἀστεροπητής,
> ἔνθα πάρος κοιμᾶθ᾽ ὅτε μιν γλυκὺς ὕπνος ἱκάνοι·
> ἔνθα καθεῦδ᾽ ἀναβάς, παρὰ δὲ χρυσόθρονος Ἥρη.

The last line splits neatly into two, opening up at first the possibility of Zeus sleeping alone on the marriage bed, only to foreclose it in the second half of the line: "and next to him was Hera of the gold throne." The break at the third foot caesura at first seems to isolate Zeus from his wife—ἔνθα καθεῦδ᾽ ἀναβάς—and then he is brought back to marital unity. Things return to normal, and whatever damage the mortal sexual entanglements of the first book cause to their world, this divine marriage continues.

So let us return to the differences between gods and mortals. Perhaps the existence of the gods is not essentially more comic and trivial than the human world. Rather, because of the contingent actions of Hephaestus, a social peace is maintained. The gods choose the peace of pleasure rather than continue with the challenge to Zeus's authority. But this peace is, in principle, perfectly conceivable for the mortal world too. Even if it is obvious that the world of divine marriages, the "exchange of women," is beset by infidelities (and the irony of Hephaestus as both the maker of marriage beds and the most infamous cuckold on Olympus drives the point home), the gods preserve the outward trappings of marital fidelity by retiring to their marriage beds. They may know that Zeus's power is arbitrary and unfair, but they choose to respect it. To return to the story of the boy who claims that the emperor has no clothes, the world of the gods is one where the tacit agreement not to challenge power holds. Divine laughter thus has a conservative function, strengthening the fictional authority of Zeus and ensuring that the social order will not change. The "unquenchable laughter" of the gods has as its counterpart the fixity of the pantheon.

Social tact, the maintenance of proper social illusions, wins out on Olympus, where no one blurts out the truth quite as readily as they do on earth. But a consequence is that even Zeus's pretensions to power run the risk of turning into a source of amusement, at least for us as we read. For laughter is a sign of the frailty of the social fictions that even the gods live by. Consider the way Zeus tries to implement the desires of Thetis and Achilles at the start of Book 2. Zeus orders a Dream to go and tell Agamemnon to marshal his troops. This simple request is not enough to guarantee that the king of gods will be understood, and so the Dream has to add to it.

> [']Keep this thought in your heart then, let not forgetfulness
> take you, after you are released from the kindly sweet slumber.'
>
> *(Il. 2.33–34)*

The tenuousness of the process of communication, under the spotlight throughout the second book, shows itself here. It will climax in the near-farcical consequences of Agamemnon's attempts to use reverse psychology to rouse his troops to war. Already the Dream realizes that even the most authoritative of divine commands might fall on deaf ears, and so has to command Agamemnon to remember. A question mark hangs over the order of the cosmos itself, since it depends on Zeus's ability to be heard and understood. We might even see significance to the poetic formula used to describe the break of day.

> Now the goddess Dawn drew close to tall Olympos
> with her message of light to Zeus and the other immortals.
>
> (*Il.* 2.48–49)

The context invites us to take literally this seeming circumlocution, "in order to speak of light to the immortals." The world is not a simple collection of natural phenomena, but thoroughly personalized, suffused with the human problem of deception. So the advent of dawn depends not only on the repetition of a natural event, but on the repetition of a speech act that up to now has worked, but need not work. What if Dawn brought her message to mortals and they didn't believe her, or they forgot what the arriving light meant, continuing mentally to slumber? The effect is the exact reverse of the customary notion that human rule should base itself on the harmony of the natural order. Because nature itself is a series of personifications, the cosmos becomes as fragile as the human world, beset by similar communicative impasses.

So the gods are more attuned to a world of social illusions, which is also one of equality under the thumb of Zeus. Then what is left of the qualitative differences between mortals and immortals? It is clear that the gods' size and strength are far greater, but this seems a difference of quantity, not quality, and even this distinction is put to the test in Book 5, where the gods and humans openly fight. The obvious remaining difference seems to be their immortality, the core truth that they do not die. But even here things are more complicated. For, we find out, the gods can die. In Book 5, when Diomedes wounds Aphrodite and she returns to Olympus for treatment, her mother comforts her, reflecting on the general vulnerability of the immortals.

> Ares had to endure it when strong Ephialtes and Otos,
> sons of Aloeus, chained him in bonds that were too strong for him,
> and three months and ten he lay chained in the brazen cauldron;
> and now might Ares, insatiable of fighting, have perished,
> had not Eëriboia, their stepmother, the surpassingly lovely,
> brought word to Hermes, who stole Ares away out of it
> as he was growing faint and the hard bondage was breaking him.
>
> (*Il.* 5.385–91)

This story offers an extraordinary rejoinder to something we take for granted in the poem, and perhaps for that reason it drew a good deal of attention in antiquity.[2] But rather than isolate this story from the main narrative, as if it were a bizarre invention of a poet prone to flights of fancy, we could see it as evidence of another illusion of the gods: that they are immortal at all. This would hint at a tragic backdrop to their apparent comedy. The gods would live their lives in "as if" mode. They know that their leader is vulnerable, but act as if his power is absolute. They know that their marriages are beset by infidelities, and yet go to bed together. Finally, they act as if they will never die, though at least one story suggests that they can experience something akin to the empty, feeble form of existence that characterizes mortals in Hades. In contrast, the world of mortals is one where difficult truths keep breaking through: the knowledge of the emptiness of social rituals, of the lack of any final justification for the social order. Husbands and wives are unfaithful, but rather than ignore it, they fight wars. They know their leaders are incompetent, but rather than bury this knowledge in the name of social peace, they split the social fabric in two and produce strife. Finally, rather than taking part in a general, social feast, they eat apart, and eating itself becomes a source of competition and social friction. Hephaestus serves all the gods, and yet Odysseus will eat separately with both Agamemnon and Achilles over the course of a few hours in Book 9.

So the comic world of the gods should be reevaluated. It is not the absence of death that makes their world comic. Rather, the constraints of comedy are reflected back into themselves, so that they keep pushing the limits of their comic universe yet fail to puncture it: they try to quarrel, to disrupt the hierarchy of power, even to kill and be killed, but seem curiously unable to succeed. Their entire world is a form of comic theater in its denial of the social fissures that appear all around them. But far from being a source of relief, the story suggests that their lives are hamstrung by this lack of meaning, as if they are gesturing toward another world to which they can have no true access. They may seem to be purely aesthetic spectators of human struggles, but these become a blueprint for the only forms of meaning that they themselves can have.

Laughter and Social Cohesion

The tragedy of Achilles is linked to the comedy of Hephaestus by what they will and will not do. But the laughter at Hephaestus is revisited, and complicated, in Book 2. Thersites, the lame, ugly mortal who provokes laughter and provides the social cohesion necessary for the Greek mission to take Troy, is a composite figure. A double of Hephaestus, the lame, ugly god whose marriage to Aphrodite is destroyed by her infidelity with the more physically attractive Ares, he also duplicates Achilles, since his exhortation to the Greeks to go home universalizes Achilles's statement in Book 1 that he will leave Troy. The Thersites episode can be seen as another instance of a more general, bathetic technique we encountered in *Iliad* 10. For just as Dolon is a cruder, caricatured version of Achilles, providing a biting commentary on the sublimity of the acts that went before, so Thersites is a comic, blunter Achilles. In Freudian terms, our laughter arises from the ease with which we understand these "simpler" characters, without any need to pay attention to the difficult, brain-troubling sublimity of what went before.[3]

But though Thersites does provide social cohesion, unlike Hephaestus he does so unwillingly. So the poet of the *Iliad* offers up an answer, albeit a temporary and unsatisfactory one, to the challenge to authority brought to the fore by Achilles. If the Greeks cannot make Achilles obey, they can force Thersites to obey. One thinks of the comic story related by Freud. There is a "Hungarian village in which the blacksmith had been guilty of a capital offence. The burgomaster, however, decided that as a penalty a *tailor* should be hanged and not the blacksmith, because there were two tailors in the village but no second blacksmith, and the crime must be expiated."[4] In Book 1, the challenge to Zeus's authority is saved, but only through Hephaestus. Here Agamemnon will indirectly retain power through the intervention of Odysseus. In both cases, the fragility of power is put on display: were it not for the intervention, it is entirely unclear what would have happened. In both cases the poem shows that an indirect propping up of power is necessary for it to continue to function. But the resistance of Thersites to this project, and the mixed reaction of the troops, suggests that maintaining power in the mortal world is far messier.

Thersites repeats the sentiment of Achilles: why not go home? But the timing of his intervention is doubly inappropriate. First, the chance of a *nostos* has already disappeared, preempted by Odysseus when he stopped the march to the ships. Even the repetition of Achilles's arguments is now senseless; authority has already been restored. Agamemnon takes control not through what he says in the argument of Book 1, but in what he does. When faced with Achilles's challenge, he gives orders to others and immediately sets in motion a communal sacrifice. When Thersites returns to Achilles's challenge against authority, the remnants of anger against the leader will be displaced onto the comic upstart. But, once again, the scene reminds us of a more fundamental displacement.

[']And now he has dishonoured Achilleus, a man much better
than he is. He has taken his prize by force and keeps her.
But there is no gall in Achilleus' heart, and he is forgiving.
Otherwise, son of Atreus, this were your last outrage.'

(*Il.* 2.239–42)

"ὃς καὶ νῦν Ἀχιλῆα, ἕο μέγ' ἀμείνονα φῶτα,
ἠτίμησεν· ἑλὼν γὰρ ἔχει γέρας, αὐτὸς ἀπούρας.
ἀλλὰ μάλ' οὐκ Ἀχιλῆϊ χόλος φρεσίν, ἀλλὰ μεθήμων·
ἦ γὰρ ἄν, Ἀτρεΐδη, νῦν ὕστατα λωβήσαιο."

We return to the diverted *cholos* of *Iliad* 1, where the attempt to kill Agamemnon directly was averted by Athena and Hera. But Achilles's anger was not so much avoided as, instead, turned onto the Greeks. In a reversal of the usual logic of scapegoats, in the *Iliad* the many will pay for the frustrated anger of the one; at first, the troops pay for Agamemnon's anger against a priest, and now they will pay for the unresolved *cholos* of Achilles. In Book 2 this logic is belatedly translated into the logic of the scapegoat. Here, someone must pay for the challenge to Agamemnon's authority, because Achilles has not killed Agamemnon, and Agamemnon chooses not to face him down. But for the masses of the Greek army, traces of the antagonism remain. They can be seen objectively in Achilles's absence, and remembered in the catalogue of ships soon to come. He remains an anomalous figure. He is not part of the catalogue and yet is too important to be ignored. But those traces can also be seen subjectively, especially in the ambivalence the troops feel toward the beating of Thersites, and the loss of a return home that it represents.

The Thersites episode also retroactively comments on the unquenchable laughter of the gods in Book 1. Their laughter is now linked to their own impotence. They too laugh at someone who is linked to political resistance to power, and whose limbs bear signs of that failure. For Hephaestus is quick to remind the gods of the failure of his previous challenge to divine authority, and the way Zeus hurled him from the heavens by the foot (*Il.* 1.590–94). They laugh at the moment something disappears from their world, the possibility of a challenge to Zeus, and thus laugh as they accept their own subordination. Their past is less forgotten than repressed, and this allows them to remain happy and subordinate. The human laughter is "troubled," broken, and points toward the possibility of freedom from the rule of Agamemnon that ties the Greeks to Troy. For all the claustrophobia of the battle on the plain, human life is sustained by the ongoing possibility of another place: a return home, for the Greeks, and a return to their past life of peace for the Trojans. But for the gods, there is no other place.

Comic Ugliness, Tragic Beauty

A common way of understanding the laughter in both these episodes is that it is the "laughter of superiority."[5] Thersites, whether of aristocratic birth or not, exhibits unseemly features, and the laughter is part of the aggression and arrogance of a warrior elite, the disdain of the beautiful for the ugly.

This was the ugliest man who came beneath Ilion. He was
bandy-legged and went lame of one foot, with shoulders
stooped and drawn together over his chest, and above this
his skull went up to a point with the wool grown sparsely upon it.

(*Il.* 2.216–19)

Just as the gods laugh at the clumsiness on display in the movements of Hephaestus, so Thersites's ugliness, an affront to an aristocratic ideology that equates moral worth with physical beauty, provokes the laughter of the troops. The laughter is enhanced, as in tendentious jokes, by the presence of sadistic desires, the troops' enjoyment of the pain of others. But because this sadism is linked to the cultural norms of a particular class, and therefore the perceived cultural deficiencies of any who do not meet these norms, the laughter has a conservative effect, policing the boundaries between mass and elite, reinforcing a specific sense of elite self even as it banishes those who do not live up to it. This is close to the going critical line on the Thersites episode, and debate has largely focused on whether the poet endorses such laughter of superiority or has a more distanced and complex attitude to it. It would be foolish to deny the power of this way of interpreting the episode. But there are other things to be said.

When the gods laugh at Hephaestus, they laugh at the obviousness of his body, the inelegance of the movements that draw attention to it. They are laughing, as we would, at the rigidity on display in serving wine with a limp. In the terms of another theory of laughter, Hephaestus's movements seem mechanical, the "mechanical encrusted onto the living" in Henri Bergson's phrase. The normal flexibility we expect from the human creature has been lost. But it is not the act itself that counts. Hephaestus's body refuses to act according to our preconceptions and instead becomes obvious, out of joint with its surroundings. Freud took these insights a step further by suggesting that we cannot help but empathize with what we see, so that we automatically compare the amount of effort exerted by the unfortunate victim to the effort that we could save were we in his place. The difference in expenditure of energy that we imagine using and so "save" becomes the source of our laughter.

This already goes beyond the "laughter of superiority" thesis. For we laugh at the clumsiness of the body as such, even as we know that we could do no differently. If we laugh as someone falls down a hole in the road by mistake, it does not mean that we could avoid the hole, or that any blame is attached to this victim of circumstance. But we still laugh. Laughter seems to coincide with the emergence of the body *qua* body, an unexpected appearance of our all-too-physical selves. It draws our attention to the cultural work we do in order to keep our body invisible, camouflaged by the normality that allows it to fit into its cultural surroundings. Indeed the crucial narrative reversal for Thersites comes when he fails to keep his body invisible. Though he wants to provoke the others' laughter, he does so in an unexpected way.

[Thersites] who knew within his head many words, but disorderly;
vain, and without decency, to quarrel with the princes
with any word he thought might be amusing to the Argives.

                                                    (*Il.* 2.213–15)

Thersites looks to find a verbal object that will make the Argives laugh. But when they laugh, it will be at him as a physical object, not at anything he says. The narrative seems to test the limits of the desires it imputes to Thersites. If he is willing to offer anything that is funny for the Argives, this will not include his own beaten body, now an instrument of others' desires. Thersites, at the episode's end, can no longer think of himself as a comic wordsmith, however imperfectly crafted and "unmeasured" those words might be. He is also a thing, an object of amusement. Yet even here, as he suffers his punishment at the hands of Odysseus, the poem sets a limit on Thersites's degradation.

['I]f once more I find you playing the fool as you are now,
nevermore let the head of Odysseus sit on his shoulders,

let me nevermore be called Telemachos' father,
if I do not take you and strip away your personal clothing,
your mantle and your tunic that cover over your nakedness,
and send you thus bare and howling back to the fast ships,
whipping you out of the assembly place with the strokes of indignity.'

(Il. 2.258–64)

This most shameless of braggarts is terrified at the prospect of his own nakedness, and feels a deep-seated shame at his own body. Odysseus will allow him to preserve some sense of self by not physically defrocking him, but only threatening to, as if his nudity would complete his abjection and make a return to the community impossible.

So what is lost, in any emphasis on the ugliness of Thersites's body, or his upstart status, is the way that he turns out to be fundamentally attached to his cultural clothing. His shamelessness has a limit. In the final tally, Thersites is less of a rebel than he thinks, and well attuned to the taboos of the social world. This dynamic spills over into how he is presented to us. For we too come to the brink of seeing Thersites as a thing, only to be spared this sight. Consider what happens after the laughter. Liberated from the hypocrisies of the social world for a moment, we return to them. Odysseus engineers both the laughter and the return to normality. But not before we have the flicker of an image of a human existing, as it were, before culture, a helpless, naked, vulnerable thing stripped of any cultural support, an image too sobering for laughter.

The length of the physical description of Thersites is worth lingering over. In general the *Iliad* delights in the physical details of the bodily deformation of its heroes, and is almost silent about beauty. We know, for example, that Achilles and Helen are the most beautiful, and that Nireus is second most beautiful after Achilles (*Il.* 2.673–74), but we are hard-pressed to find out what this beauty might consist in. Ugliness is not just a quality of the body but one that disrupts the normal invisibility of the body, whereas beauty is closer to a surface veneer that makes us forget that we have a body at all. It is the most perfect of illusions and sustains itself in silence, while ugliness, because it sticks out, provokes description.

When beauty does become visible, it is at the most tragic moments. Let us return to the body of Achilles. Only after the death of Patroclus does his body become a source of narrative interest. He first becomes aware, retroactively, of his body as inert matter, a "useless burden" on the earth as his comrades fought without him. The useless objectivity of the body has taken over his entire self. But when his body becomes reactivated in heroic struggle after Patroclus's death, and he is aware of his own impending doom, his relationship to his body changes. Consider these words to the suppliant Lycaon, whom he will soon brutally kill.

So, friend, you die also. Why all this clamour about it?
Patroklos also is dead, who was better by far than you are.
Do you not see what a man I am, how huge, how splendid
and born of a great father, and the mother who bore me immortal?
Yet even I have also my death and my strong destiny . . .

(*Il.* 21.106–10)

He comments on his beauty at the moment it is under erasure, the power of its surface appearance linked to its imminent disappearance. The poem seems to link the appearance of beauty to cosmic destruction throughout. The elders on the walls of Troy comment on Helen's beauty (*Il.* 3.155), but they tie it to the destruction she causes. When Achilles dreams that he and Patroclus will destroy the Greek and Trojan worlds, he offers an erotic image even for this. The taking of Troy will be an "unveiling" (*Il.* 16.100), a destructive rape.

Perhaps the impermanence of beauty renders its presence all the more tragic. We could link this twinning of tragedy and beauty with the thesis of Jean-Pierre Vernant about the poem's obsession with a "beautiful death."[6] For Vernant, the urge to die at the physical acme of one's life is already a desire to transmit a perfect image of oneself to eternity, the bodily correlative of the heroic belief in the need for "undying glory." Attempts to defile a corpse try to undo this cultural logic. But the reverse process is just as true. The specter of cosmic destruction not merely enhances but creates what is beautiful. So our awareness of the body's impermanence is essential for a beauty-effect. Beauty itself becomes twinned with death, but is also a last defense against its emergence, a way of keeping the nullity of our cultural fictions at bay.

Jokes and Riddles

So far we have discussed the poem's representation of laughter, and the reaction of characters within the poem to laughter. But does the poem itself make us laugh? If the *Iliad* has riddles, does it have any jokes? We can begin the search by tracing the differences between a joke and a riddle. It is a difference of degree, not kind. They both deceive. A riddle uses enigmatic language to shake up our normal ways of thinking about the world. It makes no sense, yet it suggests that there is another kind of sense to be found, even if it will take intellectual work. A joke sets up a similar difficulty, but, as Kant put it, "it deceives us only for a moment." The shortness of time and the obviousness of the solution make us laugh, as does the detour through the lost "pleasure in nonsense" of our childhood; we temporarily regress to a more pleasurable past. If the joke needs to be explained, laughter disappears. The amount of energy we expect to expend in working out a riddle's solution is, in the case of a joke, almost immediately released, and laughter is just this sudden discharge of excess energy. Jokes are understood precipitously, without effort, and this provides the laughter, whereas riddles, as a rule, are understood too late, after too much wasted effort, and this gives them an air of tragedy. By the time Croesus realizes that the kingdom referred to in the oracle is his own, his kingdom is gone. Let me offer an example of how this process might be at work in the *Iliad*. In Book 3 Menelaus proposes a duel with Paris in part in order to end the madness of collective suffering. Before they meet in combat, he prays to Zeus.

'Zeus, lord, grant me to punish the man who first did me injury,
brilliant Alexandros, and beat him down under my hands' strength
that any one of the men to come may shudder to think of
doing evil to a kindly host, who has given him friendship.'

(Il. 3.351–54)

"Ζεῦ ἄνα, δὸς τείσασθαι ὅ με πρότερος κάκ' ἔοργε,
δῖον Ἀλέξανδρον, καὶ ἐμῇς ὑπὸ χερσὶ δάμασσον,
ὄφρα τις ἐρρίγῃσι καὶ ὀψιγόνων ἀνθρώπων
ξεινοδόκον κακὰ ῥέξαι, ὅ κεν φιλότητα παράσχῃ."

Menelaus's sentiment would be straightforward, except that the entire book will revolve around the slippage of meaning of the term "friendship," *philotes*, from guest-friends to blood-relatives to sexual partners. Later, Paris will be snatched away by the goddess Aphrodite just as Menelaus is about to kill him, and the martial duel will be replaced by a different kind of duel with Helen: "Come, then, rather let us go to bed and turn to love-making" (*Il.* 3.441), where once more *philotes* is used. We could see discrete meanings of *philotes* at work in the text, first signifying friendship, later sex. But if we read the ambiguity as working from the beginning, the poem generates near farce. Menelaus complains that the Trojans behaved badly by abusing the "friendship" he offered. But perhaps Paris understood his offer only too well. Menelaus makes a blundering pun at his own expense, offering us a vignette of the foolish husband who helpfully organizes his own cuckolding.

This phrase, with its association with the limits of Menelaus's generosity, is picked up later. Menelaus has just killed the Trojan Peisandrus, and he uses his death to return to the problem of Helen.

'So, I think, shall you leave the ships of the fast-mounted Danaans,
you haughty Trojans, never to be glutted with the grim war noises,
nor go short of all that other shame and defilement
wherewith you defiled me, wretched dogs, and your hearts knew no fear
at all of the hard anger of Zeus loud-thundering,
the guest's god, who some day will utterly sack your steep city.
You who in vanity went away taking with you my wedded
wife, and many possessions, when she had received you in kindness.[']

(Il. 13.620–27)

"λείψετέ θην οὕτω γε νέας Δαναῶν ταχυπώλων,
Τρῶες ὑπερφίαλοι, δεινῆς ἀκόρητοι ἀϋτῆς,
ἄλλης μὲν λώβης τε καὶ αἴσχεος οὐκ ἐπιδευεῖς,
ἣν ἐμὲ λωβήσασθε κακαὶ κύνες, οὐδέ τι θυμῷ
Ζηνὸς ἐριβρεμέτεω χαλεπὴν ἐδείσατε μῆνιν
ξεινίου, ὅς τέ ποτ' ὕμμι διαφθέρσει πόλιν αἰπήν·
οἵ μευ κουριδίην ἄλοχον καὶ κτήματα πολλὰ
μὰψ οἴχεσθ' ἀνάγοντες, ἐπεὶ φιλέεσθε παρ' αὐτῇ."

The speech offers a fitting denouement to Menelaus's failure in Book 3. Now, after the duel, all Trojans are linked by association to the crime of Paris, and so become part of a series of generalizing second person plurals. But Menelaus is hardly in control of his own rhetoric. The problem lies in the last phrase, ἐπεὶ φιλέεσθε παρ' αὐτῇ, which Lattimore translates as "received you in kindness." The Greek has enough ambiguity to demand a somewhat defensive clarification from Walter Leaf: "φιλέεσθε, *were entertained*, as 3.207, 3.354, 6.15, etc. The gravamen of the offence lay in the outrage on the laws of hospitality."[7] The difficulty lies in working out exactly what kind of *philotes* was on offer from Helen, and how many were the beneficiaries. Menelaus's naive foolishness is multiplied, and the problem that the proposed duel tried to redress, the tragic imbalance of the suffering of the many for one, is again given a bathetic twist in the crudest of innuendos. Laughs at his own expense are, in the case of Menelaus, potentially never-ending.

The Comedy of War

Menelaus's attempt to resolve the troubled mathematics of the Trojan War is part of a wider problem of counting and classification that recurs throughout the poem. It is the central theme of Book 2, culminating in the vast intellectual effort of cataloguing the ships. But this epic feat of memory also flirts with the ridiculous. Consider the way Agamemnon urges his men to return to Greece. Agamemnon has just told the leaders, in a private gathering, of the dream from Zeus that has promised that he will take Troy. But rather than inform the troops directly, he decides to test them by suggesting that they go home. He hopes his reverse psychology will result in their demand to stay. His words return us to Achilles and his statement that he will flee Troy rather than be Agamemnon's slave.

And this shall be a thing of shame for the men hereafter
to be told, that so strong, so great a host of Achaians
carried on and fought in vain a war that was useless
against men fewer than they, with no accomplishment shown for it;
since if both sides were to be willing, Achaians and Trojans,
to cut faithful oaths of truce, and both to be numbered,
and the Trojans were to be counted by those with homes in the city,
while we were to be allotted in tens, we Achaians,
and each one of our tens chose a man of Troy to pour wine for it,
still there would be many tens left without a wine steward.
By so much I claim we sons of the Achaians outnumber
the Trojans—those who live in the city . . .

(*Il.* 2.119–30)

αἰσχρὸν γὰρ τόδε γ' ἐστὶ καὶ ἐσσομένοισι πυθέσθαι,
μὰψ οὕτω τοιόνδε τοσόνδε τε λαὸν Ἀχαιῶν
ἄπρηκτον πόλεμον πολεμίζειν ἠδὲ μάχεσθαι
ἀνδράσι παυροτέροισι, τέλος δ' οὔ πώ τι πέφανται·
εἴ περ γάρ κ' ἐθέλοιμεν Ἀχαιοί τε Τρῶές τε,
ὅρκια πιστὰ ταμόντες ἀριθμηθήμεναι ἄμφω,
Τρῶας μὲν λέξασθαι ἐφέστιοι ὅσσοι ἔασιν,
ἡμεῖς δ' ἐς δεκάδας διακοσμηθεῖμεν Ἀχαιοί,
Τρώων δ' ἄνδρα ἕκαστοι ἑλοίμεθα οἰνοχοεύειν,
πολλαί κεν δεκάδες δευοίατο οἰνοχόοιο.
τόσσον ἐγώ φημι πλέας ἔμμεναι υἷας Ἀχαιῶν
Τρώων, οἳ ναίουσι κατὰ πτόλιν . . .

Agamemnon outlines the shame of return in almost too much detail for his overall purpose. He imagines Trojan subservience in terms of wine serving. At the moment he narrates the difference in numbers between Greeks and Trojans, and reflects upon the strange failure of the rules of mathematics to apply to the current situation, his language returns us to the absence of Achilles, the Achaean who earlier refused to serve wine to Agamemnon. His words themselves provide an answer to his dilemma: the Trojans will not be slaves until a certain Greek will be a slave to Agamemnon. Agamemnon's discourse of numbers seems equally weighty, as he enumerates the troops of both sides to highlight the embarrassment of his current impasse. He previews the epic feat of memory that requires the help of the Muses, the catalogue of ships, an account that will also linger over the absence of Achilles. But a surprise comes in the way Agamemnon's counting ends.

> . . . but there are companions
> from other cities in their numbers, wielders of the spear, to help them,
> who drive me hard back again and will not allow me,
> despite my will, to sack the well-founded stronghold of Ilion.

(Il. 2.130–33)

> ἀλλ᾽ ἐπίκουροι
> πολλέων ἐκ πολίων ἐγχέσπαλοι ἄνδρες ἔασιν,
> οἵ με μέγα πλάζουσι καὶ οὐκ εἰῶσ᾽ ἐθέλοντα
> Ἰλίου ἐκπέρσαι εὖ ναιόμενον πτολίεθρον.

The Trojans have friends! This undermines all that has gone before, nullifying the embarrassing superiority of Achaean manpower. There are separate strains of defeated expectation here. First, the attempt to make the numbers add up runs into the comic knowledge that this is an impossible enterprise: those counted annoyingly refuse to remain stable; their numbers change. There is something petulant lurking in Agamemnon's footnote to the war's mathematics. Or perhaps the comedy is of the naïve sort, the amusement of the inappropriateness of the commander's failure to understand, which is in turn linked to a child-like refusal to understand how such a person could ever lose in the first place. In turn, we laugh at this inappropriateness. It shows Agamemnon's megalomaniacal narcissism, as he acts as if the mass of Trojans and their allies had gathered not to defend their city and families, but purely to frustrate him. A motif set up in the first book, the transfer of individual emotional suffering to collective physical suffering, is reversed here. In the first book, the priest Chryses demanded that Apollo make the Achaeans pay for his tears with their deaths, and the arrows of the plague became representatives of his tears. Here, Agamemnon acts as if the mass of Trojans and allies is assembled purely to make him feel perplexity, an ongoing affront to his ability to compute the permutations of war.

The poet of *Iliad* 2 is both in awe of the ability to count completely and willing to make a joke out of the absurdity of thinking, stuck in the human world of eternal flux, that one ever could. Yet to fail to try is also a possible source of amusement. The Trojan Glaucus and the Greek Diomedes meet on the battlefield in Book 6, and after a verbal exchange that is the usual precursor to a fight, they find out that their grandfathers were guest-friends. Instead of fighting, they agree to exchange gifts of armor. But in stark contrast to the emotion of their family reunion, the poet ends the interchange by remarking on the madness of Glaucus, who "exchanged gold for bronze," a line that will soon become proverbial for a bad exchange.

but Zeus the son of Kronos stole away the wits of Glaukos
who exchanged with Diomedes the son of Tydeus armour
of gold for bronze, for nine oxen's worth the worth of a hundred.

(Il. 6.234–36)

Once more any confidence that numbers could provide a sure assessment of value is comically deflated, but with a different cause. These warriors are unwittingly nostalgic and return to a world of gift exchange where the worth of the object depends on the closed orbit of its circulation between aristocratic friends and its attachment to a genealogy— not its market worth. To attempt to impose a number on the worth of this exchange would involve placing a value on Diomedes's feelings for his absent father, unknown to him since childhood, who therefore lives only in these stories of hospitality and friendship. Such an attempt would be hopelessly reductive. And this is surely part of the point. To impose the logic of market worth on armor in this exchange is absurd, just as emotions are not so easily measured. Here again, a serious point is being made through the joke. To immerse oneself in one's own world of meaning is to risk a dangerous isolation from the changing nature of the world around one, in this case the world of the market, where gold is worth more than bronze. But, on the other hand, the source of the humor comes from the recognition of the immense, invisible labor involved in maintaining family and social ties. The laughter that escapes from us at the thought of the silliness of reducing the complexity of this story to "gold for bronze" is a sign of a certain relief, a break from the pressures of civilization.

The tragic logic of the "many for the one" can also take a comic turn, and here we might see Homeric comedy commenting on the futility of war. Let us return to the exchange between Agamemnon and Achilles in the first book. With hindsight, there is the outline of a comedy of errors, as Achilles and Agamemnon fight over whether Achilles should go home, and we leave Achilles on the brink. The gathering, dispersal, and then re-gathering of the troops in Book 2 showcase an expanded version of Achilles's indecision. The vacillation is transferred to Agamemnon, but now an impasse occurs because we know that his request is ironic: he tells them to flee but does not mean it. The mass of Achaeans act out this ambiguity, at first rushing for the ships to go home, only to be pulled back again by Odysseus. Here, the vastness of the scale of events amuses, as an individual's dilemma is writ large on the movements of the masses he orders about, and with a gargantuan inefficiency. To have one man nearly go home, and orchestrate the suffering of others through his indecision, is a tragedy. To have another man know what he wants but have his desires appear inscrutable to those outside him, and as a consequence have an entire army rush hither and thither to the ships and back, is farce. One feature of the comic, as we saw on the individual level with the clumsiness of Thersites and Hephaestus, is the inflexibility of the person, the gap between the energy we know should be required to perform a task and the energy actually expended. Here, the troops' colossal waste of energy suggests a comic critique of the war that Homer tells us about, and perhaps of war as such. Is not this vast marshaling of human resources in order to solve a problem of the messiness of human emotional entanglements the ultimate form of comic farce, the most spectacular example of clumsiness?

3

The Politics of Poetry

A well-known and puzzling detail about the shield of Achilles is that it has no boss. For all the worries about its shape and the relationship of this object put together by Hephaestus to either historical shields or shields depicted elsewhere within the *Iliad*, much more striking is the absence of this central identifying feature. We are told of the shield's folds, its outer rim, and the shield-strap. We are told of the metals that Hephaestus will use to make it. But the description of its materials and accoutrements runs alongside the failure to mention its navel, *omphalos*, and the customary epithet of shields, *amphaloessai* is absent. If this is not a contingent, empty detail, then the immediate consequence is that this most fearful of objects, made by the god of fire, and soon to be party to the havoc Achilles wreaks on the Trojans, is itself fragile, held together by nothing. It is an object in suspense.

This banausic balancing act spills over into the acts depicted on the shield itself. In a city, a man on trial for manslaughter awaits a verdict. He is surrounded by a group of elders. Two talents of gold lie in the center.

and between them lay on the ground two talents of gold, to be given to that judge who in this case spoke the straightest opinion.

(Il. 18.507–8)

κεῖτο δ᾽ ἄρ᾽ ἐν μέσσοισι δύω χρυσοῖο τάλαντα,
τῷ δόμεν ὃς μετὰ τοῖσι δίκην ἰθύντατα εἴποι.

The phrase "two talents" is a verbal balancing act, caught between its obvious meaning as the material prize for the best judgment and the more usual meaning of a pair of scales, often balanced by Zeus before a judgment of life or death, most famously when he balances the scales to determine the death of Achilles or Hector (*Il.* 22.209–13). Their appearance doubles the narrative uncertainty of what this death might mean. The shield's construction delays the return of Achilles, leaving us unsure of how, even whether, the contours of his fantasies of destruction will be realized. The narrative suspense fades into a wider sense of cosmic suspense. For the power of Achilles's anger will disturb the cosmos, creating an elemental battle between fire and water that reveals the fragility of the world.

That the absence of the boss matters is suggested by the first details we are given of Hephaestus's artwork. Hephaestus first depicts heavenly bodies and ends with the depiction of the Ocean, a circle of surrounding water that is identified with the shield's outermost ring. So, tentatively, we can imagine him working outward, from inner to outer rings on the shield. As if to confirm this, Homer's description of the heavenly bodies near the center of the shield anticipates the outer ring.

> He made the earth upon it, and the sky, and the sea's water,
> and the tireless sun, and the moon waxing into her fullness,
> and on it all the constellations that festoon the heavens,
> the Pleiades and the Hyades and the strength of Orion
> and the Bear, whom men give also the name of the Wagon,
> who turns about in a fixed place and looks at Orion
> and she alone is never plunged in the wash of the Ocean.
>
> (*Il.* 18.483–89)

> Ἐν μὲν γαῖαν ἔτευξ᾽, ἐν δ᾽ οὐρανόν, ἐν δὲ θάλασσαν,
> ἠέλιόν τ᾽ ἀκάμαντα σελήνην τε πλήθουσαν,
> ἐν δὲ τὰ τείρεα πάντα, τά τ᾽ οὐρανὸς ἐστεφάνωται,
> Πληϊάδας θ᾽ Ὑάδας τε τό τε σθένος Ὠρίωνος
> Ἄρκτόν θ᾽, ἣν καὶ Ἄμαξαν ἐπίκλησιν καλέουσιν,
> ἥ τ᾽ αὐτοῦ στρέφεται καί τ᾽ Ὠρίωνα δοκεύει,
> οἴη δ᾽ ἄμμορός ἐστι λοετρῶν Ὠκεανοῖο.

In the beginning we have sea, heaven, earth, followed by the constellations. But particular attention is paid to a circumpolar constellation, *Arctos*, the Bear, which turns around an empty place in the sky, αὐτοῦ στρέφεται, and has no share in the Ocean. What seems to be a statement about a discrete object depicted on the shield is doubled as a principle of construction of the shield itself. Just as there is one constellation that never descends into the Ocean, so too there is one part of the center of the shield that will always remain separate from the outer circle that doubles as the waters of the Ocean—and therefore inside never collapses into outside. Now we know more about what holds the shield together. It is held together not by a boss, but by a principle of artistic order, a circling motion around a void that has an uneasy permanence, and that separates itself from the waters that threaten to engulf it. A consequence is that all the other elements are not discrete but are linked both to the Ocean and to each other. In the terms of the theory of Heraclitus that "all is flux," we could say that all is in flux on the shield, with the exception of one element, this constellation, and because of this constellation we can see order in the ways in which other elements flow into each other. Homer's failure to describe the boss finds its analogue in the motion of the stars at the shield's center. Just as Arctos circles not a thing but an imaginary point in the sky, so too the shield is constructed in circles around an empty space where we expect the boss to be.

The Shield's Logic of Metaphor and Metonymy

So this cosmic detail of the constellation Arctos has further significance for the construction of the shield, linking the ocean as water surrounding the earth and the Ocean as the outer rim of the shield. In providing this detail, Homer gives us an invitation to think metaphorically. A condition necessary for the existence of metaphor is the autonomy of the separate spheres that metaphor brings together. If Hephaestus is a demiurge of sorts, the craftsman's harmony in his construction mirroring the harmony of the cosmos, then craft and art must have relatively autonomous existences in order for one to be able to be grafted onto the other, and new meaning to be produced. Here, a detail from the real world, the failure of Arctos to set, shows both the separation of shield from world and also the way they overlap, one offering an allegory for the other. The single word "ocean" acts as a hinge, a verbal button joining two conceptually separate realms. If from one perspective Hephaestus creates the shield from nothing, from another his representation of Arctos not falling into the ocean suggests a moment when a cosmic principle of creation rules him, when he stumbles upon a primal rule necessary for the construction of a crafted object at all.

This principle of artistic order is picked up later in the poem, but the change of context suggests a further fading from the cosmic realm into the world of political authority. In Book 20, when Zeus demands a council of the gods, Ocean once more remains on the fringes.

But Zeus, from the many-folded peak of Olympos,
told Themis to summon all the gods into assembly. She went
everywhere, and told them to make their way to Zeus' house.
There was no river who was not there, except only Ocean . . .

(Il. 20.4–7)

Ζεὺς δὲ Θέμιστα κέλευσε θεοὺς ἀγορήνδε καλέσσαι
κρατὸς ἀπ' Οὐλύμποιο πολυπτύχου· ἣ δ' ἄρα πάντῃ
φοιτήσασα κέλευσε Διὸς πρὸς δῶμα νέεσθαι.
οὔτέ τις οὖν ποταμῶν ἀπέην, νόσφ' Ὠκεανοῖο . . .

If Ocean were present, all would indeed be flux. Note the way the absence of Ocean comments on the limits of what can reasonably be nar-
rated, a further suggestion that Hephaestus's activity in making the
shield is a window into wider principles obeyed by the imagined Homeric world, even if characters within this order (in this case, Zeus) remain unaware of it, and thus in constant danger of disrupting it. One can
imagine personified rivers, and the order of Homer's narrative stays in
place, but not the presence of the vastness of Ocean itself, which would
drag the material reality of the mass of water with it. We should also
notice another failure of Zeus's authority. We see a limit to his power
in the constraints the cosmos itself imposes on what he wants. Ocean's
absence is a necessary condition upon which he can order about, make
absent or present, the rest of the gods.

The fragility of both object and cosmos is picked up in the final image
we are left with before the shield is completed by the addition of the
Ocean. The scene is of men and women dancing, and the speed of their
feet is likened to the work of a potter.

At whiles on their understanding feet they would run very lightly,
as when a potter crouching makes trial of his wheel, holding
it close in his hands, to see if it will run smooth.

(Il. 18.599–601)

οἱ δ' ὁτὲ μὲν θρέξασκον ἐπισταμένοισι πόδεσσι
ῥεῖα μάλ', ὡς ὅτε τις τροχὸν ἄρμενον ἐν παλάμῃσιν
ἑζόμενος κεραμεὺς πειρήσεται, αἴ κε θέῃσιν.

The shield's final simile shows us the creation of another object that has
no center, though now a three-dimensional object whose manufacture
involves the creation of an empty space. If this is a further commentary
on the lack of a boss in the shield, the fragility of the object is now lingered over. The poet focuses on the moment of truth, when the object

will either stand or collapse. How can a shield, or a world, an object in suspense, hold together without a center? Just as a work of art is held together, by a kind of unexpected miracle, a θαῦμα, an event that could just as likely not have occurred. Part of the force of this simile is the suggestion that the status of the shield itself remains up in the air.

We can see the contours of an artistic manifesto in this simile. Art becomes successful only when it breaks its ties to the author, when it comes into being all at once, miraculously self-sufficient: the object must run, or fail to run, on its own, without any sign of the potter as efficient cause of its motion. To find, say, the marks of the author's handprints on a pot shows the object's lack of autonomy, its ugliness rather than its beauty. It is to lose part of the wonder of our incomprehension at the object's creation, itself filtered through our knowledge of its transience. The maker of the pot finds himself in the same situation as the viewer of the artwork: there is no secret knowledge of a creator that might help explain such an artwork to a viewer. We do not have the wonder of the audience at a conjuring trick whose secret is known to the magician, for the uncertainty also belongs to the artist. We might reverse the cliché of *ars longa, vita brevis*. The wonder of this object is the way it hovers over its non-being and flirts with complete collapse. Its power is not just in its aspirations to eternity, but rather in the way any act of creation drags the risk of a cosmic failure with it.

The beauty of the simile lies in the range of connections offered between the potter and the dance. At first, it seems to link the circling motion of the potter's wheel with the human circle made by the dancers. Both seem to be variations on the theme of turning in the same place, αὐτοῦ στρέφεται. But two metaphors within the simile complicate this. The skilled hands of the craftsman correspond to the "knowing feet" of the dancers, but both suggest the limits of human knowledge. In the case of the potter, there is a crisis of artistic knowledge as he lets the pot go, unable to guarantee its very existence. For the dancers, the ease of the dance coincides with the transfer of their knowledge to their feet. The "material" of the dancer-craftsman is the human body itself, and the success of the dance as art-object again appears at the moment the material takes on a life of its own. For us to see them directing their feet would be a sign of artistic clumsiness, not ease. In both cases what matters is the moment when, as the Greek saying goes, the wagon starts leading the ox. The separate realms are brought together in a final metaphor within the simile: "if [the pot] might run," αἴ κε θέῃσιν. The metaphor suggests an artistic rivalry, as if the potter is not simply trying to make a pot, but an object that can "run" autonomously as the dancers can. Metaphor gestures toward metamorphosis, the possible change in quality from an assortment of material elements to an independent, self-sustaining object. And this links with a wider poetic strategy of hinting at the connections between the visual and the verbal that are in tension throughout the shield's description.

So the double occurrence of the word "Ocean" sets up a logic of metaphor, the superimposition of one structure upon another, all at once, and this is premised on the single "hinge" object that guarantees the principle of separation upon which metaphor depends: the constellation Arctos. But the corresponding suggestion that Ocean does infiltrate the rest of the shield, blurring the individual identity of each object, points toward the logic of metonymy, and this helps us see the making of the shield as a narrative sequence. Let us return to the details of this at the beginning of the shield's construction.

> He made the earth upon it, and the sky, and the sea's water,
> and the tireless sun, and the moon waxing into her fullness,
> and on it all the constellations that festoon the heavens . . .
>
> (*Il.* 18.483–85)

> Ἐν μὲν γαῖαν ἔτευξ᾽, ἐν δ᾽ οὐρανόν, ἐν δὲ θάλασσαν,
> ἠέλιόν τ᾽ ἀκάμαντα σελήνην τε πλήθουσαν,
> ἐν δὲ τὰ τείρεα πάντα, τά τ᾽ οὐρανὸς ἐστεφάνωται . . .

The invitation to metaphor offers a double reading of the initial depiction of the earth, heavens, and sea. Are these heavenly bodies depicted on the shield, or are they the beginnings of the primal elements of the shield, as if Hephaestus was an atomist, molding earth, air, and water?[1] The progress of the narrative seems to foreclose this option. For though the next line does indeed begin with the missing fourth element, with fire represented by the sun, the narrative continues by pairing the sun with the moon. At this point, any ambiguity between the material cause of the shield, the physical elements that constitute it, and narrative representation of the shield seems to cease, since the moon cannot be an element and does not fit with the previous four. But we could instead see this as the moment when the logic of metonymy momentarily takes over. The sun functions, with hindsight, as a link, bridging the previous elements and the stars that follow: part of its meaning comes from its association with fire, a second part from its typical pairing with the moon, and we move from the former to the latter. As the narrative progresses, it is as if the attraction of the moon drags the sun away from its elemental bearings, allowing it to flow into what follows.

Now if this seems far-fetched, let us return to the framing ring-composition of the description of the shield, and to the simile of the potter at its end. For after the initial description of the metals that Hephaestus uses to make up the shield (bronze, tin, gold, silver), the idea of four more primal elements at work in this creation is somewhat dissonant, as if we have moved to a less complex form of creation. But what is striking is that air, earth, and water are the elements involved in making a clay pot. And what is missing from the first set of elements, the sun/fire, is picked up in the simile of the pot-maker by the analogy to Hephaestus himself, the absent creator who is also the god of fire. The process of the artist's removal from the artwork in the three-dimensional creation of the pot is mirrored in the cutting off of line 18.483, "earth, heaven, sea," from line 484, "the tireless sun and moon" within Homer's hexameter sequence. In this context, even the sun's epithet, "toiling," offers us a connection to the god whose toil we view, and who routinely shares the same epithet. The toil of the things within the world is linked to the attributes of the creator of that world.

The Shape of the Shield

Critics have persisted in trying to picture Achilles's shield, and this persistence suggests, correctly, that Homer's portrait of the shield provokes such a thought process. But it is just as clear that the narrative resists any easy transference from the verbal to the visual. An immediate problem is the lack of spatial markings on the shield that are routinely given in descriptions of other ecphrastic objects. Other poets tell us of the shape and size of the works they describe, but Homer does not. But what makes up for this, and is less often noticed, is that there is an elaborate spatial vocabulary at work in the depiction of the events on the shield. The clue to the shape of the shield lies here. Homer doesn't need to emphasize a disjunction between art object and world because the boundaries between the two are themselves in question. To talk of the shape of the world and the shape of the shield would suggest an easy separation that does not apply.

Consider the persistent vocabulary of circling, whirling, and turning at work in the shield's description. The first set of dancers whirl (κοῦροι δ' ὀρχηστῆρες ἐδίνεον, *Il.* 18.494), and the last set surround a pair of acrobats who themselves whirl (ἐδίνευον κατὰ μέσσους, 18.606). In the first city, men about to decide the lawsuit are in a circle, just as two armies encircle the second city (18.502–4). Here, the logic of metaphor and metonymy has visual analogues. We can imagine discrete, concentric circles and the events on them seen all at once, in a single glance, and allow ourselves to superimpose their meanings onto each other. On this view, the logic of the circular motion of the constellation Arctos, which turns around but always in the same place, creates ripples outward. Each wider circle repeats the movement of the constellation, but in a new context, suggesting proliferating allegorical possibilities with each ring: the movements of the stars as dancing, ploughing, surrounding a doomed city, etc. Or we can follow the events as they unfold in time, in a linear chain. On this view, the vocabulary of *dine*, whirling, suggests a single thread, proceeding from the void of the shield's center forever outward in circles, until the whorl dissolves into the final rim of the Ocean itself. If we follow Hephaestus, tracing the thread from inside to out, there is both a dilution and an expansion of meaning: the simple story of the heavens links itself to more and more of the world. Even the outer rim is not discrete but rather a point of contact with the world beyond, suggesting that the world itself is a porous and expanding entity, growing as the creative work of culture grows. That the outer rim is the flux of the Ocean is textual permission for the most frequent form of scholarly and critical speculation about the shield: its relevance to the wider narrative of the *Iliad*. But we can also follow this thread in reverse, moving from the wider world toward the central void. The events on the shield then become broken down and simplified, contracted until their meaning verges on nullity.

To make these spatial suggestions more concrete, let us look at the different ways in which acts of farming are depicted. In the case of the ploughmen, the poet clearly imagines men driving ploughs back and forth upon a field, an activity that seems to involve repeated straight lines. But this activity is overwritten by the vocabulary of circling and whirling.

> He made upon it a soft field, the pride of the tilled land,
> wide and triple-ploughed, with many ploughmen upon it
> who wheeled their teams at the turn and drove them in either direction.
> And as these making their turn would reach the end-strip of the field,
> a man would come up to them at this point and hand them a flagon
> of honey-sweet wine, and they would turn again to the furrows
> in their haste to come again to the end-strip of the deep field.

The earth darkened behind them and looked like earth that has been
    ploughed
though it was gold. Such was the wonder of the shield's forging.

(Il. 18.541-49)

Ἐν δ' ἐτίθει νειὸν μαλακὴν πίειραν ἄρουραν,
εὐρεῖαν τρίπολον· πολλοὶ δ' ἀροτῆρες ἐν αὐτῇ
ζεύγεα δινεύοντες ἐλάστρεον ἔνθα καὶ ἔνθα.
οἳ δ' ὁπότε στρέψαντες ἱκοίατο τέλσον ἀρούρης,
τοῖσι δ' ἔπειτ' ἐν χερσὶ δέπας μελιηδέος οἴνου
δόσκεν ἀνὴρ ἐπιών· τοὶ δὲ στρέψασκον ἀν' ὄγμους,
ἱέμενοι νειοῖο βαθείης τέλσον ἱκέσθαι.
ἣ δὲ μελαίνετ' ὄπισθεν, ἀρηρομένη δὲ ἐῴκει,
χρυσείη περ ἐοῦσα· τὸ δὴ περὶ θαῦμα τέτυκτο.

The back and forth of the activity is less the focus of attention than the
end of the furrow, when the plough is first whirled around (δινεύοντες)
and then successfully turned (στρέψαντε) by the twisting operations of
its handlers. The focus on this curving at the end of the straight line
makes the straight lines into an ongoing set of circles, and suggests that
the ploughmen themselves experience the force of the "whirling" vor-
tex on view on the shield, whether it is centripetal or centrifugal. But
if the description tries to compensate for the lack of verisimilitude of
ploughmen working in a circle within the shield, it also overcompen-
sates. For though we can easily imagine a series of static figures in sequence in a circle, each following the other, with a man fixed with a cup
at some random point, we now need the depiction of the man with the
cup to signify the end of the furrow. For by describing the whirl of their
ploughs, Homer has effectively molded the ploughmen into the circular
shape of the shield (or given a verbal depiction of the circle of the shield
he has in mind). But the trouble is that the straight line has disappeared,
and so requires a marker to signify where its end lies: hence the need for
the additional marker of a man with a cup as reward.

Further sophistication lies in the way these spatial problems are reflected back into the psychological aspects of the actions themselves.
The iterative and imperfect tenses that dominate the description ("they
kept turning," "the man kept giving them a cup," etc.) reflect the fixity
of these figures on the artwork, but also something of the dull repeti-
tiveness of their labor itself, the endless circle of hope's partial fulfillment, and the beginning of the task all over again. In terms of narrative,
the relief of an ending, the visual depiction of the lines of a plough
finding a *telos* (ἱκοίατο τέλσον ἀρούρης), is also swept away by the word

δόσκεν. Having turned around, they are given not the relief of an aor-
ist but a continuous action that is linked to their ongoing labor: he *kept*
giving them the cup.

So far, we have focused on the completed circles, not a whirl with any
progress to or from the center. Is there any reason to push the reading
of "whirl"? We might observe that the work of the narrator in turning
their straight line into a circle by emphasizing the turn of their ploughs
is duplicated in the "turning" involved in ploughing.

> and they would turn again to the furrows
> in their haste to come again to the end-strip of the deep field.
>
> (*Il.* 18.546–47)

τοὶ δὲ στρέψασκον ἀν' ὄγμους,
ἱέμενοι νειοῖο βαθείης τέλσον ἱκέσθαι.

This seems to be a repetition of the former sentiment. But they do not
now simply move to the end of the row; they push the plough down-
ward to churn up what seems to be the earth but is actually the gold of
the shield. The escape they seek is not the end of the labor represented
by the end of the length of the field. They seem aware, in advance, that
the poet cuts off their explicit end-point by his circling. Instead, they
follow the logic of the whirlpool and plough down, as if the only hope
of escape from this eternal circle is to burrow into the underworld itself, perhaps with the dream of finally merging into an Ocean that sustains this dream by means of its customary epithet, *bathydines*, deep-
swirling. As was the case with the dancers and the pot, the ploughmen
on the shield try to resist their maker by acting against his intentions.
But here the intentions are given a political edge. The turning up of
the field stands for a revolt against the materials of the shield itself,
its basic metals. Some of their psychic ennui, and the hopelessness of
their gestures, can even be seen in the final image of their work: the
earth is "like ploughed land." The point is not simply in the illusion
on show in the work of art, the artistic conceit that makes us think of
gold as earth, but in the despair of the actors. They plough in order
not to plough, in order to come to the end and reach a permanently
ploughed field, but each act remains perpetually unfinished: the earth
is only "like" ploughed land, a representation of an end to labor, not
the reality.

Contrast the representation of ploughmen with those at work in the
orchards. Here, there is also an elaborate description of the enclosures,
but the description removes the claustrophobia of work in the fields.

He made on it a great vineyard heavy with clusters,
lovely and in gold, but the grapes upon it were darkened
and the vines themselves stood out through poles of silver. About them
he made a field-ditch of dark metal, and drove all around this
a fence of tin; and there was only one path to the vineyard,
and along it ran the grape-bearers for the vineyard's stripping.

(Il. 18.561–66)

Ἐν δὲ τίθει σταφυλῇσι μέγα βρίθουσαν ἀλωὴν
καλὴν χρυσείην· μέλανες δ᾽ ἀνὰ βότρυες ἦσαν,
ἑστήκει δὲ κάμαξι διαμπερὲς ἀργυρέῃσιν.
ἀμφὶ δὲ κυανέην κάπετον, περὶ δ᾽ ἕρκος ἔλασσε
κασσιτέρου· μία δ᾽ οἴη ἀταρπιτὸς ἦεν ἐπ᾽ αὐτήν,
τῇ νίσοντο φορῆες, ὅτε τρυγόῳεν ἀλωήν.

The prison of the ploughmen is replaced with a single conduit that allows an escape from the doubly enfolded enclosure. The single path by means of which the grape-gatherers escape from their enclosure doubles the path of the shield's creator, but also the path of the narrator. Rather than repetition, we have a series of discrete acts, as each place is created and left behind. The path doubles the constraints of narration itself, the need for a single story-thread to be taken rather than another, but also some of the relief of narrative. Later we are told that Hephaestus creates a dancing floor, just as Daedalus, a craftsman whose name becomes identified with craftsmanship itself, once made one for Ariadne. But the belated nod to the creator of the spatial puzzle of the labyrinth is a key to how we are to read the contrasting scenes of farming: on the one hand, the endless puzzlement of the ploughmen's eternal confusion and repetition, as if a work without end mirrors the experience of being lost in a labyrinth; on the other, the juxtaposed "solution" to the riddle, the offer of the single exit of linear narrative.

The Twin Cities

Let us keep the logic of metaphor and metonymy in mind as we approach the descriptions of urban life on the shield. Consider the strangeness of the first city.

On it he wrought in all their beauty two cities of mortal
men. And there were marriages in one, and festivals.
They were leading the brides along the city from their maiden chambers

under the flaring of torches, and the loud bride song was arising.
The young men followed the circles of the dance, and among them
the flutes and lyres kept up their clamour as in the meantime
the women standing each at the door of her court admired them.

(Il. 18.490–96)

Ἐν δὲ δύω ποίησε πόλεις μερόπων ἀνθρώπων
καλάς. ἐν τῇ μέν ῥα γάμοι τ᾽ ἔσαν εἰλαπίναι τε,
νύμφας δ᾽ ἐκ θαλάμων δαΐδων ὕπο λαμπομενάων
ἠγίνεον ἀνὰ ἄστυ, πολὺς δ᾽ ὑμέναιος ὀρώρει·
κοῦροι δ᾽ ὀρχηστῆρες ἐδίνεον, ἐν δ᾽ ἄρα τοῖσιν
αὐλοὶ φόρμιγγές τε βοὴν ἔχον· αἳ δὲ γυναῖκες
ἱστάμεναι θαύμαζον ἐπὶ προθύροισιν ἑκάστη.

The first surprise is the plurality of weddings, as if to emphasize that this is no normal city, but one used to symbolize the meaning of the marriage process. The description of the weddings brings further problems. Maidens are ready to marry, married women on their household thresholds are desperate to watch, young people dance, and the wedding cry stirs forth. But there is a striking absence of adult men. There are no grooms, no fathers of the brides. They are hinted at in the verb ἠγίνεον, but their identities disappear in the lack of subject provided for this third person plural verb: "some people were leading them."

The absence of grooms can be explained because the weddings are suspended, frozen in time, as the poet tips his cap to the narrative problem of depicting a process on a thing. The absence of the men would thus be anticipatory rather than a simple error. This interpretation allows us to linger over another aspect of the wedding's suspense. For we have not just the images but the sounds of a wedding: αὐλοὶ φόρμιγγές τε βοὴν ἔχον.

The interest lies in the difficulty of the phrase βοὴν ἔχον; the context suggests that it means "produced a shout," though the metaphor was unusual enough to cause Nauck to emend ἔχον to χέον, and so translate "were pouring out their sounds." For now, let us translate it literally: "the flutes and lyres were holding/having a shout." Most editors have rejected Nauck's suggestion and printed the reading of the manuscripts, offering a parallel phrase at *Il.* 16.104–5. Here, the poet returns to the battle narrative after the conversation between Achilles and Patroclus ends.

and around his temples the shining helmet
clashed horribly under the shower of strokes . . .

δεινὴν δὲ περὶ κροτάφοισι φαεινὴ
πήληξ βαλλομένη καναχὴν ἔχε, βάλλετο δ᾽ αἰεὶ . . .

Walter Leaf's note *ad loc* learns from this that the phrase "give a clang-ing" is a model for "give a sound" on the shield. But one might notice something entirely different here. For crashing is one of the few sounds a shield, as a metal object, is capable of making.

What we have stumbled upon is another part of the shield's balanc-ing act. We have the image of a wedding, and the start of the wedding song (πολὺς δ᾽ ὑμέναιος ὀρώρει), but the poet immediately confronts a problem: what will it sound like when we remember that we have only the representation of a wedding on a shield? The narrative's answer lies in the phrase βοὴν ἔχον. First we can read ἔχον as not *producing* a shout, but *holding* it. The wedding song has started, and yet nothing is heard, for the shout remains within the voices of the singers, in the metal of the instruments, and ultimately in the metal of the shield itself, which does not yet crash. We can thus see the failure of the flutes and lyres to play as concurrent with the holding back of the singers' voices, and thus not read "shout" as a metaphor at all. And what we are spared, as we lose ourselves in the representations on the shield, and forget the status of shield as shield, is precisely the "crash" the shield might make. The suspense of the pot in the simile toward the end of the description of the shield, its future success or failure, here occurs at the level of sound: will the sound of this wedding song be heard as pleasure or pain, harmony or cacophony?

But if the wedding is suspended, frozen at a crucial moment of tran-sition for females from maidens to wives, we are also offered an ex-tended look at the significance of the point of transition itself, when female identity is neither that of wife nor that of virgin maiden. This indeterminacy spills over from the brides themselves and onto women currently married, since the wives are attracted away from their fixed position in the household by the spectacle and back to the threshold they once crossed. The marriages on the shield are not just a transition for a particular woman or set of women; since they zero in on a moment of change, they open up the question of what the identity of a woman could be. With this in mind, let us follow the narrative into the further events in this city.

The people were assembled in the market place, where a quarrel
had arisen, and two men were disputing over the blood price
for a man who had been killed. One man promised full restitution

in a public statement, but the other refused and would accept nothing. Both then made for an arbitrator, to have a decision . . .

(*Il.* 18.497–501)

λαοὶ δ' εἰν ἀγορῇ ἔσαν ἀθρόοι· ἔνθα δὲ νεῖκος
ὠρώρει, δύο δ' ἄνδρες ἐνείκεον εἵνεκα ποινῆς
ἀνδρὸς ἀποφθιμένου· ὃ μὲν εὔχετο πάντ' ἀποδοῦναι
δήμῳ πιφαύσκων, ὃ δ' ἀναίνετο μηδὲν ἑλέσθαι·
ἄμφω δ' ἱέσθην ἐπὶ ἴστορι πεῖραρ ἑλέσθαι.

The city's plurality of weddings is now contrasted with a single legal dispute that demands the attention of its male population. The city is divided into a female sphere of weddings, itself described in such a way as to showcase the way in which marriage enacts the transition from *oikos* to *oikos*, and a male sphere of justice and politics. Both are frozen in moments of uncertainty, even as the troubled interaction between men threatens to break down into a far broader and more destructive conflict. We can now see that this gendered split in the city answers to a narrative problem set up in the description of the weddings. If it was tempting to fill in a male subject for the people we presumed were escorting the brides at *Il.* 18.492, the second scene in this divided city invites us to think again. For we retroactively find out that the men are elsewhere, pulled away from the weddings into the dispute over a blood price.

What is the political significance of this? If we were to try to relate this divided city to the stories of epic itself, we might put on hold the connections to the wider problems of Troy and turn instead to the *Odyssey*. For at the center of that poem is a woman suspended between loyalty to a past wedding, almost annulled by the passing of time, and a social injunction to remarry. Penelope too is on the brink of a wedding that never seems to arrive, and in conflict with the suitors over this. And the source of this conflict is the uncertainty of a "man who has died," or perhaps who has not, but whose status as a figure of authority able to put an end to any uncertainty about her social role has definitely disappeared. The suitors indefinitely prolong a feast and seem to desire a permanently postponed wedding, offering one answer to the suspended happiness of the wedding feasts of the shield. And even the women about to marry, frozen in the public sphere for a moment until the ritual is complete, double the dangerous position of Penelope, earning great fame for herself by her control of the men in her household, as Eurymachus says of her when he taunts Telemachus with his impotence. The suspended scenes of this visual object are a key to the plot of this great poem. For the *Odyssey* obsesses over these moments of transition, and constructs a prolonged thought experiment into what might happen when figures of authority (in this case, Odysseus) are absent. Finally, what is most clear about the suitors, for all their pretensions to power, is that they do not try to move into Odysseus's position, but keep as safe a distance from Penelope as Agamemnon does from Briseis. They remain tied to the general suspense, as if their world is a social analogue of the bossless shield, social actors circling around the void left by the departure of the king, pulled toward the power vacuum at the center of Ithaca without ever seriously trying to seize power.

We earlier referred to the two talents on display next to the litigants. Their normal referent as the balancing scales used to decide upon life or death is perfectly appropriate here. The representation of wealth stands there, as if to promise a resolution to the conflict with material recompense. But if the scene is aware of Achilles's challenge to any logic that would equate a man's life with goods, then we can explain another puzzle. The talents are not to be given to either of the litigants, but instead to the best speaker, moving the problem out of the realm of economics and into the realm of rhetoric. This makes it easier to understand the nature of the dispute, which has produced extensive scholarly debate within the field of legal history. The difficulty lies in the translation of lines 499–500. Is one party refusing recompense, or denying that he has received any? (The phrase ὃ δ' ἀναίνετο μηδὲν ἑλέσθαι can clearly mean both.) Is the other claiming that he has paid, or that he has the right to pay? (Again, ὃ μὲν εὔχετο πάντ' ἀποδοῦναι can mean both.) But rather than presuming some hidden clarity here, consider that the description of the dispute itself, suspended between two equally viable meanings of the words, mirrors the visual suspense of the shield and finds a symbol of that suspense in the reward—the two talents that can also represent scales. The judges are called up to find a limit, an end to the ambiguity of words that makes resolution impossible. So once more the poem traces a point of connection: the concerns of those on the shield seep into the worries of critics as they interpret the meaning of the shield. For how, in this case, can we separate the interpretative act of the critic from the moral act of the judge, even as the spectators of this judicial conflict flow into the minds of us as interpreters of the poem?

The ambiguity of language thus forms an analogue to the suspension

of the epic universe. The desire for a limit, and for an arbitrator, is itself
already an allegory for the difficulty of understanding a work of art precisely because of its autonomy. It is the desperate desire for the revela-
tion of an author's intentions, for a remedy against the anarchy of over-
interpretation. But the dilemma belongs not merely to the proliferation
of third parties to this suit; it is a dilemma for the litigants themselves.
We can take no comfort in the possibility that the case is a simple misunderstanding, where each party knows what is true and maintains his
own point of view but is nevertheless willing for pragmatic reasons to
turn to a third party. The litigants turn to a third party because they do
not know what they are saying; the ambiguity of the language falls back
on them. And as allegory for the work, they seem to voice a demand of
the art object itself. Severed from its creator, it provokes us, cries out for
us as litigants, as judges, as critics, to tell it what it means.

But ambiguity in words and the enigmatic potential of a suspended
image is not the only correspondence between words and visual object
suggested here. For in the male world, the word for the quarrel itself,
ἐνείκεον, doubles the crucial spatial activity of the female sphere of the
city, the "whirling" of the wedding dances.

> They were leading the brides along the city from their maiden chambers
> under the flaring of torches, and the loud bride song was arising.
> The young men followed the circles of the dance, and among them
> the flutes and lyres kept up their clamour as in the meantime
> the women standing each at the door of her court admired them.
> The people were assembled in the market place, where a quarrel
> had arisen, and two men were disputing over the blood price . . .
>
> (*Il.* 18.492–98)

νύμφας δ' ἐκ θαλάμων δαΐδων ὕπο λαμπομενάων
ἠγίνεον ἀνὰ ἄστυ, πολὺς δ' ὑμέναιος ὀρώρει·
κοῦροι δ' ὀρχηστῆρες ἐδίνεον, ἐν δ' ἄρα τοῖσιν
αὐλοὶ φόρμιγγές τε βοὴν ἔχον· αἳ δὲ γυναῖκες
ἱστάμεναι θαύμαζον ἐπὶ προθύροισιν ἑκάστη.
λαοὶ δ' εἰν ἀγορῇ ἔσαν ἀθρόοι· ἔνθα δὲ νεῖκος
ὠρώρει, δύο δ' ἄνδρες ἐνείκεον εἵνεκα ποινῆς . . .

The word ἐνείκεον replaces ἐδίνεον: both four-syllable words, both in
the same point in the line before the bucolic diaeresis as they bring the
fourth foot to a close. The overlay of "quarrel" on "whirl" suggests that
whirling is a metaphor for quarrel, as if a quarrel is a frantic, persistent

turning around the absence of any true answer to their dilemma. And can we not also see an elemental whirling doubled in the rearrangement of the letters, with ἐνείκεον a near anagram of ἐδίνεον? The details of the quarrel drag us back to the strangeness of the wedding. The dispute over a man who has died is linked to the absence of a husband at the wedding's center. The wordplay is returned to later, as the battle begins to rage outside the second city. Once more, we have words of four syllables ending before the bucolic diaeresis.

and Hate was there with Confusion among them, and Death the
    destructive;
she was holding a live man with a new wound, and another
one unhurt, and dragged a dead man by the feet through the carnage.
The clothing upon her shoulders showed strong red with the men's blood.
All closed together like living men and fought with each other . . .

(*Il.* 18.535–39)

ἐν δ᾽Ἔρις ἐν δὲ Κυδοιμὸς ὁμίλεον, ἐν δ᾽ ὀλοὴ Κήρ,
ἄλλον ζωὸν ἔχουσα νεούτατον, ἄλλον ἄουτον,
ἄλλον τεθνηῶτα κατὰ μόθον ἕλκε ποδοῖιν·
εἷμα δ᾽ ἔχ᾽ ἀμφ᾽ ὤμοισι δαφοινεὸν αἵματι φωτῶν.
ὡμίλευν δ᾽ ὥς τε ζωοὶ βροτοὶ ἠδ᾽ ἐμάχοντο . . .

The quarrel of two men, ἐνείκεον, a conflict that threatens to spiral into war, is now replaced by the harmony of two cosmic forces, Strife and Tumult, ὁμίλεον, whose agreement nevertheless paradoxically signifies the expanded quarrel of war itself. Finally, the series of verbs in the imperfect, from whirling to conflicting, ends in an adjective, δαφοινεὸν. This is a different part of speech, an adjective and not a verb, and yet it rhymes with the previous string of verbs before the diaeresis. So we can read motion into the static depiction of the cloak—less a bloody garment and more a continual spattering of blood in the frenetic killing.

Scholars name these cities on the shield cities of war and peace, the pleasure of the weddings in the first city fueling the belief in the possibility of the peaceful resolution of the conflict of the manslaughter dispute, and both scenes contrasting with the strife of the city at war. But what is so marked about the first city is the depiction of suspense itself. We do not know what will happen, though of course the creation of this suspense in part invites critical projections of the city's future. The contrast might cause us to miss the other ways in which the cities mirror each other.

and between them lay on the ground two talents of gold, to be given
to that judge who in this case spoke the straightest opinion.
        But around the other city were lying two forces of armed men
shining in their war gear. For one side counsel was divided
whether to storm and sack, or share between both sides the property
and all the possessions the lovely citadel held hard within it.
But the city's people were not giving way, and armed for an ambush.
Their beloved wives and their little children stood on the rampart
to hold it, and with them the men with age upon them . . .

                                                                    (*Il.* 18.507–15)

κεῖτο δ' ἄρ' ἐν μέσσοισι δύω χρυσοῖο τάλαντα,
τῷ δόμεν ὃς μετὰ τοῖσι δίκην ἰθύντατα εἴποι.
        Τὴν δ' ἑτέρην πόλιν ἀμφὶ δύω στρατοὶ ἥατο λαῶν
τεύχεσι λαμπόμενοι· δίχα δέ σφισιν ἥνδανε βουλή,
ἠὲ διαπραθέειν ἢ ἄνδιχα πάντα δάσασθαι,
κτῆσιν ὅσην πτολίεθρον ἐπήρατον ἐντὸς ἔεργεν·
οἳ δ' οὔ πω πείθοντο, λόχῳ δ' ὑπεθωρήσσοντο.
τεῖχος μέν ῥ' ἄλοχοί τε φίλαι καὶ νήπια τέκνα
ῥύατ' ἐφεσταότες, μετὰ δ' ἀνέρες οὓς ἔχε γῆρας . . .

    The two talents of gold, a symbol of balance and division, are picked
up in the first curious detail of the second city: that it is surrounded by
two encamped armies who themselves are divided as to what to do.
The separation of "us" and "them," besieger and besieged, is fractured
further as the besiegers become human personifications of the scales
themselves, two sides unsure what to do. In the first city, a primal uncertainty at the center of the social world spirals outward, drawing the
city into factions and possible war. In the second city, the uncertainty
is already civic, splitting the people in two, whereas in the center of
the besieged city, our expectation is defeated by the surprise of certainty: the people arm for action. But even this unity divides this city
into worlds of male and female just as surely as the first; the wives go
to the walls, a double of the wives on the threshold of the doors in the
marriage ceremonies. We can map this besieged city onto Troy, where
any confidence in resistance acts out an illusion; they cannot believe
that the race is run, the city is lost. On this reading, the entire besieged
city forms a double of the dead man at the center of the first city, and
the debate of those around it is a telling sign that at least they know it.
As such, the women left behind have in their futures not the hope for
the empty, manless weddings to their kinfolk on show in the first city,
but rather the customary fate of female victims of war.

A World of As If

The representation of the war in the second city invites us to contemplate the different permutations of illusion on the shield.

> and Hate was there with Confusion among them, and Death the
>   destructive;
> she was holding a live man with a new wound, and another
> one unhurt, and dragged a dead man by the feet through the carnage.
> The clothing upon her shoulders showed strong red with the men's blood.
> All closed together like living men and fought with each other . . .
>
> (*Il.* 18.535–39)

How are we to understand the phrase "as living mortals"? The comment at first seems to be on the power of the work of art, a representation so persuasive that we treat as alive what is merely inanimate metal. But once more the illusion of art fades into other kinds of illusion. The phrase comments upon the content of the art, the mortal warriors who double the heroes of the poem itself. For they are victims of a similar illusion: they act "as if" they are alive, but in reality the specter of fate is all around them. The image draws out the paradox of living mortals, beings who are destined to die, yet act as if they are not, strangely unaware of the fate that is dragging them off. The representation on the shield defines all humans, regardless of the status of their wounds, as doomed to death. The distinctions of newly wounded or unwounded become pointless, swallowed up in the deeper truth of the impermanence of mortal existence: "as if they were living." The tripartite division is a strange version of the riddle of the sphinx, reminding us that the number of limbs at stake in that ruse is itself a form of denial of the ultimate goal of humans, the limbless state of death itself. And this has especial point within the *Iliad*, a poem so full of figures on the threshold of death without knowing it.

A final possibility would see the phrase "as if living mortals" as referring to the divine figures of Tumult, Eris, and Fate. For by joining the realm of mortals and leaving the world of the gods, the divine forces fight "as if" they are mortal. So we have the reverse of a process I noted earlier about the Homeric gods. By portraying gods anthropomorphically, the poem struggles to think of them as anything other than mortal creatures; their immortality itself becomes an illusion, turning them into doubled, larger-than-life forms of humans themselves. But the shield comments on this process. These depictions of Eris, though we have no idea what pictorial form they take, do not matter much. For whatever the form, we try to gentrify these allegories of the dissolution of our world and treat them as if they belong to the order of our mortal, living universe. But this too is an illusion. They are utterly alien, foreign to us, and to make images of them is another way of deluding ourselves.

The question of fate opens up one last, crucial question: what is the relationship of the scenes on the shield to the story of Achilles, the figure who has defined himself as precariously balanced between two fates?

For my mother Thetis the goddess of the silver feet tells me
I carry two sorts of destiny toward the day of my death.

(Il. 9.410–11)

μήτηρ γάρ τέ μέ φησι θεὰ Θέτις ἀργυρόπεζα
διχθαδίας κῆρας φερέμεν θανάτοιο τέλοςδέ.

The choice finds itself represented in the second city of the shield, where the horror of war abruptly ends, and the description then switches to the scenes of ploughs and orchards.

and Hate was there with Confusion among them, and Death the
    destructive . . .

(Il. 18.535)

ἐν δ᾽Ἔρις ἐν δὲ Κυδοιμὸς ὁμίλεον, ἐν δ᾽ ὀλοὴ Κήρ . . .

The special relevance of this personified "Death" to Achilles is worth lingering over. He is not subject to the illusions of the other men who die. Not only is he aware of his mortality from the poem's beginning, but by this point he actively seeks it out, welcoming it as the answer to his current view of the worthlessness of his life. So when Achilles, in contrast to the rest of the Myrmidons, exults in the shield while they turn away in horror, we see his willingness to cast his cold eye on Fate itself. The poem dramatizes Achilles's difference from the rest of mortals by showing him looking at, and taking delight in, the illusions about death that blind the rest of us.

But we can also see the contours of the choice Achilles does not make, his would-be life in Phthia, traced out in the shield's depiction of agricultural life. We can return to the conceit at work in the vocabulary of repetition in these scenes in the orchards and fields, both a commentary on the work of art itself, motionless in its apparent frozen movement, and also an oblique hint at human revulsion at the endlessness of the labor. As such, this apparent scene of joy, the image of an ordered world presided over by a happy king, is a sharp shift in narrative perspective, a turning away from the viewpoint of the workers and toward that of the supervisor of the work. At only one other place in Homer does such a cluster of frequentatives occur. It is in the picture of the torments of those in the underworld, and particularly those of Tantalus and Sisyphus, at *Odyssey* 11.582–600. The endlessness of the work of peacetime functions as a composite of the stories of endless punishment applied to Tantalus and Sisyphus. For the former, the earth keeps vanishing as he bends down to drink; for the latter the labor of the rock is an endless pushing. The utter stupidity of the laborers' repeated, senseless acts turns life into the image of punishments in Hades and the endless torments there. In the ordering of the action, in the rhythmic back and forth of their repetitions, no further purpose seems apparent. There is no path to an elsewhere, no anticipation of a story yet to come, no other place to travel. Our exultant king is the equivalent of the lords of the underworld, Minos and Rhadamanthus, who supervise this kind of punishment. Life becomes vegetal, a labor for nothing other than the senseless continuation of the means to live. And is this not one way of imagining the other possible choice of Achilles, the choice for peace? The *Iliad* has already punned on the name of Achilles's homeland, the locus for this road not taken. Phthia suggests *phthisis*, the word for the perishing of all biological things.[2] The shield offers up a vision of the kind of world that Achilles will reject, and the manner of the description is as close as the poem gets to commentary on the choice that is offered to him. The choice of peace is no utopia, but a living version of the darkest corner of Hades, a short circuit to a living death in the name of avoidance of a biological one.

Art, Kant famously argued, has a purposeless purposefulness. It has form, obeys some principles of balance and rationality, but cannot be reduced to any other form of discourse. The moment an art object has a useful purpose and can be subordinated to that external end, it is no longer an art object. The shield does not reject such an idea, nor does it divorce itself entirely from the search for a meaning beyond the lifespan of a single human. But by lingering on the darkness of what human purposelessness might mean, its beauty is also terrifying. Whereas Keats, in his own reflections on the permanence of a work of art, sees in the scenes of a Grecian urn a twinning of truth and beauty, other images of permanent purposelessness creep onto the shield. As for Achilles, for all his delay and failure to choose, he can never escape the darkness of this vision of peace, and so turns back to the world of war and death.

4

The Poetry of Politics

Homer returns to the illusions of the shield, the "as if" mode on display in the representations of life, in the funeral games of Book 23. The games are not just "play," but play as politics. They take the form of politics, but without the direct political consequences for social life that occur in the real world. Male equals compete publicly, the distribution of prizes doubles the distribution of war prizes, and the process of distribution itself is argued over and ultimately resolved. But the power structure outside the games stays the same. Here Achilles will distribute prestige, but he does so as an arbitrator, not a king, a temporary surrogate for Agamemnon. The visions on the shield freeze social life, allowing us to see the social fissures of the real world. Here, the detachment from the official world allows the games to function as a social science laboratory. Conflict creation and resolution are an ongoing experiment.

From this perspective, the crucial events of the games preserve this space of quasi-politics, of detachment from the real world. When Ajax meets Diomedes in hand-to-hand combat, the form of the contest threatens to undermine the logic of the games themselves. If all the games have affiliation with martial skills, and are thus simultaneously both competition and practice, the "game" of fighting blurs the distinction. Games must be an allegory of social life, not the thing itself, and this contest pushes the logic of games to the brink. The watchers, at first in wonder at the prospect of this encounter, end up in terror, and have to bring the contest to a halt.

The son of Tydeus, over the top of the huge shield, was always
menacing the neck of Aias with the point of the shining

94

spear, but when the Achaians saw it in fear for Aias
they called for them to stop and divide the prizes evenly.

(Il. 23.820–23)

Τυδεΐδης δ᾽ ἄρ᾽ ἔπειτα ὑπὲρ σάκεος μεγάλοιο
αἰὲν ἐπ᾽ αὐχένι κῦρε φαεινοῦ δουρὸς ἀκωκῇ.
καὶ τότε δή ῥ᾽ Αἴαντι περιδείσαντες Ἀχαιοὶ
παυσαμένους ἐκέλευσαν ἀέθλια ἶσ᾽ ἀνελέσθαι.

The contest, though Diomedes will be tacitly awarded the greater prize, has to be a draw, because the obvious form of victory in such a contest, the life of one contestant and the death of another, would disrupt the exercise of social solidarity between friends that the funeral games display. The actors, Ajax and Diomedes, forget that they are acting out battle, not actually trying to kill each other, and so the external intervention is a sign that this particular experiment in aesthetic play has failed. To return to the simile of the potter and his clay, the spectators' wonder is fueled by the extreme daring of this work of art, as armed combat flirts with the failure of death itself. So the spectators' intervention ensures that collapse does not happen, but also represents a failure of nerve on their part: when the possibility of collapse becomes too real, their wonder turns into terror, and they usurp the role of the artist in halting the experiment. Death itself must not proceed "beyond the shield," ὑπὲρ σάκεος μεγάλοιο, but must be folded back into its play of illusions of social solidarity.

Consider also the final event. When Agamemnon steps forward to take part in the spear-throwing contest, Achilles stops him.

'Son of Atreus, for we know how much you surpass all others,
by how much you are greatest for strength among the spear-throwers,
therefore take this prize and keep it and go back to your hollow
ships; but let us give the spear to the hero Meriones . . .[']

(Il. 23.890–93)

"Ἀτρεΐδη· ἴδμεν γὰρ ὅσον προβέβηκας ἁπάντων
ἠδ᾽ ὅσσον δυνάμει τε καὶ ἥμασιν ἔπλευ ἄριστος·
ἀλλὰ σὺ μὲν τόδ᾽ ἄεθλον ἔχων κοίλας ἐπὶ νῆας
ἔρχευ, ἀτὰρ δόρυ Μηριόνῃ ἥρωϊ πόρωμεν . . ."

A specific kind of artificiality is guaranteed by this act. There will be no enmity to the death in the games. But the players compete for power only in a wider world where the merit and power of the king are not questioned. The final game returns us to the central theme of the poem, the *eris* generated between Agamemnon and Achilles. But Achilles's deference to Agamemnon suggests not just the power of Agamemnon, but that Achilles is aware of the need for the illusion of merit that props that power up. If Agamemnon took part and lost, the games would once more become overtly political.

The Shape of the Funeral Games

The emptiness at the center of the shield finds a double in the juridical scene in the first city. The circle of elders surrounds two litigants, but the absent third man, recently killed, is the cause of their particular grouping. In Book 23, the games take place because of a man who has died in strange circumstances, and though the Greeks are certain that Hector has killed him, the poem has gone to some length to complicate the identity of the killer. But the manner of description of Patroclus's funeral again returns us to the shield.

> He spoke, and all of them assembled moaned, and Achilleus led them.
> Three times, mourning, they drove their horses with flowing manes about
> the body, and among them Thetis stirred the passion for weeping.
>
> (*Il.* 23.12–14)

Ὣς ἔφαθ᾽, οἳ δ᾽ ᾤμωξαν ἀολλέες, ἦρχε δ᾽ Ἀχιλλεύς.
οἱ δὲ τρὶς περὶ νεκρὸν ἐΰτριχας ἤλασαν ἵππους
μυρόμενοι· μετὰ δέ σφι Θέτις γόου ἵμερον ὦρσε.

The extended weeping (*myromenoi*) involves a punning on the name of Achilles's people, the Myrmidons, mentioned twice in the run-up to this emotional outburst. The pun is elaborated as Homer describes the scale of their mourning. They weep in the thousands (*myrioi*) near Achilles's ship: κὰδ δ᾽ ἷζον παρὰ νηῒ ποδώκεος Αἰακίδαο / μυρίοι (*Il.* 23.28–29). The Myrmidons, excluded from the epic for too long by Achilles's actions, are finally allowed to fight, but find their true epic identity only here, their names an anagrammatic amalgam of weeping and excess, as they become vast, sublime embodiments of the loss felt at a single human death. This collective mourning returns us to the tears of Achilles by the seashore in the poem's first book. Grief proliferates from individual to ethnic group. But the tears also have material, almost cosmic consequences.

The sands were wet, and the armour of men was wet with their tears. Such
was their longing after Patroklos, who drove men to thoughts of terror.

(*Il.* 23.15–16)

δεύοντο ψάμαθοι, δεύοντο δὲ τεύχεα φωτῶν
δάκρυσι· τοῖον γὰρ πόθεον μήστωρα φόβοιο.

This contingent detail, the moisture of the sand, is picked up later in one of the most curious events of the funeral. The funeral pyre fails to light, and Achilles is forced to summon the winds to dry it. This apparently unmotivated act returns us to the excess of weeping: if the pyre does not light, it is because tears suffuse everything. We return to the cosmic tensions of the shield, surrounded by the Ocean and yet kept in balance because of the failure of the central ring to dip into the Ocean. Here, the balance is upset by the presence of humans themselves. Water soaks the earth, the earth refuses to permit fire, and it requires "air," the working of the winds, to restore enough equilibrium to let the pyre burn. The battle of Hephaestus and the rivers from Book 21 is now doubled, but with different sources, and the funeral games stall because a second kind of Ocean, the flood of tears, overwhelms them. Now the watery element is not external to humans but produced by them, suggesting that human grief undermines any simple opposition between inside and outside. The mass of Myrmidon mourning throws the world off kilter.

The question mark over the circumstances of the death of the man killed in the dispute on the shield also returns in the description of Patroclus's funeral. For the riddle of Patroclus's death, the possibility of his manslaughter at the hands of Achilles, makes itself felt in the preliminaries to the ritual. Achilles begins the mourning and puts his "man-slaying" hands on his friend.

Peleus' son led the thronging chant of their lamentation,
and laid his manslaughtering hands over the chest of his dear friend . . .

(*Il.* 23.17–18)

τοῖσι δὲ Πηλεΐδης ἁδινοῦ ἐξῆρχε γόοιο,
χεῖρας ἐπ᾿ ἀνδροφόνους θέμενος στήθεσσιν ἑταίρου . . .

Physical contact between these two friends occurs only after Patroclus's death. Neither in Patroclus's supplication of Achilles in Book 16 nor when Achilles sings the "songs of men" in Book 9 do their hands actually meet. This moment doubles the first touch of Book 19, when Achilles's hands first get hold of Patroclus's corpse. But if the first touch is all too solid, the second touch is nothing but air. When he meets the *psyche* of Patroclus in a dream, the insubstantial shadow of the man slips through his fingers.

The epithet "manslaughtering" is far better known from its appearance in Book 24, when the wonder of Priam's gesture lies in the kissing of Achilles's man-slaying hands.

[He] caught the knees of Achilleus in his arms, and kissed the hands
that were dangerous and manslaughtering and had killed so many
of his sons.

(Il. 24.478–80)

χερσὶν Ἀχιλλῆος λάβε γούνατα καὶ κύσε χεῖρας
δεινὰς ἀνδροφόνους, αἵ οἱ πολέας κτάνον υἷας.

In Book 24 the epithet is expanded upon and explained by the hands' physical role in killing Priam's sons. But here, it is the asymmetry between the usual work of Achilles's hands and his intimate history with Patroclus that matters. Not only does this most bloodthirsty of warriors indulge in a gesture of tenderness, but whatever his role in Patroclus's death, it was not a physical one: his hands are clean, even if his mind is not. The touching threatens to narrow the gap between cause and effect (the cause being Achilles's words, "murder the Greeks," the effect Patroclus's death). The killing becomes material, even at the moment that a longed-for physical intimacy is both granted and denied, and tenderness melds into manslaughter.

The split between the mystery of Patroclus's death and the brutal simplicity of Achilles's killing is on show in the form that Patroclus's funeral pyre will take. The 12 Trojans whom Achilles pulled from the river, direct victims of his man-slaying hands, are placed around the body of Patroclus, providing a different version of the manslaughter trial represented on the shield. In both cases, the trauma at the center is one of uncertainty, and it spirals outward into the wider world, bringing confusion and further deaths. In this context, the appearance of Patroclus's ghost is a forerunner of the famous scene in Akira Kurosawa's *Rashomon* where a murder victim is brought back to life by a medium in order to clarify the circumstances of his death, but his return only brings further mystery, since he too is ignorant. In the case of Patroclus, his return to the upper world in no way enlightens him, and Achilles's role in his death, though it remains on the outskirts of our knowledge, is still a taboo subject for them both. But Patroclus's own story of his past nevertheless flirts with the solution of this puzzle, returning us to the problem of manslaughter and hinting at a broader necessity at work.

There is one
more thing I will say, and ask of you, if you will obey me:

do not have my bones laid apart from yours, Achilleus,
but with them, just as we grew up together in your house,
when Menoitios brought me there from Opous, when I was little,
and into your house, by reason of a baneful manslaying,
on that day when I killed the son of Amphidamas. I was
a child only, nor intended it, but was angered over a dice game.

(Il. 23.81–88)

ἄλλο δέ τοι ἐρέω καὶ ἐφήσομαι, αἴ κε πίθηαι·
μὴ ἐμὰ σῶν ἀπάνευθε τιθήμεναι ὀστέ᾽, Ἀχιλλεῦ,
ἀλλ᾽ ὁμοῦ, ὡς τράφομέν περ ἐν ὑμετέροισι δόμοισιν,
εὖτέ με τυτθὸν ἐόντα Μενοίτιος ἐξ Ὀπόεντος
ἤγαγεν ὑμέτερονδ᾽ ἀνδροκτασίης ὕπο λυγρῆς,
ἤματι τῷ ὅτε παῖδα κατέκτανον Ἀμφιδάμαντος,
νήπιος, οὐκ ἐθέλων, ἀμφ᾽ ἀστραγάλοισι χολωθείς . . .

The curious detail that Patroclus himself came to Peleus's house while fleeing a charge of manslaughter becomes heartbreakingly relevant. An irony (or necessity?) lies here. In fleeing the circumstances of his past, he ends up in the same scenario, but as victim. The form of that manslaughter previews the central question of the funeral games: when can and should competition become deadly? But it also offers a pithy, retroactive summary of the *Iliad*'s plot. For, with the hindsight of Book 23, is not the whole story of Briseis the story of the anger of men over a simple game? Briseis, as object of this game, proved with hindsight to be worthless to them.

The Geometric Patterns of the Games

A superficial resemblance between the geometrical description of the funeral games and the design of the shield is easy to see, though the craftsman has changed. There are the circuits of the chariot and foot races, the whirls of discus and wrestlers, but all this in a wider order maintained by Achilles as master of ceremonies. He takes on the role of Hephaestus, but presides over a living, moving work of art. The correspondences between their geometries can shed some light on the puzzling details of the games themselves.

Consider the chariot race, and the curious advice Nestor gives his son Antilochus before the race begins. He suggests the need to use cunning, *metis*, so that his horses can overcome others that are by nature superior. The form this cunning must take is clear: Antilochus is to round the turning post more tightly than his rivals. But the narrative defies our expectations. We are never told whether Antilochus takes this advice. Instead, in a complicated passage, he seems to win a stare-down with Menelaus by refusing to budge from his tracks as the road narrows. Can we explain this anomaly? Let us begin with Nestor's advice.

but make your left-hand horse keep hard against the turning-post
so that the hub's edge of your fashioned wheel will seem to be
touching it, yet take care not really to brush against it,
for, if so, you might damage your horses and break your chariot . . .

(*Il.* 23.338–41)

ἐν νύσσῃ δέ τοι ἵππος ἀριστερὸς ἐγχριμφθήτω,
ὡς ἄν τοι πλήμνη γε δοάσσεται ἄκρον ἱκέσθαι
κύκλου ποιητοῖο· λίθου δ᾽ ἀλέασθαι ἐπαυρεῖν,
μή πως ἵππους τε τρώσῃς κατά θ᾽ ἄρματα ἄξῃς . . .

A difficulty lies in the phrase κύκλου ποιητοῖο, which has troubled philologists. It is generally agreed that what must be meant here is the "circle" of the chariot's wheel, and the phrase is thus a subjective genitive, dependent on πλήμνη. But the trouble is that the distance from πλήμνη seems too great for this meaning to be comfortable. So let us translate literally, and "nonsensically": "so that the wheel-nave might seem to come to the edge of a crafted / poetic circle." If we read this advice with the patterns of the shield in mind, we get closer to Nestor's idea. Nestor's *metis* is a geometrical one: he asks his son to turn the corner in such a way as to come to the edge of a "made circle." The poetic circle doubles a noetic circle, the vision Nestor has of what a perfect turn would look like. This game doubles the turning of the ploughmen on the shield. Both concentrate on the moment when a straight line turns into a circle.

But the geometry of this *metis* also harbors an ethical dimension. The command to "avoid touching the stone" returns us not simply to the turning post but to Nestor's previous description of it, and what it might signify.

I will give you a clear mark and you cannot fail to notice it.
There is a dry stump standing up from the ground about six feet,
oak, it may be, or pine, and not rotted away by rain-water,
and two white stones are leaned against it, one on either side,
at the joining place of the ways, and there is smooth driving around it.
Either it is the grave-mark of someone who died long ago,

or was set as a racing goal by men who lived before our time.
Now swift-footed brilliant Achilleus has made it the turning-post.

(Il. 23.326–33)

σῆμα δέ τοι ἐρέω μάλ' ἀριφραδές, οὐδέ σε λήσει.
ἕστηκε ξύλον αὖον ὅσον τ' ὄργυι' ὑπὲρ αἴης,
ἢ δρυὸς ἢ πεύκης· τὸ μὲν οὐ καταπύθεται ὄμβρῳ,
λᾶε δὲ τοῦ ἑκάτερθεν ἐρηρέδαται δύο λευκὼ
ἐν ξυνοχῇσιν ὁδοῦ, λεῖος δ' ἱππόδρομος ἀμφὶς·
ἤ τευ σῆμα βροτοῖο πάλαι κατατεθνηῶτος,
ἢ τό γε νύσσα τέτυκτο ἐπὶ προτέρων ἀνθρώπων,
καὶ νῦν τέρματ' ἔθηκε ποδάρκης δῖος Ἀχιλλεύς.
τῷ σὺ μάλ' ἐγχρίμψας ἐλάαν σχεδὸν ἅρμα καὶ ἵππους . . .

There has been a great deal of sophisticated commentary on these lines, and a wide range of attempts to link them with the general ideology of the poem's heroism.[1] If the poem takes for granted an ethics of glory as a means of prolonging one's fame past death, this passage seems to question that strategy and emphasize the unreliability of fame. Fame depends upon the legibility of signs, *semata*, and *semata* are relentlessly effaced by time itself. But one can link this notion more specifically to the chariot race. For Nestor's speculation on the turning post as tombstone is a veiled warning to Antilochus: to "touch the stone" means to risk death, for the chariot is liable to collapse away from the balance of its circular path and in on itself, and thus crash. So Antilochus is asked to skirt a double danger: on one hand the possibility of a life of obscurity, on the other the brutal consequence of gaining a name in the form of an immediate epitaph. By touching the stone, by crashing and dying at the turning post, Antilochus becomes the answer to the riddle of this unnamed person's stone: a cenotaph will be filled. So too the circle Nestor asks Antilochus to construct becomes a temporary work of art, like the shield, circling around death's void.

Now we are in a better position to understand why the narrative seems to abandon these words of advice. For Antilochus will indeed best Menelaus, but not in the way foreshadowed.

There was a break in the ground where winter water had gathered
and broken out of the road, and made a sunken place all about.
Menelaos shrinking from a collision of chariots steered there,
but Antilochos also turned out his single-foot horses
from the road, and bore a little way aside, and went after him;
and the son of Atreus was frightened and called out aloud to Antilochos:

'Antilochos, this is reckless horsemanship. Hold in your horses.
The way is narrow here, it will soon be wider for passing.
Be careful not to crash your chariot and wreck both of us.'
        So he spoke, but Antilochos drew on all the harder
with a whiplash for greater speed, as if he had never heard him.

                                                        (*Il.* 23.420–30)

ῥωχμὸς ἔην γαίης, ᾗ χειμέριον ἀλὲν ὕδωρ
ἐξέρρηξεν ὁδοῖο, βάθυνε δὲ χῶρον ἅπαντα·
τῇ ῥ' εἶχεν Μενέλαος ἁματροχιὰς ἀλεείνων.
Ἀντίλοχος δὲ παρατρέψας ἔχε μώνυχας ἵππους
ἐκτὸς ὁδοῦ, ὀλίγον δὲ παρακλίνας ἐδίωκεν.
Ἀτρεΐδης δ' ἔδεισε καὶ Ἀντιλόχῳ ἐγεγώνει·
"Ἀντίλοχ' ἀφραδέως ἱππάζεαι· ἀλλ' ἄνεχ' ἵππους·
στεινωπὸς γὰρ ὁδός, τάχα δ' εὐρυτέρη παρελάσσαι·
μή πως ἀμφοτέρους δηλήσεαι ἅρματι κύρσας."
        Ὣς ἔφατ', Ἀντίλοχος δ' ἔτι καὶ πολὺ μᾶλλον ἔλαυνε
κέντρῳ ἐπισπέρχων, ὡς οὐκ ἀΐοντι ἐοικώς.

The narrative is notoriously obscure here. Still, it is generally agreed
that the pathway, normally wide enough for two chariots, is artificially
narrowed by the wasting away of part of it because of rain, creating a
gully. Antilochus moves off the track when it is still safe to do so, when
the ground remains even, and presumably closes in on Menelaus. When
they reach the narrow part, he cuts in, and Menelaus has a choice: to
continue straight risks a crash, to move inside risks falling off into the
gully. So he withdraws and yields his place to Antilochus. Antilochus
rejects Nestor's explicit advice to make the turn tightly. But he also rejects Nestor's implied ethical injunction to come close to death but to
avoid it. Nestor urges a circling of death; Antilochus chooses a direct
confrontation with it, and in doing so he confronts Menelaus with his
inability to confront it. The game stages the beginnings of the battle for
prestige that jumpstarts Hegel's master-slave dialectic. For Hegel, the
master and slave are initially distinguished by nothing more than the
ability of the master not to buckle before the threat of the "Absolute
Master," death itself, and the slave's work for the master is the consequence. The divergence from his father's advice also has a spatial analogue on the shield. Nestor's advice returns us to the endless circles of
ploughing, whereas Antilochus's assumption of the single path is a continuation of the orchard scene, where there was also a single path, μία δ'
οἴη ἀταρπιτὸς (*Il.* 18.565). This part of the story of the chariot race picks

up the description of the path from the shield. On the shield, the single path functioned as an escape, a way out of an abyss. Here, the single-ness of the path suggests a zero-sum conflict, an either-or confrontation that demands gain and loss, a refusal of compromise or mediation. This is a path from which there is *no turning*: ἀ-ταρπιτὸς. It previews another conflict on another path in Greek literature, where neither father nor son will give way despite the possibility of a third way, and which also involves goads, κέντρα. It is beautifully appropriate that this father-son conflict, in which the father is the arch-mediator, turns out to be a con-flict between the tactics of avoidance and confrontation.

Politics, Competition, Death

But the shield and games occur at different times in the narrative of the poem. The suspense of the shield comes when the major questions of the poem remain in doubt. Four books later the races of the funeral games start when all the major races of the poem have been run: Hector is dead, both Achilles and Troy are doomed beyond any possibility of salvation, and Achilles's wrath has all but run its course. So when the games offer allegories for avoiding violent political conflict, there is an element of tragedy. We have a social version of the individual motif of "a fool understands too late," a place where the lessons of the poem are worked through but only at the price of remembering the lessons' belatedness. In these games, because of a series of timely interventions, friends will indeed remain friends, and no stolen prize will wreak havoc with Greek solidarity.

We will turn to some of these lessons shortly. But before doing so, a prior question suggests itself. If the funeral games effectively banish the distinction between friends and enemies, is there anything left of the concept of the political at all? In Carl Schmitt's influential attempt to specify the terrain of politics, the distinction between friends and en-emies is paramount. The role of the state is to maintain this distinction, to protect the group life of the community while policing the line that separates enemy from friend. Politics is existential, concerned less with the ways life is spent and more with the art of preserving communal life itself. To imagine a world without this external threat to life runs the risk, for Schmitt, of destroying politics entirely, reducing it to mere entertainment.

A world in which the possibility of war is utterly eliminated, a completely pacified globe, would be a world without the distinction of friend and enemy and hence a world without politics. It is conceivable that such a world might contain many very interesting antitheses and contrasts, competitions and intrigues of every kind, but there would not be a meaningful antithesis whereby men could be required to sacrifice life, authorized to shed blood, and kill other human beings. For the definition of the political, it is here even irrelevant whether such a world without politics is desirable as an ideal situation. The phenomenon of the political can be understood only in the context of the ever present possibility of the friend-and-enemy grouping, regardless of the aspects which this possibility implies for morality, aesthetics, and economics.[2]

But as soon as you define questions of death as all that matter, the only locus for meaning, you end up in the perverse scenario where any act, however trivial, in order to be endowed with meaning requires a facedown with death. To return to Jacques Lacan's critique of existentialism, it offers "a personality that achieves self-realization only in suicide; and a consciousness of the other that can only be satisfied by Hegelian murder." But for all this, Schmitt's worry that the realm of the political, without the specter of death, could reduce social life to a soap opera is useful for thinking through issues central to the Homeric poems. The funeral games are a test case, a space where "antitheses," competitions, and intrigues continue, with death formally banished. Yet the games could hardly be any more intense; every event matters almost too much, and violent internal conflict threatens to erupt at every moment. Even the most trivial act can spiral into deadly rivalry. The chariot race causes a fight between spectators, when Oilean Ajax and Idomeneus argue over who sees which of the teams of horses is in first place (*Il.* 23.456–98). If anything, there is an overabundance of meaning, where nothing in public is "mere entertainment," and one is accountable for one's every word and deed.

But Schmitt's worry is not absent in Homer. For the funeral games contrast with a second set of games in Homer, and these *are* mere entertainment. At the beginning of the *Odyssey*, Penelope's suitors inhabit a world where politics is formally banished and entertainment has taken over. They feast, they enjoy the near-limitless supply of goods offered up by Odysseus's *oikos*, and they play a game, *pessoi*, which is some form of draughts. But the narrator gives us neither a catalogue of winners and losers nor any sense that winning or losing matters to the competitors. The form of the suitors' deaths is a perfect reversal of the lives they led. We start with games that mean nothing and where death is banished, empty intellectual trifles where the body is not involved and life is taken for granted. We end with a bow contest that links physical to social worth and where the specter of death, formally banished in the previous non-contests, erupts. What has been repressed in the suitors' daily lives returns in every deadly arrow Odysseus shoots. So what distinguishes these two very different sets of games: the empty displays of the suitors and the intense competition at Patroclus's funeral?

The stakes are high here and ultimately relate to the relationship between politics and competition. For we have two kinds of utopia on view, which will provide the contours for the future democratic experiments of the Greeks. In both cases we have not politics but an organized "pretend" community that acts as a provocation to political thinking. The lack of politics proper is due in both cases to an absence: Agamemnon neither supervises the games nor takes part in them, just as Odysseus's absence is the *sine qua non* for the strange form of social organization among the suitors on Ithaca. Finally, both worlds presume the equality, even if this is obviously artificial, of all the participants. The Greeks in the funeral games compete from the same starting point regardless of intrinsic worth (there is no handicapping). In the case of the suitors, their supposed competition for Penelope is on permanent hold, leaving them as *de facto* equals because of the absence of the man recognized as best, Odysseus himself.

But the differences are equally important. To help elucidate this, let me turn to some speculations of Nietzsche on the significance of competition for the formation of the Greek state, and his provocative attempt to rethink the logic of democratic ostracism. "Contest culture," he argues, was central to Greek political organization, and this culture in turn produced an ambivalence toward anyone who seemed to be the best.

If one wants to observe this conviction—wholly undisguised in its most naïve expression—that the contest is necessary to preserve the health of the state, then one should reflect on the original meaning of ostracism, for example, as it is pronounced by the Ephesians when they banish Hermodorus: 'Among us, no one shall be the best; but if someone is, then let him be elsewhere and among others [Heraclitus]'. Why should no one be the best? Because then the contest would come to an end and the eternal source of life for the Hellenic state would be endangered. Later on ostracism receives quite another position with regard to contests; it is applied, when the danger becomes obvious that one of the great competing politicians and party-leaders feels

himself urged on in the heat of the conflict towards harmful and destructive measures and dubious coups d'état. The original sense of this peculiar
institution however is not that of a safety-valve but that of a stimulant. The
all-excelling individual was to be removed in order that the contest of forces
might re-awaken, a thought which is hostile to the 'exclusiveness' of genius
in the modern sense but which assumes that in the natural order of things
there are always several geniuses which incite one another to action, as much
also as they hold one another within the bounds of moderation. That is the
kernel of the Hellenic contest-conception: it abominates autocracy, and fears
its dangers; it desires as a preventive against the genius—a second genius.[3]

At first it seems that the suitors, and in particular Antinous, must learn
this political lesson. The suitors' games of *pessoi* are a double of a more
fundamental game that links them as a community, the presumed competition for the right to marry Penelope. Yet when the bow contest begins, Antinous, in a doubling of the strategy of deferral made famous
by Penelope's raveling and unraveling of Laertes's shroud, makes sure
that it does not end. He refuses to compete himself and tries to prolong it into the next day (*Od.* 21.257–68). The contest is deferred, and
Antinous suggests that they replace it with the more customary act of
feasting, without ever putting his own strength on the line. Antinous's
failure to compete is a way of keeping this game alive, but as an empty
ritual without closure, games without end, as if to have any winner at
all is to offer up the dangers of a "best man." From this perspective,
whether he succeeded or failed in stringing the bow, the result would
have exactly the same effect: it would end the protracted contest for
the hand of Penelope, end the uncertainty over who was best. Either
the suitors would condemn themselves to the knowledge of their own
impotence, a contest where all have lost and no one has won, or they
would be forced to crown Antinous victor. Even the form of the contest
emphasizes the equal status of the community of insiders.

'Take your turns in order from left to right, my companions
all, beginning from the place where the wine is served out.'

(*Od.* 21.141–42)

"ὄρνυσθ' ἑξείης ἐπιδέξια πάντες ἑταῖροι,
ἀρξάμενοι τοῦ χώρου, ὅθεν τέ περ οἰνοχοεύει."

The bow is passed around as wine is passed around in the communal
feasts, in a show of equality between drinkers that becomes formalized
in the Greek symposium. This is, perhaps, a hint that we should not be
looking for a resolution to the contest in victory, but that its significance

lies in the egalitarian way each is invited, in turn, to take part. Antinous preserves the ignorance of who is best, and this, he hopes, will allow their peculiar society to continue.

For all the moralizing hatred of the suitors that the *Odyssey* seems to delight in, it does so by identifying with the aristocratic position of Odysseus. When one brackets this identification, the world of the suitors begins to look strikingly proto-democratic. Yet even so, from the perspective of democratic hindsight, there is something wrong with the suitors' world. For in banishing knowledge of the "best" man, far from fostering competition, they banish the contest itself. Instead of a plurality of geniuses, we have a plurality of near nonentities, engaged in endless consumption but no production, fear of crowning a victor producing pseudo-action rather than a spur to action. For this reason their group inferiority complex remains all too real. Though Odysseus is physically removed from their world, he is with them all the time, a constant reminder of someone they formally aspire to replace, while their actions belie these aspirations. So two entirely different critiques of the suitors are available: one from an aristocratic and the other from a democratic perspective. From the former, they are essentially inferior to the aristocrat Odysseus, their presence in his palace an affront to the genetic order of things. From the latter, their sense of inferiority produces their own impotence, and their loss in the bow contest is a symptom of the feebleness of a society that long ago ceased to compete.

We can now see what is so different about the funeral games. In the *Odyssey*, the best man is physically absent but all the more present as a fantasy organizing the lives of the suitors. But by the end of the *Iliad* the "best" of the Greeks, Agamemnon, is physically present, but without any grip on the imaginations of those around him. His status as leader is a formality, his merit nothing more than a fiction, adhered to but not believed in. So when Agamemnon fails to throw a spear, he becomes an embodied reminder of the idiocy of thinking that permanent excellence could ever reside in one person, and so the contests are real. Far from a restoration of aristocratic power, the funeral games suggest that Agamemnon, and the aristocratic *primus inter pares* ideology he represents, is dead, even if he does not yet know it.

We can also see the different kinds of equality at work in both communities. In the funeral games, an artificial equality is a spur to competition, an invitation both to take part and to differentiate oneself from the rest, until the next game reestablishes that equality once more. In the case of the suitors, their failure to participate in meaningful competition ensures an equality of nobodies, both theoretically and practically—theoretically because the suitors are committed to the collective need not to know who is the best among them, and this is the central truth that keeps them together; practically because this taboo, and the concomitant lack of competition, condemns them to become statically equal, to lose any link to the practice of social virtues that might distinguish them.

Conflict Management

There is one other obvious difference between the funeral games and the competition of the suitors. Book 23 presents a series of games, and an array of different prizes for each one, and the poem lingers over the difficulty of the process of distribution. The Greeks continue to try to match material value to social worth. For the suitors, the contest is to be won by the single man who can string the bow, and it is a lone contest for an object of incalculable value, Penelope. The funeral games preserve a social peace by distributing gifts with flexibility; they avoid the all-or-nothing nature of the bow contest on Ithaca. But even the funeral games nearly stumble at the first hurdle. Fighting over the prizes for the first event almost brings an end to everything. And if the fight will not be over a woman, it will be over a proxy for a woman.

The prizes for the chariot race are named by Achilles in advance of the race, and seem unexceptional.

[Achilleus] brought prizes for games out of his ships, cauldrons and tripods,
and horses and mules and the powerful high heads of cattle
and fair-girdled women and grey iron. First of all
he set forth the glorious prizes for speed of foot for the horsemen:
a woman faultless in the work of her hands to lead away
and a tripod with ears and holding twenty-two measures
for the first prize; and for the second he set forth a six-year-old
unbroken mare who carried a mule foal within her.
Then for the third prize he set forth a splendid unfired
cauldron, which held four measures, with its natural gloss still upon it.
For the fourth place he set out two talents' weight of gold, and for
the fifth place set forth an unfired jar with two handles.

(*Il.* 23.259–70)

νηῶν δ' ἔκφερ' ἄεθλα, λέβητάς τε τρίποδάς τε
ἵππους θ' ἡμιόνους τε βοῶν τ' ἴφθιμα κάρηνα,

ἠδὲ γυναῖκας ἐϋζώνους πολιόν τε σίδηρον.
Ἱππεῦσιν μὲν πρῶτα ποδώκεσιν ἀγλά᾽ ἄεθλα
θῆκε γυναῖκα ἄγεσθαι ἀμύμονα ἔργα ἰδυῖαν
καὶ τρίποδ᾽ ὠτώεντα δυωκαιεικοσίμετρον,
τῷ πρώτῳ· ἀτὰρ αὖ τῷ δευτέρῳ ἵππον ἔθηκεν
ἑξέτε᾽ ἀδμήτην, βρέφος ἡμίονον κυέουσαν·
αὐτὰρ τῷ τριτάτῳ ἄπυρον κατέθηκε λέβητα
καλὸν, τέσσαρα μέτρα κεχανδότα, λευκὸν ἔτ᾽ αὔτως·
τῷ δὲ τετάρτῳ θῆκε δύω χρυσοῖο τάλαντα,
πέμπτῳ δ᾽ ἀμφίθετον φιάλην ἀπύρωτον ἔθηκε.

The list begins with a woman, but it is the detail of the mare, pregnant with a mule, that will later be picked up by the poet. When the race is over, Achilles suggests that Admetus, who came last despite having the best horses, should be given second place. A worry endemic to games themselves, that short-term luck can override merit, is brought into focus. But Antilochus quickly rejects the solution.

[']But if you are sorry for him and he is dear to your liking,
there is abundant gold in your shelter, and there is bronze there
and animals, and there are handmaidens and single-foot horses.
You can take from these, and give him afterwards a prize still greater
than mine, or now at once, and have the Achaians applaud you.
But the mare I will not give up, and the man who wants her
must fight me for her with his hands before he can take her.'
So he spoke, but brilliant swift-footed Achilleus, favouring
Antilochos, smiled . . .

(Il. 23.548–55)

"εἰ δέ μιν οἰκτίρεις καί τοι φίλος ἔπλετο θυμῷ,
ἔστί τοι ἐν κλισίῃ χρυσὸς πολύς, ἔστι δὲ χαλκὸς
καὶ πρόβατ᾽, εἰσὶ δέ τοι δμῳαὶ καὶ μώνυχες ἵπποι·
τῶν οἱ ἔπειτ᾽ ἀνελὼν δόμεναι καὶ μεῖζον ἄεθλον,
ἠὲ καὶ αὐτίκα νῦν, ἵνα σ᾽ αἰνήσωσιν Ἀχαιοί.
τὴν δ᾽ ἐγὼ οὐ δώσω· περὶ δ᾽ αὐτῆς πειρηθήτω
ἀνδρῶν ὅς κ᾽ ἐθέλῃσιν ἐμοὶ χείρεσσι μάχεσθαι."
Ὣς φάτο, μείδησεν δὲ ποδάρκης δῖος Ἀχιλλεὺς . . .

The horse's sex reminds us here of the same phrase, used by Agamemnon, when he refused to return Chryseis: I will not give her up. Achilles smiles as if to acknowledge this, and the tragedy of the first book returns here as near comedy. The event parades itself as a crisis, but the emotional involvement, from the perspective of Achilles, is hardly necessary because this story has already been told.

The elevating of a mare to the position of woman as object of su-
preme value is part parody, but it casts light on the conditions that
produce judgments of value. In the primary list of gifts, we start with
a woman, but it is the mare, pregnant with an offspring of a different species, with all the baggage that this entails, that will replace the
woman in the fight.[4] The contest allegorizes the problem of a woman's
value, the mare's pregnancy voicing a fear, never explicitly uttered,
about Helen and what happens to wives who sleep with foreigners. We
also see the genesis of value itself, for the worth of objects is far from
intrinsic, but instead linked to the events of the competition, and the
risks Antilochus has run to win this object. Without his staring down
of death, the mare would be worth less to him. Antilochus's risking of
his own life in the chariot race becomes a double of Achilles's own risks
for his spear-prizes, and these feelings are transferred into the importance placed on mare, Briseis, and Helen alike. It is common to point toward the women in this poem as largely objects, things to be exchanged
rather than human subjects who themselves control exchange, as part
of the poem's patriarchal fabric. But one reason for the epic's tragedy is
that they are not treated enough as objects. Women become the privi-
leged site for the transference of the contradictory feelings of the warriors around them. This has nothing to do with women themselves, but
everything to do with the role they play in the male psychic economy.
Nor does this provide any ultimate solution to the problems posed by
the episode. Is it deflationary, a bathetic downgrading of the sublime
fight over a woman into one over a mare? Or is it instead a suggestion of
the way the most apparently ordinary of everyday prizes can suddenly
become elevated in status?

But this conflict between Menelaus and Antilochus will be solved
more elegantly than the one of the first book, and with two different
kinds of flexibility. We can term them objective and subjective flexibility,
though, as we will see, the worlds of subjects and objects thoroughly
interpenetrate each other. At the level of objects, Achilles simply acquiesces to Antilochus's suggestion, and adds a gift.

[']if you would have me bring some other thing out of my dwelling
as special gift for Eumelos, then for your sake I will do it.'

(*Il.* 23.558–59)

The zero-sum contest is undermined, and once more we are reminded
of Briseis's role in Book 1. For zero-sum conflict turns out not to be
something objective, but to be dependent on the desire for such a con-

flict. If competitors fight over a finite amount of gifts, they must in part be committed to provoking such a fight, and not simply because of attachment to the objects themselves. There is no necessity limiting their number. Achilles's actions here are a retroactive critique of Agamemnon: he acts out the generosity of a king and empties his own coffers in an act of largesse that allows social solidarity to be preserved. But we can also remember his own suggestion that Chryseis cannot be replaced because there is no store of public booty available for distribution. For the largesse he now shows was also available to him then. If it is true that there are no public goods, there is certainly an excess of private goods he once chose to keep private in order to keep the conflict alive.

Let us now turn to our characters' subjective feelings. The distribution of objects changes, but Menelaus still considers himself cheated by Antilochus. But this too is resolved. First, Antilochus retracts.

[']You know how greedy transgressions flower in a young man, seeing
that his mind is the more active but his judgment is lightweight. Therefore
I would have your heart be patient with me. I myself will give you
the mare I won, and if there were something still greater you asked for
out of my house, I should still be willing at once to give it
to you, beloved of Zeus, rather than all my days
fall from your favour and be in the wrong before the divinities.

(*Il.* 23.589–95)

Antilochus's speech is a triumph of diplomacy. Without admitting responsibility directly, he turns his own specific situation into a generalized truth. All young men are greedy, though the rest of the syllogism (I am young man, therefore I am greedy) is left unspoken. He acknowledges his former self, and yet distances his present self from past acts, as if the man in the chariot race is a third person distant from the one who now dishes out gnomic wisdom about the folly of young men. Antilochus gives in without any of the humiliation associated with capitulation.

But he also shifts the frame of reference of the conflict toward the generosity associated with gift exchange. Not only the mare will be returned, but the mare as representative of "something still greater." But it is here that the poem once more flirts with the antinomies of such generosity. For, as we take up our imaginary invitation inside Antilochus's house, what is the most valuable item there? A mare has metamorphosed into Helen, and returned us to the poem's earlier joke on Menelaus: that he was willing to "offer his guests 'dearness,'" *philotes.*

Antilochus's act is impossible to read, an act of generosity that threatens to disrupt the particular fabric of the life of the *oikos*, but also an act of subservience that flirts with ridicule, either a double of Menelaus's own unwitting generosity or a parody.

Menelaus's response takes up the challenge, and the poet continues the allegory of the causes of the Trojan War.

> 'Antilochos,
> I myself, who was angry, now will give way before you,
> since you were not formerly loose-minded or vain. It is only
> that this time your youth got the better of your intelligence.
> Beware another time of playing tricks on your betters.
> Any other man of the Achaians might not have appeased me.
> But you have suffered much for me, and done much hard work,
> and your noble father too, and your brother for my sake. Therefore
> I will be ruled by your supplication. I will even give you
> the mare, though she is mine, so that these men too may be witnesses
> that the heart is never arrogant nor stubborn within me.'
>
> (*Il.* 23.602–11)

Menelaus is sure to fill out Antilochus's syllogism. He even reshapes the implied significance of the loss of Helen. Menelaus's generosity gets him in trouble; the war itself has become a series of labors on his behalf. The language of uniqueness, and thus of flattery, "I only accept from you," is simultaneously the language of threat and of one-upmanship: "Anyone else but you would have died, and I choose to spare you."

The entire episode is a theoretical reflection on the nature of gift exchange, perhaps even an attempt to transfer manners into a code of law. The mule, though never changing hands in reality, and still belonging to Antilochus, has been stamped, in the minds of all, with the ownership seal of Menelaus. Instead of a gift freely given, the kind of gift that embeds the person receiving it in a web of reciprocal relations, this object takes with it the sign of someone else's ownership. In Antilochus's house, it nevertheless belongs to Menelaus. Antilochus can use it, but at the price of its not belonging to him. So the question arises: could this technical sophistication have stopped the Trojan War? Could Helen have stayed with Paris, if Paris had been willing publicly to renounce his claims on her, and if Menelaus, in exchange for Paris's recognition of his property rights, allowed her to? Paris could have her only on the condition that he realizes she can never be properly his.

The mare is perfectly appropriate. Antilochus and Menelaus fight over the division of an object that cannot be divided physically and yet already bears the marks of division—like Helen of Troy, Helen of Sparta, born of a god, born of man—and this division could prolong itself into the next generation by means of her mule offspring. Yet the episode also shows how so much changes even as the world of objects stays the same: Antilochus begins and ends with the mare in his possession. At first, with hindsight, it seems as if Antilochus finds a perfect solution to his problem. For the only way to keep the mare without creating a social catastrophe is by letting it go. He must give her up in order to keep her. But Menelaus's intervention adds a footnote: Antilochus will only be able to have her the second time around at the price of publicly admitting that she is not his.

5

Couples
The *Iliad* on Intimacy

The *Iliad* creates a crescendo of couples. Agamemnon and Chryseis, Achilles and Briseis, Helen and Paris, Hector and Andromache, Achilles and Patroclus—all move in and out of narrative focus, bringing with them their different versions of love. So when Hector and Achilles duel to the death in Book 22 in their long-awaited brief encounter, it is not surprising that it takes an erotic turn. Rather than fight, Hector imagines a way out. What if they could talk to each other as a boy and girl, speaking the language of love? Hector rejects the idea as utopian, and asks for something more manageable. He suggests that they return to the civilized rules of warfare, the mutual respect for either corpse after one of them dies. But Achilles brutally rules this out.

'Hektor, argue me no agreements. I cannot forgive you.
As there are no trustworthy oaths between men and lions,
nor wolves and lambs have spirit that can be brought to agreement
but forever these hold feelings of hate for each other,
so there can be no love between you and me, nor shall there be
oaths between us, but one or the other must fall before then
to glut with his blood Ares the god who fights under the shield's guard.[']

(*Il.* 22.261–67)

If the *Iliad* is a story about the defeat of intimacy, about the replacement of social bonds with an inhuman disdain for them, this is its crowning moment. Achilles lauds the victory of the logic of heroism and war, the zero-sum brutality of "'kill or be killed,'" over everyday, domestic peace. As Hector put it earlier, this is the erotic language, the "'sweet invitation'" in Lattimore's translation, the *aoristus*, of war.

Therefore a man must now turn his face straight forward, and perish
or survive. This is the sweet invitation of battle.

(*Il.* 17.227–28)

τῷ τις νῦν ἰθὺς τετραμμένος ἢ ἀπολέσθω
ἠὲ σαωθήτω· ἢ γὰρ πολέμου ὀαριστύς.

But though the romantic solution is ruled out, the language of *eros* suffuses Homer's description of their duel. Hector and Achilles will meet "'apart from the others'" (οἶος ἄνευθ' ἄλλων, as Priam fears at *Il.* 22.39) in an isolated togetherness that mirrors the intimacy of lovers. Such intimate separation from all others is rare in the poem. When Hector and Andromache meet on the walls of Troy, for example, they are not alone but accompanied by a servant, and this surely removes much of the *eros* from their encounter. By way of contrast, when Aphrodite escorts Helen to Paris's bedroom and leaves them alone, the implications are clear. Some of the dangerous, erotically charged connotations of two alone together are glimpsed in Glaucus's "'Potiphar's wife's tale'" of his grandfather Bellerophon's encounter with his guest-friend's wife, Anteia (*Il.* 6.160–96). Their momentary intimacy, alone apart from others, lasts long enough for Anteia to make her advances and Bellerophon to refuse, but the doubt spawned by the secrecy of the encounter will soon have fatal consequences. As with Achilles and Thetis, there is an atmosphere of secrecy and possible betrayal as these couples spend time "'alone together,'" but now erotic desire becomes part of the mix.

Achilles also looks Hector up and down for a point of weakness in his own armor, now worn by his foe (*Il.* 22.321–23), conceptually undressing his most intimate enemy. When the Greeks will later take turns stabbing his corpse, we are given a martial allegory of the violent sexual acts that Homer elsewhere spares us. When Paris sees Helen, for example, he feels desire, and then the narrator rushes to the euphemism of their going to bed together (3.447–48). The killing of Hector transfers the language of sex onto the battlefield.

Hector in Love

This prevalence of the erotic should encourage us to look in more detail at Hector's utopian thought experiment (*Il.* 17.227–28). Exactly what kind of romantic scenario does he imagine, and why is it so impossible? For though Hector's intuition is surely right, the reasons for it are complex.

> [']Or if again I set down my shield massive in the middle
> and my ponderous helm, and lean my spear up against the rampart
> and go out as I am to meet Achilleus the blameless
> and promise to give back Helen, and with her all her possessions,
> all those things that once in the hollowed ships Alexandros
> brought back to Troy, and these were the beginning of the quarrel;
> to give these to Atreus' sons to take away, and for the Achaians
> also to divide up all that is hidden within the city,
> and take an oath thereafter for the Trojans in conclave
> not to hide anything away, but distribute all of it,
> as much as the lovely citadel keeps guarded within it;
> yet, still, why does my heart within me debate on these things?
> I might go up to him, and he take no pity upon me
> nor respect my position, but kill me naked so, as if I were
> a woman, once I stripped my armour from me. There is no
> way any more from a tree or a rock to talk to him gently
> whispering like a young man and a young girl, in the way
> a young man and a young maiden whisper together.
> Better to bring on the fight with him as soon as it may be.
> We shall see to which one the Olympian grants the glory.'

(*Il.* 22.111–30)

> "εἰ δέ κεν ἀσπίδα μὲν καταθείομαι ὀμφαλόεσσαν
> καὶ κόρυθα βριαρήν, δόρυ δὲ πρὸς τεῖχος ἐρείσας
> αὐτὸς ἰὼν Ἀχιλῆος ἀμύμονος ἀντίος ἔλθω
> καί οἱ ὑπόσχωμαι Ἑλένην καὶ κτήμαθ' ἅμ' αὐτῇ,
> πάντα μάλ' ὅσσά τ' Ἀλέξανδρος κοίλης ἐνὶ νηυσὶν
> ἠγάγετο Τροίηνδ', ἥ τ' ἔπλετο νείκεος ἀρχή,
> δωσέμεν Ἀτρεΐδησιν ἄγειν, ἅμα δ' ἀμφὶς Ἀχαιοῖς
> ἄλλ' ἀποδάσσεσθαι, ὅσα τε πτόλις ἥδε κέκευθε·
> Τρωσὶν δ' αὖ μετόπισθε γερούσιον ὅρκον ἕλωμαι
> μή τι κατακρύψειν, ἀλλ' ἄνδιχα πάντα δάσασθαι
> κτῆσιν ὅσην πτολίεθρον ἐπήρατον ἐντὸς ἐέργει·
> ἀλλὰ τίη μοι ταῦτα φίλος διελέξατο θυμός;
> μή μιν ἐγὼ μὲν ἵκωμαι ἰών, ὃ δέ μ' οὐκ ἐλεήσει
> οὐδέ τί μ' αἰδέσεται, κτενέει δέ με γυμνὸν ἐόντα
> αὔτως ὥς τε γυναῖκα, ἐπεί κ' ἀπὸ τεύχεα δύω.
> οὐ μέν πως νῦν ἔστιν ἀπὸ δρυὸς οὐδ' ἀπὸ πέτρης
> τῷ ὀαριζέμεναι, ἅ τε παρθένος ἠΐθεός τε,
> παρθένος ἠΐθεός τ' ὀαρίζετον ἀλλήλοιιν.

βέλτερον αὖτ' ἔριδι ξυνελαυνέμεν ὅττι τάχιστα·
εἴδομεν ὁπποτέρῳ κεν Ὀλύμπιος εὖχος ὀρέξῃ."

The poet contrasts the violence of war and a peaceful erotic discourse of
domesticity. Love and war are opposed to each other, the latter a nega-
tion of the former. The language of a maiden and young man, about to
embark upon the first stages of an erotic partnership, doubles the way
the poet lingers over the domestic chores of washing that went on in the
streams outside Troy. Hector and Achilles have just run round a world
that is lost, and yet still visible (*Il.* 22.147–56). His fantasy is of peace,
and the lovers' conversation merges into the peace before the Achaeans came. The contrast seems greater when we recognize that the verb
used here, ὀαριζέμεναι, is used by the poet to describe the interchange
between Hector and Andromache in Book 6.

[Paris] came on brilliant Hektor, his brother, where he yet lingered
before turning away from the place where he had talked with his lady.

(*Il.* 6.515–16)

Ἕκτορα δῖον ἔτετμεν ἀδελφεὸν, εὖτ' ἄρ' ἔμελλε
στρέψεσθ' ἐκ χώρης ὅθι ᾗ ὀάριζε γυναικί.

This meeting, even as it ties Hector up in a series of social relations at
Troy, will be their last.

But rather than dilute Hector's fantasy of love-talk, we should bring
it into greater focus. The word ὀαριζέμεναι can help. Though of uncer-
tain etymology, it is most likely linked to the verb ἀραρίσκω, "'to fit together.'"[1] This fits well with the most common use of ὀάρ as a noun,
which seems to mean not "'lover,'" but rather "'spouse'" or "'companion.'" Hector's metaphor of "'the love-language of war'" would suggest that when two men fight, there is a different kind of commitment
than that of marriage, but one that echoes marriage: the agreement to
kill or be killed, to turn two into one, mixed up in the strange physical
intimacy of the face-to-face encounter, takes the place of an agreement
to produce one out of two, and the ensuing intimacy of sex that leads
to an expanded family unit. So when Hector imagines a way out of this
language of war, and turns instead to two lovers, it is not just their flirtation that he imagines, but flirtation preceding their promises. In this
language of love, promises become a commitment for a shared life, and
at the center of a culture of "'making,'" not "'unmaking'"—of creation,
not destruction.[2]

But the metaphor works both ways, as the zero-sum commitment of war also colors the poem's view of marriage. Let us return to Hector and Andromache. For all the tender and comforting words uttered between husband and wife, their parting ends with an order. Hector demands that she return to the domestic interior even as he departs from the city into the plain: "'Go therefore back to our house, and take up your own work'" (*Il.* 6.490). Book 22 remembers this command, for Andromache, embedded in the interior of the palace, faithful to his command to weave indoors, as a result becomes the last to find out about Hector's death (*Il.* 22.440–66).

But why was such a command necessary? When Hector returned in Book 6 from the battlefield to try to find her, she was not in her place; she had gone with a maid and her son to the battlements. This mini-drama, spanning Book 6 and Book 22, begins by attempting to return a woman to her place, but it overshoots the mark, forcing her so far into the interior of the house that she loses all contact with the social world around her. This too is part of the "'conversation'" between husband and wife, the language of *aoristus*. Her obedience to Hector distances her all too far from him, divorcing her from the most elementary kind of participation in his life.

The domestic drama between Hector and Andromache is not the glamorized tale of private intimacy it is often taken to be. There is pathos to the episode, the tragic suffering of the isolated Andromache and the way her discourse invokes her helplessness and dependence. But Andromache flits between an extreme of helplessness and a disturbing independence. And these two things are causally related. Because she is in an anomalous position in terms of her kin, because she is socially embedded entirely by way of her husband and not in a broader set of family relations, she is strangely freer from the usual constraints. Let us turn to her speech to Hector.

['']Hektor, thus you are father to me, and my honoured mother,
you are my brother, and you it is who are my young husband.
Please take pity upon me then, stay here on the rampart,
that you may not leave your child an orphan, your wife a widow,
but draw your people up by the fig tree, there where the city
is openest to attack, and where the wall may be mounted.
Three times their bravest came that way, and fought there to storm it
about the two Aiantes and renowned Idomeneus,
about the two Atreidai and the fighting son of Tydeus.
Either some man well skilled in prophetic arts had spoken,
or the very spirit within themselves had stirred them to the onslaught.'

(*Il.* 6.429–39)

Consider the marked contrast between the opening and closing of the speech. First, she outlines her tragic family history, the loss of her close family members one by one, and so her pathetic dependence. But it is the close of her speech that shocked the most famous editor of Homer in antiquity, Aristarchus, who believed Homer could not have written those lines. For, as he puts it, Andromache is "'opposing him [Hector] as a general,'" something impossibly inappropriate for a woman.[3] The battle advice is also ignored in the rest of the poem. A scholiast tries to motivate the lines by suggesting that they refer to the things that she has seen from the wall, as if she is excitedly reporting a recent discovery. This quaint remark, called "'absurd'" by a recent commentator, looks for a narrative rationale to explain the anomaly of Andromache's advice.[4] Yet the absurdity hints at an explanation. A momentary view from the wall cannot explain Andromache's advice; it is hardly likely that, in the few moments that she has been on the wall, this series of attacks has occurred. Only a long-term presence on the wall could provide the perspective for this long-term strategy. But what if Homer suggests this? What if this single trip to the wall is not quite so isolated, and her constant observation is what leads to this attempt to "'be a general'"? Certainly Hector seems aware of it, with a riposte that is strangely defensive, replacing strategy with the sexual apartheid of the code of honor.

['']Go therefore back to our house, and take up your own work,
the loom and the distaff, and see to it that your handmaidens
ply their work also; but the men must see to the fighting,
all men who are the people of Ilion, but I beyond others.'

(*Il.* 6.490–93)

Andromache's advice is a problem, something that sticks out and cannot be easily integrated into the story. In terms of narrative, there is the unmotivated and isolated mention of the Greek attack on a single part of the wall; in terms of social mores, her "'opposition as a general'" that so perplexed Aristarchus. The only way to get rid of the narrative problem is by making the social problem all the more acute. It makes sense as advice if she has been a regular visitor to the wall, and if she has regularly been putting herself in the position of a general, but this is to dare to imagine Andromache differently, not as idealized, submissive wife. The notion that she saw the attack on this single visit solves this dilemma, but at the price of narrative absurdity.

The situation of Penelope at the opening of the *Odyssey* offers an instructive double. For when Telemachus returns her to the domestic interior in the opening book, at the point when he is coming of age and gives orders for the first time, we might ask: where has she been for the last twenty years? The absence of a man in charge of the house has consequences for social life in Ithaca and the role of free women, though we are given only a glimpse of them. *Iliad* 6 gives us a compressed version. The men are still removed, though only to the space outside the walls. And yet Andromache's husband's absence still allows a freedom to maneuver. Even the triangle formed between husband, wife, and son is doubled. In the *Odyssey*, we see the moment when a wife loses her freedom of movement but gains the pleasure of seeing her son grow to maturity and regain control of the household. This is the bribe she is offered for a return to Greek cultural norms.

This is also the lurking logic of Hector's doomed fantasy for the future of their son, Astyanax. For when Astyanax cries at his father's helmet, the tears threaten the cultural logic of the heroic world. The child is "'unmanly,'" offering up a natural reaction to his father's gore-filled helmet, failing to see the person he naively believes to be his father beneath the mask. But he must learn that there is more truth in this gore-spattered mask than in the face behind it. He will have to become the kind of warrior who does not shrink from blood, because this is exactly the kind of man his father is. His coming of age will also be tied to a sexual hierarchy: he will bring back spoil to delight his mother. What Andromache will be allowed, in the possible gap opened up between the eclipse of the father and the maturation of the son, is the hope for the son's emergence as a warrior, and eventual pride in his martial exploits. But what disappears is both the possibility for another kind of son and another kind of identity for Andromache.

Yet we also witness a duplication of wedding vows between Hector and Andromache, a second commitment between husband and wife to the idea of commitment itself. The feel of intimacy comes from the *form* of this language: if Hector commands and Andromache obeys, this ties them together as husband and wife. The tragedy lies in the content of the commitment. Andromache's separation from Hector, her inability to persuade him of her military insight, guarantees both their dooms.

Let us return to Hector's fantasy of Book 22. There is a contrast between the word for "'woman/wife'" in 22.125—"he might kill me naked, like a *gyne*, 'woman/wife'"—and the switch to the word *parthenos*, "'virgin,'" "'maiden,'" in 22.127. Hector first imagines himself as a helpless, isolated woman before Achilles, the very situation he imagined for Andromache in Book 6. There, he morosely imagined the day Troy would be taken and Andromache dragged off, only to hope that he might die before ever witnessing it (*Il.* 6.447–65). In response to this image of an isolated woman, he imagines himself a young girl, but only insofar as he is the possible future bride of Achilles. The first image, a naked woman soon to be the possession of her male conqueror, highlights a pure asymmetry of power, and his response is to go back in time, to imagine these same figures as a young man and women talking to each other in the words of commitment, turning from a moment when discourse has no meaning to one where the language of promise means everything.

This gives context for Hector's prior offer of all the possessions of Troy. The speech returns us to the pivotal speech of Achilles in Book 9, where he claims that no amount of goods from Agamemnon can bring him back to the war, for they are not worth his life. Here, no amount of goods will be worth Hector's life. But, in the case of Agamemnon, it was not simply a string of commodities that was offered, but gifts linked to kinship ties, including marriage and subordination to Agamemnon as son-in-law. Here, the offer of all that Troy can materially give is not just the sign of an impossible generosity, but an imaginary presentation of bridal gifts, one that seeks recompense all at once for quite discrete problems that have haunted the entire poem.

First, there is the attempted recompense for the cause of the war, the abduction of Helen. Hector imagines reversing the effects of the capture of a bride and her household goods by the opposite process, a wedding of perfect generosity, where the city empties itself out as a bride price. In response to the negotiations over what the Trojans might offer to end the war, Hector contemplates a gift giving that goes hand in hand with surrender. In Book 6 Hector chases Andromache, eventually catching up with her on the wall. She surrenders to the role of good wife. This is played out once more in Book 22, but here it is Hector who is chased and finally tricked into facing Achilles, only to imagine a life-saving surrender to which he cannot commit.

Second, there is the isolation of Achilles. One symptom is the poem's failure to embed him in the bond of marriage. Three possible marriages stretch out before him in the poem, with three separate fathers imagined organizing them. First we have Briseis. Though it begins as a relationship of conqueror to concubine, we later find out that he flirts with marriage, and with Patroclus as instigator (*Il.* 19.295–99). This marriage would effectively tie Achilles to the sets of relationships that have defined him for the previous decade in Troy, and it points to the sign of Patroclus's power over Achilles there, in the makeshift situation of Greeks in Troy that has become more and more permanent. There are two competitors for the marriage arrangement in Greece. Agamemnon offers a daughter as bride in Mycenae, but Achilles himself imagines a Greek alternative, a return to Phthia, where his father, Peleus, would arrange the marriage. But Achilles remains free of all these attachments. Hector's speech operates with these problems as background, and since he cannot come up with a pragmatic solution, he conjures up a utopian one, an impossible wedding that would return Achilles to the social world and also repair the damage caused by Helen's abduction. Because there is no worthy bride, he puts himself in the place of one, only to deny this as impossible: "'There is no way to talk to him.'" His fantasy is a neat, imaginary solution to a real problem. The only difficulty, much as in the closing scene of Billy Wilder's *Some Like It Hot*, when the millionaire finds out that his future bride is a man in drag, is that in the world they live in, men do not marry men. Because *Some Like It Hot* is a comedy, the millionaire can drolly respond to his future bride's confession that he is a man with the retort "'Nobody's perfect.'" The *Iliad* follows a more tragic path.

One further displaced erotic desire haunts Books 6 and 22. Why does Hector choose to face Achilles in the first place? He claims that he cannot return to Troy after the destruction of lives he has caused, that he would feel shame in front of the Trojan women (*Il.* 22.105–7). But the form of his death suggests a second possibility. In Book 6 Hector leaves his comrades on the battlefield and goes back to the city, but he will soon return to them, leaving his wife and family behind. In Book 22 he once more splits off from his Trojan comrades to fight Achilles. But this time they will not reunite, and none come to help him. Did he expect them to? The trick Athena plays upon him suggests that the narrative is alive to the problem.

Athene left him there, and caught up with brilliant Hektor,
and likened herself in form and weariless voice to Deïphobos.
She came now and stood close to him and addressed him in winged words:
'Dear brother, indeed swift-footed Achilleus is using you roughly
and chasing you on swift feet around the city of Priam.
Come on, then; let us stand fast against him and beat him back from us.'
        Then tall Hektor of the shining helm answered her: 'Deïphobos,
before now you were dearest to me by far of my brothers,
of all those who were sons of Priam and Hekabe, and now
I am minded all the more within my heart to honour you,
you who dared for my sake, when your eyes saw me, to come forth
from the fortifications, while the others stand fast inside them.'

                                                        (*Il.* 22.226–37)

What is at stake in the fight with Achilles now changes. Less an attempt to win *kleos* and to avoid shame, it becomes a test of love offered up to his fellow Trojans. Athena cruelly allows Hector the illusion, for a moment, that at least one of his comrades loved him enough to risk his life at the hands of Achilles. Hector's language makes the cruelty all the more awful. He speaks of Deiphobus, for the first time in the poem, as "'by far the dearest'" of his kinsmen, leaving us to ponder the absence of *philoi* from his current predicament. He imagines Deiphobus unable to endure seeing him die, preferring to risk death outside the wall, and turns every Trojan into a willing watcher of his death, rooted to the spot by their individual cowardice. Perhaps, in a turn of the screw, Athena deliberately chooses to take the name of a Trojan who has the word "'fear'" emblazoned across his name, Dei*phobos*. He stands in for the fears that everyone behind the walls of Troy feels in the face of Achilles.

But this test of love also picks up a crucial scene from Book 6. For when Hector encounters Helen in Book 6, and she tries to persuade him to take a seat in her room at Troy, he refuses not only because of his duty to his comrades. Rather, it is their longing for him.

> 'Do not, Helen,
> make me sit with you, though you love me. You will not persuade me.
> Already my heart within me is hastening me to defend
> the Trojans, who when I am away long greatly to have me.[']
>
> (*Il.* 6.359–62)

"μή με κάθιζ᾽, Ἑλένη, φιλέουσά περ· οὐδέ με πείσεις·
ἤδη γάρ μοι θυμὸς ἐπέσσυται ὄφρ᾽ ἐπαμύνω
Τρώεσσ᾽, οἳ μέγ᾽ ἐμεῖο ποθὴν ἀπεόντος ἔχουσιν."

Hector displaces Helen's barely concealed desire for him. Her implied longing (ποθὴν) means little compared to the longing felt by his fellow Trojan warriors. But Athena's trick in Book 22 will show him, and us, that the desire remains unreciprocated. The Trojans do not feel the longing for him when he is absent that he felt for them.

Love Arriving Too Late

Hector is surely right that his imaginary proposal to Achilles would have failed. But there is a specific reason: Patroclus. The problem is not just that Hector has killed Patroclus. As we have seen, this is a dubious proposition at best. Rather, Hector's fantasy of a symmetrical lover's discourse with Achilles forgets that Achilles already has had this fantasy, but with Patroclus. Hector's utopia is far more out of place than he realizes. He articulates a possible relationship between himself and Achilles that takes the place of a relationship between Achilles and Patroclus that has long been foreshadowed. So Hector's fantasy of the future is thus a vision of a lost opportunity between Achilles and Patroclus.

The nature of Achilles's love for Patroclus is a notorious problem. Were they lovers? Is Homer's silence on the question an example of his tact, or is Homer silent because they are only friends? At the very least, Achilles's mother thinks that they were lovers. As she sees him writhing in sleepless agony over Patroclus's death, "'longing for his manliness'" (ποθέων ἀνδροτῆτά, *Il.* 24.6), she reminds him of the virtues of sleeping with a woman. "'It is a good thing to mingle in intimacy with *even* a woman'" (ἀγαθὸν δὲ γυναικί περ ἐν φιλότητι / μίσγεσθ', *Il.* 24.130–31). As James Davidson has recently argued, to deny the force of the particle περ, "'with *even* a woman,'" in the name of cleansing any sexual sense from Thetis's words seems perverse.[5] But this does not mean that Patroclus and Achilles were lovers, only that Thetis interprets Achilles's writhing as he remembers his dead companion as a symptom of a belated sexual longing. It remains possible that Achilles's sexual desire only appears after Patroclus is dead. Achilles desires the unattainable.

But an emphasis on sex might cause us to miss something more radical. For the peculiar kind of symmetrical relationship that Homer imagines for Patroclus and Achilles is closer to marriage than simply sex. The motif begins in *Iliad* 9, when Phoenix offers up the parallel of Meleager's anger at his mother, and his refusal to fight on behalf of his people because of it (*Il.* 9.529–99). He withdraws together with his wife, Cleopatra, and chooses not to fight again until she supplicates him. Cleopatra's supplication not only foreshadows the later supplication of Patroclus (her name in reverse) in Book 16, but also suggests that Phoenix imagines Patroclus supplicating Achilles *as his wife*, just as Meleager's withdrawal into the domestic space with his wife mirrors Achilles's withdrawal with Patroclus. As Thetis can imagine the two as lovers, so their peculiar domestic arrangement allows Phoenix to think of them as a couple.

But they are a strange kind of couple. Let us return to Achilles's eerie wish in Book 16 that the two of them will be the only survivors of the sack of Troy, with all other Greeks and Trojans dead. Behind this strange scenario lies another mythic marriage. In the *Homeric Hymn to Demeter*, after Hades has abducted Persephone, Hermes eventually calls upon him to let her return to her mother, Demeter, on earth, in order to appease the maternal wrath (*menis*) that threatens all life. Hades relents and tells Persephone that she can return to her mother, but then reminds her of his suitability as a future husband.

for I shall be no unfitting husband for you among the deathless gods, that am own brother to father Zeus. And while you are here, you shall rule all that lives and moves . . .

(Hymn to Demeter 363–65)[6]

οὔ τοι ἐν ἀθανάτοισιν ἀεικὴς ἔσσομ' ἀκοίτης,
αὐτοκασίγνητος πατρὸς Διός· ἔνθα δ' ἐοῦσα
δεσπόσσεις πάντων ὁπόσα ζώει τε καὶ ἕρπει.

There is a well-known problem in these lines. Where exactly will Persephone be queen, and over the living or the dead? Hades seems to be congratulating her on her return to the earth, and Persephone seems to want to return there. So if he were offering her a marriage in Hades, this proposal would seem to have little chance of success. A reasonable solution is self-conscious ambiguity in the lines. One can imagine Persephone at first understanding that they refer to her dominion on *earth*, especially as the phrase "'all that lives and moves'" seems to refer to living creatures, not those of the underworld. But what can it mean to be queen of all that is alive? From Hades's perspective, is this not an apt description of the realm of death itself? To rule the dead is to have the ultimate control over the living, the certainty that any independence from death is only temporary, since life is lived on borrowed time. Hades's promise thus enigmatically straddles the world of earth and the underworld, articulating a relation between them rather than simply separating them. Even on earth death always has its implied dominion.

This conceptual relationship between the living and the dead, articulated through the vision of a marriage that entails dominion over all living things, can help us understand the fantasy implied in Achilles's final words to the living Patroclus.

[']Father Zeus, Athene and Apollo, if only
not one of all the Trojans could escape destruction, not one
of the Argives, but you and I could emerge from the slaughter
so that we two alone could break Troy's hallowed coronal.'

(Il. 16.97–100)

"αἲ γὰρ, Ζεῦ τε πάτερ καὶ Ἀθηναίη καὶ Ἄπολλον
μήτέ τις οὖν Τρώων θάνατον φύγοι, ὅσσοι ἔασι,
μήτέ τις Ἀργείων, νῶϊν δ' ἐκδῦμεν ὄλεθρον,
ὄφρ' οἶοι Τροίης ἱερὰ κρήδεμνα λύωμεν."

The universality of destruction suggests that Achilles imagines an authority over life and death. But although human lives are once again the spoils, he wants to share them equally. Even the erotic image of them "'loosening the veils'" of Troy, though usually understood as a rape fantasy suggested by the destruction of a town, seems just as appropriate to the loss of a maiden's virginity on her wedding night. If so, then Achilles's fantasy would follow the common Homeric practice of displacing a sexual desire. Achilles's fantasy of a wedding night with Patroclus is uttered only in the form of a metaphor, in the defloration imagined for Troy.

Patroclus's ghost later picks up this obscure motif as he imagines the kind of togetherness outlined by Achilles.

No longer shall you and I, alive, sit apart from our other
beloved companions and make our plans . . .

(*Il.* 23.77–78)

οὐ μὲν γὰρ ζωοί γε φίλων ἀπάνευθεν ἑταίρων
βουλὰς ἑζόμενοι βουλεύσομεν, ἀλλ' ἐμὲ μὲν κὴρ . . .

The lines point toward the secret that has separated them for the whole *Iliad*, and that Patroclus continues to remain unaware of: Achilles's request to his mother to kill Patroclus, his "'plan'" made apart not only from the Greeks, but from Patroclus too. But the fantasy of them alive "'apart from the companions'" suggests not just that Patroclus refers to his own irreversible death, but that he imagines the two of them as *the only two alive*, as if picking up the last words Achilles spoke to him.

But for all the fantasy of togetherness and symmetry in Achilles's relationship with Patroclus, the reality remains starkly different. Achilles's fantasy uses the dual form (νῶϊν) to highlight their imagined togetherness. But throughout the poem these heroes never do anything as a pair. Their togetherness occurs only in a fantasized future that will never arrive. Their failure to appear as a couple might also add something to our analysis of the most famous couples in the poem, at least in scholarly discourse: the duals of *Iliad* 9.

So these two walked along the strand of the sea deep-thundering
with many prayers to the holder and shaker of the earth, that they
might readily persuade the great heart of Aiakides.
Now they came beside the shelters and ships of the Myrmidons
and they found Achilleus delighting his heart in a lyre, clear-sounding,
splendid and carefully wrought, with a bridge of silver upon it,
which he won out of the spoils when he ruined Eëtion's city.

With this he was pleasuring his heart, and singing of men's fame,
as Patroklos was sitting over against him, alone, in silence,
watching Aiakides and the time he would leave off singing.
Now these two came forward, as brilliant Odysseus led them . . .

(Il. 9.182–92)

Τὼ δὲ βάτην παρὰ θῖνα πολυφλοίσβοιο θαλάσσης
πολλὰ μάλ᾽ εὐχομένω γαιηόχῳ ἐννοσιγαίῳ
ῥηϊδίως πεπιθεῖν μεγάλας φρένας Αἰακίδαο.
Μυρμιδόνων δ᾽ ἐπί τε κλισίας καὶ νῆας ἵκέσθην,
τὸν δ᾽ εὗρον φρένα τερπόμενον φόρμιγγι λιγείῃ,
καλῇ δαιδαλέῃ, ἐπὶ δ᾽ ἀργύρεον ζυγὸν ἦεν,
τὴν ἄρετ᾽ ἐξ ἐνάρων πόλιν Ἠετίωνος ὀλέσσας·
τῇ ὅ γε θυμὸν ἔτερπεν, ἄειδε δ᾽ ἄρα κλέα ἀνδρῶν.
Πάτροκλος δέ οἱ οἶος ἐναντίος ἧστο σιωπῇ,
δέγμενος Αἰακίδην, ὁπότε λήξειεν ἀείδων.
τὼ δὲ βάτην προτέρω, ἡγεῖτο δὲ δῖος Ὀδυσσεύς . . .

Notice that the arrival of these "'two'" ambassadors, regardless of their
identity, frames a far clearer pair: Achilles and Patroclus. They are spoken of as if alone: Patroclus is οἶος ἐναντίος, and no other attendants
are present. But whereas those who arrive are in the dual, Achilles and
Patroclus most emphatically are not. Achilles sings. Patroclus waits for
him to finish the song. The forged togetherness of those arriving contrasts with the asymmetry and separation of the two they have come
upon, who are alone, together. The full description of the pair, between
the duals of lines 182 and 192, takes eleven lines, and the central line between the pairs of duals, 9.187, involves the description of the lyre that
joins them, which itself happens to be "'bridged,'" "'yoked'" together,
and artfully contrived. Regardless of where these troubling duals origi-
nated, whether from a merging of different versions of the embassy or
a simple aberration in oral performance, is it not clear that the way they
have been used to frame this other couple, Achilles and Patroclus, is
itself perfectly arranged? The artful contrivance of the yoked lyre comments on the contrivance of the poetic lines themselves, two forms in
the dual eleven lines apart, framing a central image of a yoke that both
holds Achilles and Patroclus together in song, and yet also separates
them: one sings, the other listens.

But what kind of a yoking together, in music, is this? Greg Nagy
suggests that this encounter offers us insight into the construction of
Homeric poetry itself.

Both the plural usage here of *klea andron* 'glories of men' (as opposed to the singular *kleos* 'glory') and the meaning of the name Patroklees are pertinent to the rhapsodic implications of this passage: it is only through Patroklees 'he who has the *klea* [glories] of the ancestors' that the plurality of performance, that is, the activation of tradition, can happen. So long as Achilles alone sings the *klea andron* 'glories of men', these heroic glories cannot be heard by anyone but Patroklos alone. Once Achilles leaves off and Patroklos starts singing, however, the continuum that is the *klea andron*—the Homeric tradition itself—can at long last become activated. This is the moment awaited by Patroklees 'he who has the *klea* [glories] of the ancestors'. In this Homeric image of Patroklos waiting for his turn to sing, then, we have in capsule form the esthetics of rhapsodic sequencing.[7]

The recourse to performance helps explain the text as we have it. But these lines also articulate the peculiar dynamic of the plot of the *Iliad*, bound up as it is in the relationship between Achilles and Patroclus. For now, and until Book 11, when he sends Patroclus to find out the identity of the wounded Machaon, it will be Achilles's turn. His singing duplicates his control of the narrative, his absence from the battlefield, his orchestration of Greek deaths. Achilles's performance of this song doubles the control he exerts over the field of glory, and over Patroclus. Sent off to battle by Achilles, Patroclus will nevertheless act for himself, have his moment in the heroic sun, disobey Achilles's orders, and try to kill Hector. He will not fight with Achilles, but he threatens to replace him, presumptively moving toward Achilles's narrative encounter with Hector, hinted at by Odysseus in Book 9 (*Il.* 9.304—"'for now you might kill Hector'"). The asymmetry of their musical performance mirrors the asymmetry of the relationship traced in the poem's plot.

Book 9 dramatizes the asymmetry of their roles even further. Far from acting together, Achilles orders Patroclus to prepare food and make sacrifice, and Patroclus obeys. He fulfils domestic functions more normally associated with a wife. But buried in Achilles's most significant order to his friend, when he demands that his companion sacrifice to the Greek gods, is another riddle.

he himself sat over against the godlike Odysseus
against the further wall, and told his companion, Patroklos,
to sacrifice to the gods . . .

(Il. 9.218–20)

αὐτὸς δ᾿ ἀντίον ἷζεν Ὀδυσσῆος θείοιο
τοίχου τοῦ ἑτέροιο, θεοῖσι δὲ θῦσαι ἀνώγει
Πάτροκλον, ὃν ἑταῖρον . . .

Achilles orders his own companion to sacrifice to the gods. But the strange emphasis on "'his own companion'" (ὃν ἑταῖρον) hints at a darker implication. What if, instead of ordering his companion to sacrifice to the gods, he is also giving orders to the gods to sacrifice his own companion?[8] The ethics of sacrifice, what it means to pray to the gods, is hopelessly colored by his prayer to Thetis in Book 1. Even as Achilles imagines sharing a future with Patroclus, he uses him as a sacrificial object, the ultimate sacrifice he unwittingly makes to cause the Greeks pain.

6

Flirtations

The commitment of war shadows the commitment of marriage. The latter is a primal act of trust, and cultural making, which bridges the gap between two people but also attaches them to the broader world. Hector and Andromache's marriage-talk fades into the sexual apartheid that becomes the content of their agreement: she will do women's work, while he will take care of the business of men. Yet the utopian moment of promise and agreement remains. War, by contrast, is a zero-sum destruction of one warrior by another, which fades into the destruction of one group by another. A process of "'unmaking'" rather than making, its contract involves a perverse act of trust in the all-or-nothing game of death. It rules out in advance any other communicative pact. In this context Hector's desire for marriage-talk with Achilles is as appropriate as it is destined to fail: an imaginary marriage intended not only to restore communication between a Greek and a Trojan, but to reverse the ethnic dividing lines that appeared after the rape of Helen.

But *Iliad* 6 offers us the example of the exact opposite of this discourse, an encounter between warriors where war-commitment is temporarily suspended. The Trojan Glaucus and the Greek Diomedes are about to fight, but they find out that their grandfathers were once guest-friends, embark on a personal peace, and exchange gifts to cement it. We have the epic's version of the "'Christmas peace'" of the First World War, where the rival armies halted the killing long enough to play soccer with each other before a return to the business of death, or the fantasy of the war-weary Dicaeopolis from Aristophanes's *Acharnians*, who proposes his own, personal peace in response to the stubbornness of a community committed to war. Long thought to be out of place in *Iliad* 6, Glaucus and Diomedes are out of place in the entire poem, an exception to the poem's discourse of death. Yet in Book 6 the instability of inside and outside, domestic and public, friend and enemy, is always on show.

Their encounter offers a preemptive answer to the problem faced by Hector in *Iliad* 22. How can warriors who have embarked on a battle to the death talk themselves out of death? They find a way, and so shake up all that is taken for granted in the poem's war culture. Instead of a shared assurance in what each knows of the other, their conversation highlights the depths of their mutual ignorance, a space where they can talk, think, and desire differently. Their encounter is more than a resolution of conflicting principles: for example, the universal rules of *xenia*, guest-friendship, pitted against the ethnic rivalry of war. It offers a glimpse into an uncertainty that shadows all principles and produces an exchange of gifts rather than an exchange of life for death. What follows is a selective, literary commentary on this episode, but one that tries to bring out what is at stake for the entire poem.

The Ignorance of War

> Now Glaukos, sprung of Hippolochos, and the son of Tydeus
> came together in the space between the two armies, battle-bent.
> Now as these advancing came to one place and encountered,
> first to speak was Diomedes of the great war cry:
> 'Who among mortal men are you, good friend? . . .[']
>
> (*Il.* 6.119–23)

> Γλαῦκος δ᾽Ἱππολόχοιο πάϊς καὶ Τυδέος υἱὸς
> ἐς μέσον ἀμφοτέρων συνίτην μεμαῶτε μάχεσθαι.
> οἳ δ᾽ ὅτε δὴ σχεδὸν ἦσαν ἐπ᾽ ἀλλήλοισιν ἰόντε,
> τὸν πρότερος προσέειπε βοὴν ἀγαθὸς Διομήδης·
> "τίς δὲ σύ ἐσσι, φέριστε, καταθνητῶν ἀνθρώπων; . . ."

At first Diomedes's question seems straightforward. He fights for glory, pure prestige, so finding out the name of the opposing warrior is crucial. To fight a person with no patronymic or heroic identity is to waste effort, for the conquest cannot increase one's fame. This logic is at work in the ritual of supplication. When defeated, a warrior renders himself prone and helpless, as if to say to his conqueror: "'I am nothing, there remains no glory in removing my biological life; your victory has already been symbolically registered by my open recognition of your superiority.'" But the more famous and accomplished the opponent, the greater glory to be gained. The heroic context suggests specific reasons for Diomedes's question and denies the possibility that it is motivated by a genuine desire to find out any personal information about his opponent, the kind of thing "'who are you?'" might suggest in another context.

But, in the first irony of the episode, this is exactly the kind of question it will end up being. The banal normalcy of "'who are you?'" is first transformed by the logic of war into a game of glory, but it will later reassert itself. It comes to mean no more, or less, than this, the relic of a past era of peace when knowledge of identity could be an opening to friendship rather than a marker of the gap between "'us'" and "'them,'" a preliminary death rite. The encounter, as it moves from war to peace, also moves from a closed to a more open question. Diomedes seems to know very well what he wants to find out, and yet, by the end of the episode, it will turn out that he asked for something quite different.

Hindsight also complicates Homer's introduction to their encounter. They come "'into the middle,'" to a space that is neither Greek nor Trojan, yet driven by a martial desire that suggests it will soon be a space of violent collision. They enter in the dual (συνίτην μεμαῶτε μάχεσθαι), grammatically linked together only for a moment, until the logic of killing or being killed will separate them, and only one will leave. But the narrative stops short of this, σχεδόν, and this "'nearly'" takes over the place of conflict between groups and makes instead a place for a strange and surprising intimacy. The geographical no-man's-land allows an exchange of sequential stories. Information cannot come all at once but requires some form of alternation, waiting, as if to allow the uncertainty of desire to inhabit their words.

> Since never
> before have I seen you in the fighting where men win glory . . .
> (*Il.* 6.123–24)

οὐ μὲν γάρ ποτ' ὄπωπα μάχῃ ἔνι κυδιανείρῃ . . .

Diomedes's clarification of his own question confirms that the request is hardly serious. To speak to an enemy on the battlefield is already to be fighting, engaged in the to and fro of verbal abuse to gain a psychological advantage, the discourse of "'flyting words.'" To say that he has never seen Glaucus fight insults Glaucus in an elegant syllogism. Who do not fight in the front lines? Cowards. Therefore Glaucus is a coward. Diomedes may know very well who Glaucus is. His question is war's way of saying "'you are a nobody,'" expressing a fighter's contempt at the arrogance of an inferior's challenge. Yet we cannot rule

out the possibility that this bluster-filled clarification might suggest uncertainty in his initial question. To utter the words "'who are you?'" is
to identify with a position of ignorance and vulnerability, if only for a
moment. Once more, the narrative information conveyed by this bluster
will end up being of greater significance than the insult: we have an
encounter between men who do not yet quite know each other.

> yet now you have come striding far out in front of all others
> in your great heart, who have dared stand up to my spear far-shadowing.
> Yet unhappy are those whose sons match warcraft against me.
> But if you are some one of the immortals come down from the bright sky,
> know that I will not fight against any god of the heaven,
> since even the son of Dryas, Lykourgos the powerful, did not
> live long; he who tried to fight with the gods of the bright sky,
> who once drove the fosterers of rapturous Dionysos
> headlong down the sacred Nyseian hill, and all of them
> shed and scattered their wands on the ground, stricken with an ox-goad
> by murderous Lykourgos, while Dionysos in terror
> dived into the salt surf, and Thetis took him to her bosom
> frightened, with the strong shivers upon him at the man's blustering.
> But the gods who live at their ease were angered with Lykourgos,
> and the son of Kronos struck him to blindness, nor did he live long
> afterwards, since he was hated by all the immortals.
> Therefore neither would I be willing to fight with the blessed
> gods . . .

> (*Il.* 6.125–42)

The emergence of Glaucus becomes less an idiotic challenge than a
troubling puzzle. No longer a nobody, he is anomalous, strangely out
of place, at first staying too far away from the front lines, now fighting
too far to the front. In a foreshadowing of the status of Andromache,
both subservient and yet ready to give orders, Glaucus too is everything and nothing, an utter coward and yet rashly brave. So we open
up the possibility that this out-of-place figure is a god. The ethics of
xenia, guest-friendship, demand that you treat strangers well, since any
human you meet could be a god. *Xenia* depends on an uncertainty principle commanding humans to look beyond themselves, and not take
what they know for granted. This sets up the miraculous encounter
that will occur.

> [']but if you are one of those mortals who eat what the soil yields,
> come nearer, so that sooner you may reach your appointed destruction.'
> Then in turn the shining son of Hippolochos answered:

'High-hearted son of Tydeus, why ask of my generation?
As is the generation of leaves, so is that of humanity.
The wind scatters the leaves on the ground, but the live timber
burgeons with leaves again in the season of spring returning.
So one generation of men will grow while another
dies.[']

(*Il.* 6.142–50)

Glaucus's reply is another puzzle. In response to the question about identity, he offers up one of the most famous and poignant similes in the *Iliad*, a wry reflection on the general insignificance of human life. But how are we to read it? The simple question on the battlefield prompts some homespun philosophy. Diomedes surely never had this in mind when he asked "'who are you?'" The power of the simile threatens to condemn all the acts of the poem to meaninglessness, dwarfing any single, named human amid the thousands of leaves, all destined to reproduce themselves, then die, in an endless cycle. Human identity loses significance as it spirals into the yawning chasm of infinity. Yet even this simile could be part of the flyting words. Glaucus could be trying to knock Diomedes off balance by showing the intellectual idiocy of thinking that human identity could ever matter. Are these lines a kind of supra-poetic sublimity, a gallows humor that mocks the warrior's attempt to win a name for himself against the ravages of mortality and time? If so, do they also attack the epic's own project of remembering? Or is this already a tactic of combat, an attempt to gain an edge?

Yet if you wish to learn all this and be certain
of my genealogy: there are plenty of men who know it.

(*Il.* 6.150–51)

εἰ δ' ἐθέλεις καὶ ταῦτα δαήμεναι, ὄφρ' ἐῢ εἰδῆς
ἡμετέρην γενεήν, πολλοὶ δέ μιν ἄνδρες ἴσασιν . . .

Even here there is a further surprise. For how would we expect Glaucus to continue? If the quest for human identity is truly meaningless, one might imagine an immediate fight, or perhaps a retreat. But Glaucus backtracks. With hindsight, the simile's knowing disdain for any attempt at finding individual meaning in life now seems a prelude to this, a brash show of confidence designed to hide, and then perhaps allow, this elementary sharing of information, as if pretending not to care is a necessary prelude to caring.

He asks if Diomedes wants to learn of *hemeteren geneen*, "'our generation.'" What does "'our'" mean here? One could read it as the common

use of plural for singular, meaning nothing more than "'my generation.'" Perhaps it refers to the family that Glaucus belongs to, which
would have the effect of splitting the world into two groups, Glaucus's
family and everyone else. But there are further possibilities. The power
of the simile of dying leaves might leave its mark here. Insofar as both
Diomedes and Glaucus are part of this universal dying and coming to
be, they are part of a single, human *genos*. The division into "'us'" and
"'them'" founders against the stark truth of the cycle of life and death
they both share, even as it points toward a different kind of knowledge
that humans share. But "'our generation'" also looks forward to what
will soon happen, and the different kind of link they share because of
the friendship of their ancestors. Not just their knowledge of death, but
shared guest-friendship links them.

"'Many men know it,'" says Glaucus. This seems to be a "'flyting'"
response to Diomedes's initial question. Diomedes hinted that Glaucus was a coward, since he was a stranger to the front lines. Glaucus
reverses this; not to know his name, when so many do, means that Diomedes is the buffoon. But the difference between "'many'" and "'all'"
opens up a gap. Glaucus can now tell his own story. The almost universal fame of Glaucus's autobiography makes the possibility of telling it
to someone new all the more exciting; it is as if a wonderful joke had
become obsolete through being told to everyone—and then someone
new arrived. A new audience means that one's story may not be a cliché for them; it may be different from what "'many know'"—and in
this space a friendship will soon be formed. The episode becomes a
felicitous reverse of a mini-tragedy related at the beginning of the book
concerning the hero Axylus.

> Diomedes of the great war cry cut down Axylos,
> Teuthras' son, who had been a dweller in strong-founded Arisbe,
> a man rich in substance and a friend to all humanity
> since in his house by the wayside he entertained all comers.
> Yet there was none of these now to stand before him and keep off
> the sad destruction . . .
>
> (*Il.* 6.12–17)

Axylus practices a utopian version of guest-friendship, treating all as
friends and trying to compensate for the vast indifference of the world
of leaves by making friends one by one, at every opportunity. But in
the world of the *Iliad*, this seems hopelessly naive—a futile, preemptive
defense measure against the dangers of the battlefield, where such rules

have no place. Diomedes is no friend, and Axylus's lifework of making friends means nothing here. Glaucus and Diomedes at first seem to lack this openness to another person, constrained as they are by their commitment to kill or be killed. Yet they manage to find an opening in the discourse of war, and so escape death. For all his hospitality and displays of generosity, Axylus's world remains one of friend and enemy. He can turn strangers into friends, but only in the context of *xenia*; he has no power over the world of war. But Glaucus and Diomedes undermine our sense of friend and enemy, and show that the division into "'us'" and "'them'" is unreliable. We can even see the tree simile as retroactively giving meaning to Axylus's name. For depending on whether the alpha in *A-xylos* is privative or intensifying, his name means either "'very woody'" or "'lacking in wood.'" But this is ominously appropriate, at first signifying his intense link to every relationship of *xenia*— "'very woody'"—and later signifying his utter loneliness at the point of death, a situation where he is separated from all such relations as he faces Diomedes.

Let us return to Glaucus's speech.

There is a city, Ephyre, in the corner of horse-pasturing
Argos; there lived Sisyphos, that sharpest of all men,
Sisyphos, Aiolos' son, and he had a son named Glaukos . . .

(*Il*. 6.151–54)

When you are asked to talk about your genealogy, how much information should you offer? Glaucus has already surprised us with his initial evasion of the question, and his philosophical rejoinder to it. But now he comes to the point. As we listen, we finally meet "'Glaucus'" (the man Diomedes might know), his town, his father, and his grandfather. But this will not be *our* Glaucus. The common practice of naming grandchildren after grandfathers will be at work in this family too. So in order to tell the rest of the story of his background to Diomedes, to join the genealogical dots linking grandfather to grandson, sixty more lines of narrative will be required.

Homer seems to be joking, though in doing so he raises series issues already outlined in Glaucus's simile. How much of one's story is enough to identify a person? How much of one's family background is necessary to allow someone to know you? The additional story offered by Glaucus will be the difference between life and death, offering details that tie him to Diomedes. But, in principle, the opening simile suggests that, were there world enough and time, they should be able to find *some* point of contact between them. In Book 2, the poet was unable to count out the Trojan and Greek soldiers, and so turned the task over to the Muses. Here, the superhuman knowledge is not of numbers, but of the myriad links that connect leaf to leaf, branch to branch, a knowledge that could convert enemy into friend.

Amusement comes from identifying with the perspective of the listener, Diomedes: for how long, with how much patience, should one listen to another's tale when one has only asked for a name? The tale goes on too long, teases us with the relief of an answer to the question, only to frustrate. Does this not reflect the initial frustrations of the warrior Diomedes? Glaucus veers into the comic territory of Nestor, whose never-ending speeches are central to the construction of a shared heroic culture. Yet despite the length of Glaucus's reply, there remains something fortuitous and random about the encounter. To patiently chart all of each other's stories, to explore all the possible links that might connect us to strangers, is a truly endless, Sisyphean task. Within this context, Glaucus's own heritage, with Sisyphus as his great-grandfather, might be significant. Sisyphus is given his rock to push as a punishment for his attempt to cheat death. His great-grandson finds himself in a world where death is actively embraced. For the episode juxtaposes the difficulty of the search for identity with the ease of the answers heroic ideology offers. Later, in Book 12, the Trojan Sarpedon also answers the question "'why fight?'" One fights to give meaning to mortal life by achieving fame, the best hope of prolonging one's name beyond one's mortal span. But the length of Glaucus's speech points at something else. Do heroes fight to avoid the endless labor of the quest for identity, lacking the patience required to listen to and understand properly the trivia offered up by others that could, at some point, link them to you?

The Slippage of Signs

['A]nd Glaukos in turn sired Bellerophontes the blameless.
To Bellerophontes the gods granted beauty and desirable
manhood; but Proitos in anger devised evil things against him,
and drove him out of his own domain, since he was far greater,
from the Argive country Zeus had broken to the sway of his sceptre.
Beautiful Anteia the wife of Proitos was stricken
with passion to lie in love with him, and yet she could not
beguile valiant Bellerophontes, whose will was virtuous.

So she went to Proitos the king and uttered her falsehood:
"'Would you be killed, o Proitos? Then murder Bellerophontes
who tried to lie with me in love, though I was unwilling.'"
So she spoke, and anger took hold of the king at her story.
He shrank from killing him, since his heart was awed by such action,
but sent him away to Lykia, and handed him murderous symbols,
which he inscribed in a folding tablet, enough to destroy life,
and told him to show it to his wife's father, that he might perish.[']

(*Il.* 6.155–70)

"αὐτὰρ Γλαῦκος τίκτεν ἀμύμονα Βελλεροφόντην·
τῷ δὲ θεοὶ κάλλός τε καὶ ἠνορέην ἐρατεινὴν
ὤπασαν· αὐτάρ οἱ Προῖτος κακὰ μήσατο θυμῷ,
ὅς ῥ' ἐκ δήμου ἔλασσεν, ἐπεὶ πολὺ φέρτερος ἦεν,
Ἀργείων· Ζεὺς γάρ οἱ ὑπὸ σκήπτρῳ ἐδάμασσε.
τῷ δὲ γυνὴ Προίτου ἐπεμήνατο δῖ' Ἄντεια,
κρυπταδίῃ φιλότητι μιγήμεναι· ἀλλὰ τὸν οὔ τι
πεῖθ' ἀγαθὰ φρονέοντα, δαΐφρονα Βελλεροφόντην.
ἥ δὲ ψευσαμένη Προῖτον βασιλῆα προσηύδα·
'τεθναίης, ὦ Προῖτ', ἢ κάκτανε Βελλεροφόντην,
ὅς μ' ἔθελεν φιλότητι μιγήμεναι οὐκ ἐθελούσῃ.'
ὣς φάτο, τὸν δὲ ἄνακτα χόλος λάβεν οἷον ἄκουσε·
κτεῖναι μέν ῥ' ἀλέεινε, σεβάσσατο γὰρ τό γε θυμῷ,
πέμπε δέ μιν Λυκίηνδε, πόρεν δ' ὅ γε σήματα λυγρὰ,
γράψας ἐν πίνακι πτυκτῷ θυμοφθόρα πολλά,
δεῖξαι δ' ἠνώγειν ᾧ πενθερῷ, ὄφρ' ἀπόλοιτο."

Glaucus continues with a tale of love that doubles the situation between him and Diomedes. The failed sexual tryst offered by Anteia
causes her to construct a zero-sum conflict between two men. Anteia's
failure of intimacy with Bellerophon means someone must die: her husband must kill Bellerophon or be killed himself. Our two warriors must
find a way of defusing their situation in the manner of Bellerophon. In
both cases signs defuse the conflict. Between Glaucus and Diomedes,
the stories of their background increasingly buffer them from deferred
death at each other's spears. In the case of Proitus and Bellerophon, the
signs are the mysterious σήματα λυγρὰ inscribed on a tablet that defer the
immediate murder, and create another zone of uncertainty.

These signs, *semata lugra*, have provoked much scholarly interest,
in part because of the vexed question of Homer's relationship to the
technologies of writing. Since the Homeric poems crystallized around
the time of the emergence of writing in Greece, are these written signs

a hint that the poem is aware of the power of the written word? But all the emphasis on the form that these signs may or may not have taken, whether pictograms, alphabetic writing, or a remnant of the Linear B script, evades something that is crucial to their role in the story Homer gives us: we never find out *what* they say, only how they say it. Glaucus's embedded love story is the *Iliad*'s version of Edgar Allan Poe's "'The Purloined Letter.'" In that story, the content of the letter that circulates among king, minister, and wife is also left empty. We witness instead how the protagonists relate to it, and how they read others as they relate to the letter. The minister, for example, sees the queen's anxiety about the letter, and this is enough for him to assess its power to compromise her, regardless of what it says. So too in Bellerophon's tale we do not find out what the *semata* signify, but we hear about the social scenes where people read them.

The signs first appear in response to Proitus's own vacillation. He reacts to his wife's "'kill-or-be-killed'" not with an act but with signs that seem to demand Bellerophon's death and yet delay it. The *semata* are symptoms of the doubt Proitus felt about Bellerophon's crime, a compromise between his wife's command and his own desire to avoid a rash and irrevocable act. In the phrase "'he shrank from killing him,'" the poet also comments on the state of affairs between Glaucus and Diomedes. Diomedes's "'who are you?'" at first seems a ritualized prelude to death, but it turns into another way of "'shrinking from killing.'" Let us follow the signs on their journey.

Bellerophontes went to Lykia in the blameless convoy
of the gods; when he came to the running stream of Xanthos and Lykia,
the lord of wide Lykia tendered him full-hearted honour.
Nine days he entertained him with sacrifice of nine oxen,
but afterwards when the rose fingers of the tenth dawn showed, then
he began to question him, and asked to be shown the symbols,
whatever he might be carrying from his son-in-law, Proitos.
Then after he had been given his son-in-law's wicked symbols
first he sent him away with orders to kill the Chimaira
none might approach; a thing of immortal make, not human,
lion-fronted and snake behind, a goat in the middle,
and snorting out the breath of the terrible flame of bright fire.
He killed the Chimaira, obeying the portents of the immortals.
Next after this he fought against the glorious Solymoi,
and this he thought was the strongest battle with men that he entered;

but third he slaughtered the Amazons, who fight men in battle.
Now as he came back the king spun another entangling
treachery; for choosing the bravest men in wide Lykia
he laid a trap, but these men never came home thereafter
since all of them were killed by blameless Bellerophontes.
Then when the king knew him for the powerful stock of the god,
he detained him there, and offered him the hand of his daughter . . .

(*Il.* 6.171–92)

The *semata* are not read until the norms of guest-friendship have been established, the stranger embedded in the new household. The *semata*, signs of the compromised desire of Proitus, are further compromised by this established friendship, as the conflicting emotions spiral. Anteia's father refers to them strangely. He asks to see not signs but simply the "'evil sign,'" and plural becomes singular. Does he believe that the message must be simple and unambiguous? Perhaps he refers to the entire package of folding tablets. Yet his use of the singular becomes stranger with hindsight. As if in response to his contraction of signs into a single sign, he allots a single task, presumably one he believes will be enough to kill Bellerophon. But it will not be. The tests, and his commands, proliferate, producing a second, a third, a fourth quest.

This unexpected sequence might return us to the conflict between husband and wife, and in particular their names. "'Proitus'" seems to echo *protos*, first, whereas "'Anteia'" suggests her "'opposite'" character, as if in the beginning, in this primal marriage, there is no more than assertion and denial, one and "'not one.'" Their marriage is constructed in base two, where only the absolute values of "'yes'" and "'no'" exist. Bellerophon's entrance produces a triangle, causing a rift between husband and wife, but also a series of stories that are a consequence of this rift and take the form of a numerical sequence. These signs are generated by the uncertainty opened up by the lie between husband and wife, as if only the outside world can now say who is lying, who is telling the truth. Each story of Bellerophon's success becomes a message back to Proitus that this man does not deserve to die; his heroism keeps pronouncing his innocence of the rape. Bellerophon's quests are a response to, and confirmation of, the initial doubt of the husband.

Bellerophon's acts are inversely symmetrical to the tale of deceit between husband and wife. Exiled from the intimacy of *xenia* with his host, his first task lands him in the nonhuman world of the Chimaira, but the ones that follow return him ever closer to his host's hearth. First a monster; then the killing of an alien group of men, the Solymoi; then the Amazons, females who seem to draw the hero closer to the battle between the sexes that launched the quest. When he finally defeats his host's men in an ambush, Bellerophon is on the verge of invading his host's own home. If the *semata lugra* at first propel Bellerophon away from the domestic intimacy and intrigue of one household, his response to the commands brings him closer and closer to the intimacy of his host's household, so that the offer of the daughter's hand in marriage in order to halt the killing makes poetic sense. The marriage tries to heal the wound of failed intimacy between Anteia and Bellerophon. The logic of "'kill or be killed,'" opened up by Anteia's demand that her husband kill Bellerophon, stops at the moment it threatens to invade her father's space. The *semata lugra*, produced in response to a lie, will find their answer in the fundamental promise that anchors marriage.

Can we draw any conclusions from these Iliadic tales of flirtation and commitment—both the failures and the successes? Intimacy has a rhythm. Individuals rush away from it only to return to it, as if the narrative itself is in search of a compromise. The external world of symbols can provide some breathing space away from the suffocation of domestic ties, and yet each sign from that world links heroes to their own past, both its joys and its traumas. The arena that should offer the greatest contrast to erotic domesticity, the hand-to-hand combat of warriors for glory, eerily doubles its intimate dilemmas. Even the poem's most utopian moments are hardly to be trusted. Glaucus and Diomedes agree not to fight, but instead to exchange armor. But their agreement's utopianism is colored by pragmatic compromise. Their own exceptional discourse must remain precisely that: an exception. They will find others to kill and will strip them of their weapons rather than exchange them. Nevertheless, from now on we see that every martial encounter between enemies could, had the combatants exchanged a few stories, have been one between distant friends. Their success even haunts the failure of communication between Hector and Achilles. But lest optimism carry us away, we should remember why such an exchange of armor is impossible in Book 22. Hector's armor is already Achilles's own, and linked to the death of Patroclus. Any sign of mutual solidarity can just as easily become a sign of hopeless separation.

7

The Afterlife of Homer

Mimnermus, the seventh-century poet from Colophon, at the end of a poem about the impermanence of life offers the following image. Two men, both at death's door, are afflicted by different kinds of misery.

Many evils beset our souls; sometimes the household
is worn away, and there are the painful works of poverty.
Another lacks children, and desiring these most of all
he journeys below the earth to Hades.

(Frag. 2.11–14)[1]

πολλὰ γὰρ ἐν θυμῶι κακὰ γίνεται· ἄλλοτε οἶκος
  τρυχοῦται, πενίης δ᾿ ἔργ᾿ ὀδυνηρὰ πέλει.
ἄλλος δ᾿ αὖ παίδων ἐπιδεύεται, ὧν τε μάλιστα
  ἱμείρων κατὰ γῆς ἔρχεται εἰς Ἀΐδην.

The poem fits well with what remains of Mimnermus's poetry. He obsesses over aging and death while celebrating beauty and transient youth, though even this is tinged with melancholy. The gloomy view from the end of a life reflects on lost desires that promised to give life meaning: a flourishing household, a healthy set of children, wealth and the living progeny to supervise that wealth.

Homer's Disappearing Households

But if we imagine these lines as a commentary on the final books of the *Odyssey* and the *Iliad*, they offer further poetic power. At first, the prospect of a household materially ruined seems to be the shared terror of Laertes and Odysseus when they meet in the orchard in *Odyssey* 24. The "hard works of poverty" make us focus on Laertes, and the kind of life he has chosen for himself in the absence of his son. But the image of a man on the threshold of death, lacking children, returns us to the situation of Priam. Hector is dead, and though Priam's other children are biologically alive, he acts as if they were not.

'Make haste, wicked children, my disgraces, I wish all of you
had been killed beside the running ships in the place of Hektor.
Ah me, for my evil destiny. I have had the noblest
of sons in Troy, but I say not one of them is left to me . . .[']

(*Il.* 24.253–70)

The living children are an embarrassment; they insult the memory of the virtuous sons now gone. For Priam the quantity of surviving sons means nothing when measured against the quality of sons lost, and this awareness comes with the death of Hector. He sunders his sons into two groups; the dead have value, the living none. Their presence is a sign of his impotence and loss of hope. He sees only what they are not: Hector.

   This Mimnerman vignette of Priam at first seems to exaggerate Priam's plight. Priam does not lack sons, but only noble sons. He at least recognizes the ignoble sons that remain, if only by rebuking them. But in the tent of Achilles he talks of them differently.

'Achilleus like the gods, remember your father, one who
is of years like mine, and on the door-sill of sorrowful old age.
And they who dwell nearby encompass him and afflict him,
nor is there any to defend him against the wrath, the destruction.
Yet surely he, when he hears of you and that you are still living,
is gladdened within his heart and all his days he is hopeful
that he will see his beloved son come home from the Troad.
But for me, my destiny was evil. I have had the noblest
of sons in Troy, but I say not one of them is left to me.
Fifty were my sons, when the sons of the Achaians came here.
Nineteen were born to me from the womb of a single mother,
and other women bore the rest in my palace; and of these
violent Ares broke the strength in the knees of most of them,
but one was left me who guarded my city and people, that one
you killed a few days since as he fought in defence of his country,
Hektor; for whose sake I come now to the ships of the Achaians
to win him back from you, and I bring you gifts beyond number.[']

(*Il.* 24.486–502)

We know that some sons survive. Yet in his words to Achilles Priam discounts this: only one was left, unbroken by Ares, and he is gone. Priam takes his earlier rhetoric at face value. His desire for his sons' death, his verbal disowning of them, is now registered in the image of his own completed paternity offered to Achilles: a father lacking children. Hector's death changes Priam's notion of what a son is. No longer concerned with a world where "son" means "biologically descended from father," he seeks a deeper concept of what a son might be. In the terms of Plato, we could say that he seeks the form of a son. He frees himself from kinship ties to his living family, and this freedom allows him to brave biological death in the trip to Achilles's tent, where his new search begins.

But the second part of Mimnermus's phrase is equally suggestive. The old man "goes to Hades." It is now well accepted that Priam's journey in *Iliad* 24 has the structure of a descent into the underworld, a *katabasis*.[2] His guide is Hermes, the god who has the duty, as *psychopompos*, of escorting the souls of the dead to Hades. Priam goes to Achilles's tent "as if to death" (*Il.* 24.328), and Achilles is the consummate figure of death. Mimnermus can thus lay claim to being the first ancient interpreter of Book 24 as a descent into the underworld. But in selecting the image of the aging Laertes and Priam out of these final books, Mimnermus invites us to read the endings of these two poems against each other, narrating different kinds of confrontation with aging and death, and from the perspective of the two elders, Priam and Laertes, rather than from the perspective of the poems' heroes, Achilles and Odysseus. If Priam desires a son, then Achilles's tent becomes the place where he can find one. First, in the dead body of Hector, his son reduced to brute material leftover. But if he seeks the form of a son, then this can only lie in Achilles himself, this figure of martial excellence who doubles the excellence of Hector. Priam finds in Achilles a truer double of his son's last hours, the hero who chose heroic combat with Achilles instead of the defense of Troy. Achilles offers Priam the sight of the heroic part of Hector that Priam had earlier denied.

Michael Lynn-George has emphasized the gap that remains between Priam and Achilles, and this sets limits to any fantasy of a father-son reunion. When Achilles first addresses Priam, he calls him *deile*, wretched: "That opening vocative is significant in terms of what it is not, for Achilles and Priam never articulate the associative relation rehearsed by Hermes and Priam just prior to this encounter in their addressing of one another as *pater* and *philon tekos*, 'father' and 'dear child.'"[3] But this verbal tact is part of the eerie mix of realism and magical otherworldliness that structures the close of the poem. In this dark, metaphorical Hades, the rules and customs of the outside are momentarily suspended, allowing a clarity of perception unavailable in the heroic daytime. Yet this makeshift, philosophical tent is fragile, and the reality of the outside world is always on the verge of breaking through.

Consider some of the intrusions of realism. At the start of the descent, Hermes suggests that Priam's wagonload of goods is a sign of a pathetic attempt to rescue the city's treasure from the doom that now hangs over it. At the episode's end, Hermes returns Priam to the world of his biological sons by reminding him of how much they would have to give in ransom for him once captured. From the side of Achilles, the suicidal bravery that motivates Priam's trip is dismissed by the brusque claim that only a god could have brought him within the Greek's tent. But alongside his wonder also sits the uneasy knowledge that Priam's presence is a scandal, a second betrayal of the Greeks by Achilles that he needs to keep secret. The encounter thus becomes a double of that other secret rendezvous—the one by the shore with his mother in Book 1. Hector's body threatens to return Priam to the sets of identifications with his city, people, and sons that he has been forced to forget in order to kiss Achilles's hands.

Yet these moments also trace in sharper relief the wonder of the encounter. When Hermes imagines Priam escaping with the wealth of Troy, he discounts the power of this good shepherd, whose desire leads him to squander what remains of his family's wealth in search of a lost son. When he tells Achilles that he is bringing him "gifts beyond number," *apoina apereisia*, we return to the ransom that began the poem, but by now "limitless" means much more than when we heard it uttered by Chryses. Priam symbolically makes good on the fantasy of emptying all of Troy in exchange for reconciliation with Achilles, the fantasy Hector imagined only to cast it aside as impossible. The material limitations of goods piled on a cart fail to represent the depth of Priam's desire. "Limitless," *apereisia*, is not a different way of saying "very much" but signifies his true desire. The body of Hector is worth the rest of the world to him, until the discourse of realism intrudes and the ransom becomes simply "great" (*Il.* 24.556). When the time for departure arrives, his other sons come alive again.

You have ransomed now your dear son and given much for him.
But the sons you left behind would give three times as much ransom
for you, who are alive . . .

(*Il.* 24.685–87)

Priam returns to life to witness the final act of the war, one beyond the scope of the epic. But the poem also suggests why this end is not worthy of narration. Priam has succeeded in recovering the corpse of his son, and its burial and the preemptive songs of mourning that it will provoke from Hecabe, Andromache, and Helen stand in for the imminent death of the city itself. If we continue to identify with Priam, the father who returns to a world that no longer has a meaning, Troy's fall is irrelevant. From the perspective of the father, Hector was not just the protector of Troy, but the essence of Troy. When he is gone, Troy becomes a collection of buildings and nobodies. The poem's ending is tragically understated. We know Troy is doomed, but we see only its representative warrior perish. To see the city itself destroyed would be too gruesome, too painful. But to identify with Priam is to undermine this mathematical logic. For feelings of loss destroy the living world in advance. The poem begins and ends with two supplications of old men, the failure of Chryses, the success of Priam. But in Chryses's willingness to wish victory to the Greeks in exchange for his daughter we have a precursor of Priam. For in Achilles's tent the corpse of his son means more than all of Troy.

Two Descents to Hades, Two Love Stories

Achilles's tent, where threats of biological death lurk, also becomes a place of symbolic death. The encounter between Achilles and Priam is possible because they have separated themselves from their other meaningful attachments. Priam's family fail to convince him to stay because they place a value on his biological life that he does not share. Another descent to an outlying region, from the *Odyssey*, might help give these Iliadic events greater focus. Again, let us turn to Michael Lynn-George and the way in which he contrasts the ends of the poems.

Whereas Odysseus goes down finally into the orchard of an outlying estate, Priam is a voyager who descends into what is almost the land of the dead, 'death's other kingdom', an outlying site in which an impossible reunion of father and son is restructured by the possibilities of relations between other fathers and other sons.[4]

Let us keep these critical coordinates but focus instead on what these episodes have in common, beginning with the shared vocabulary of "descent."

The others went from the city, and presently came to the country
place of Laertes, handsomely cultivated. Laertes
himself had reclaimed it, after he spent much labor upon it.
There was his house, and all around the house ran a shelter . . .

(*Od.* 24.205–8)

οἱ δ' ἐπεὶ ἐκ πόλιος κατέβαν, τάχα δ' ἀγρὸν ἵκοντο
καλὸν Λαέρταο τετυγμένον, ὅν ῥά ποτ' αὐτὸς
Λαέρτης κτεάτισσεν, ἐπεὶ μάλα πολλὰ μόγησεν.
ἔνθα οἱ οἶκος ἔην, περὶ δὲ κλίσιον θέε πάντῃ . . .

He did not
find either Dolios, as he came into the great orchard . . .

(*Od.* 24.221–22)

οὐδ' εὗρεν Δολίον, μέγαν ὄρχατον ἐσκαταβαίνων . . .

The *Odyssey* shifts the scene from the real descent of the dead suitors
into Hades, the second Nekyia, to a descent to a land where, for Laertes,
nothing has changed since Odysseus left. There is even an intertextual
joke as Odysseus's descent is described: on this trip, he does not meet
Dolion, the servant of Laertes, but also, by a letter, fails to meet Dolon,
the Trojan spy he encountered and killed in the *Iliad*'s other metaphorical descent into the land of the dead, the Doloneia of Book 10. Where
Priam comes to Achilles's tent, *klisie* (*Il.* 24.431, 448, etc.), Odysseus
approaches the outbuildings of the servants that surround the *oikos* of
Laertes, the *klision*.

There are more general similarities. The *Odyssey* reverses the *Iliad*'s
story of an old man who comes to a son who represents death. Here
the son comes to the father, but his lying words about his encounter
with the traveler Odysseus bring his father's sorrow close to death ("the
black cloud of sorrow closed on Laertes," *Od.* 24.315) as the poem flirts
with a symbolic parricide. Each traveler arrives to break up a seemingly
endless labor, and one that destroys the dignity of the laborer: the nur-
turing of the orchard, the constant dragging of Hector's body around
the walls of Troy. These shadowy, repetitive acts themselves evoke the
Homeric Hades. Figures in the underworld are wraiths, mirages lacking the substance that made their former selves feel alive, but the truly
unfortunate ones, such as Sisyphus or Tantalus, engage in senseless,
perpetual labor. Laertes becomes wraithlike as his body suffers from
his labor. Achilles's failed labor of defilement causes him to ignore the
food that normally fortifies humans, and his physical wasting away is
avoided only by the magical intervention of the gods, who feed him

nectar and ambrosia (*Il.* 19.347–48). Their repetitions seek to freeze time. Achilles's doomed attempt to defile a body that the gods refuse to let rot suspends normal biological decay, while Laertes strives to maintain the form of his orchard, and thus the illusion that time has stood still since the moment Odysseus left.

Yet their motives are different. Achilles drags Hector as a way of clinging to the lost Patroclus, a melancholia that refuses to give up its attachment to a lost love-object. What of Laertes's labor of love? Much depends on the reading of a passage that has received some superb scholarly commentary. Laertes works because of a promise he once made to Odysseus, a promise Odysseus recalls in order to help his father remember. Here are the lines in question, with Pietro Pucci's translation.

'Let me tell the trees in the well-tilled orchard, which you once gave, when I, being still a child, asked you for each detail, as I followed around the garden; we were passing among these trees and you named them and explained every detail. You gave me thirteen pear-trees, ten apples, forty figs. And here you promised to give fifty rows of vines, and each one was maturing in successive seasons—there are bunches of grapes of all sorts—whenever Zeus' seasons loaded them up on high.'

(Od. 24.336–44)[5]

"εἰ δ' ἄγε τοι καὶ δένδρε' ἐϋκτιμένην κατ' ἀλωὴν
εἴπω, ἅ μοί ποτ' ἔδωκας, ἐγὼ δ' ᾔτευν σε ἕκαστα
παιδνὸς ἐών, κατὰ κῆπον ἐπισπόμενος· διὰ δ' αὐτῶν
ἱκνεύμεσθα, σὺ δ' ὠνόμασας καὶ ἔειπες ἕκαστα.
ὄγχνας μοι δῶκας τρεισκαίδεκα καὶ δέκα μηλέας,
συκέας τεσσαράκοντ'· ὄρχους δέ μοι ὧδ' ὀνόμηνας
δώσειν πεντήκοντα, διατρύγιος δὲ ἕκαστος
ἤην· ἔνθα δ' ἀνὰ σταφυλαὶ παντοῖαι ἔασιν,
ὁππότε δὴ Διὸς ὧραι ἐπιβρίσειαν ὕπερθεν."

Notice the translation of ἐγὼ δ' ᾔτευν σε ἕκαστα, "he asked for each *detail.*" The translation is reasonable and seems to be justified by Laertes's response: "you named them and explained every detail." But this commits Pucci to the following story. A curious child, who wants to know, asks questions about the kinds of trees there are, and his father answers his questions. This proto-scholar, proto-environmentalist, pays attention to the details that his later critics also care about. The curiosity of Odysseus finds its counterpart in the knowledge of Laertes, whose explanations are already tied up in the care of the plants themselves. Knowledge is poured from one to another, as if from a full jug to an empty cup, and curiosity and care reciprocate each other.

But we can translate differently. "I kept asking *for* each thing," rather than "asking *about* each thing." We have the usual double accusative construction with the verb of asking: asking someone for something. Here, the child does not first want to know each thing; he wants to *have* each thing, and knowledge enters the scene belatedly. The boy, full of childish arrogance and expectation, wants everything, and asks for everything. We can imagine the conversation. "Can I have this?" "Yes, it's a pear tree." "Can I have this?" Yes, it's a fig tree." Rather than an exchange of information, we have a playful contract and a promise, and the knowledge of the father intervenes only to clarify exactly what is being exchanged. Perhaps the remembered encounter is full of the frivolous promises a father makes to his son. But the circumstances at the poem's end make us take them all too seriously.

Though Laertes promises each fruit, things become more complicated when the boy approaches the vines that do not yet bear fruit. Laertes can no longer promise a thing, but only a thing to come that involves labor.[6] To give the property to a child is to exchange an object, but not the care of the object. Laertes promises more at the moment when he confronts the transience of the object, the fact that vines are subject to growth and decay. After a series of requests, and affirmative answers, the father becomes embarrassed by the paucity of the next object, the vine without fruit, and teaches the child about the seasons. But he now implicitly makes a different promise. He gives not simply to pass on possession of this object to his son, but to guarantee its future identity. The discourse of future plenitude is set in motion by an absence, the missing harvest of grapes.

His compulsion to care for the garden begins here, as the father's care of the orchard is set in motion by the desire of the son. A platitude of psychoanalytic theory is that "desire is desire of the other": the idea that our desires do not belong to us but come to us from without, modeled on the desires and enigmas that we confront in those closest to us. One model for this identity crisis is the child who realizes one day that his desires are not his, that he is a prisoner of his parents' desires and hopes for him. But the end of the *Odyssey* reverses this commonplace, for the father is the slave of his son's desires. This also provides the shock of this final recognition scene. Since Odysseus's first footsteps back on Ithaca when he was confronted with the strangeness of the place, this epic has shown us that recognition can never be taken for granted. The effects of time mean that there is always something different to be recognized. Recognition itself needs to negotiate the flux that time produces. But Book 24 offers us the bizarre sameness of the garden. Odysseus uncannily steps into the same orchard twice.

In the childhood conversation in the orchard, the poem lingers over Laertes's shift from giving what he already has, the trees and the dead labor that has gone into their current state, to giving what he does not have: the promise of the care to come, which will turn a king into a slave. This would hardly have mattered if Odysseus had taken over the orchard's keeping when he became a man. But he disappears to Troy, while the care of the orchard remains. The father turns into nothing other than a man faithful to the promise made to a child. We shift from a father who uses gifts as power (in the grand tradition of Agamemnon and his gifts to Achilles) to a father who shows his *love*. Consider the world of difference between Agamemnon's persistent forms of giving (Agamemnon's offer of gifts to Achilles in *Iliad* 9 is littered with statements that he will give, δώσω), the presumption of an endless store of goods that endlessly extend his power, and the turnaround brought about by Laertes's declaration: "I will give." What Agamemnon refuses to give, his own person, is the precise opposite of the gift of Laertes. The signs of decay on his body become the price he has paid for the orchard's perfection. The gift of the orchard is not a sign of power. Laertes has no desire to enlarge it. After all, the riches of the household, preserved elsewhere by the gruesome slaughter of the suitors, make it clear that this garden carries no more than sentimental value. So one shock, at the end of this poem of economy and thrift, so obsessed with the fiscal importance of the *oikos*, is its willingness to make its social value thoroughly relative. The poem turns a household into a vehicle for paternal love. The *Odyssey*'s end, with the contrast between Agamemnon's gifts and Laertes's selfless care, perhaps also answers the question of what Achilles wanted from Agamemnon in *Iliad* 9. Not objects, but love, not signs of what Agamemnon had, but of what Agamemnon lacked: a gesture of good faith from a different kind of father.

This gives added poignancy to the care of the orchard. This regal old man, who acts like a slave but looks like a king, and cares for everything around him but himself, lives the paradox of a voluntary servitude. The honor of a promise made and kept stands out against the poem's string of uncertainties. The promise in part suggests that Laertes is no longer the patriarchal head of the household, only the guarantor of an estate that is no longer his for a son who may, or may not, come home. He is the opposite of Odysseus, who acts in *Odyssey* 24 as he has always acted, returning to someone else's property with the arrogance of one who already owns it. The walk to the orchard doubles the approach to the Cyclops, that other homestead where his arrogance allowed him to help himself—an arrogance perhaps explained here by the story of the father's too-eager generosity in giving his son what he wanted, as if Odysseus's megalomania is the corollary of a premature inheritance. But in *Odyssey* 24, when Odysseus acts as if the land is his own, he has no sense of what that means until he sees his father. We can begin to see the depth of Homer's challenge to identity; mastery and servitude are less signs of an unchanging social essence and more a symptom of the depths of one's love. Property, as in the *Iliad*, is never a sure mark of prestige, but is caught up in the paradoxes of how humans organize their desires.

Family Truths and Reconciliations

We might also note Odysseus's hesitation as he remembers: "Am I to tell of . . . ?" The difficulty of remembering registers the painful awareness of the toll his childish request has taken on his father. Here there is a marked contrast with that other love story of the poem, the recognition scene with Penelope and the olive tree bed. For, despite general critical agreement that "the bed's immovability symbolically implies Penelope's loyalty and that the reciprocal recognition suggests the renewal of their secret marital *eros*," there is more to be said.[7] As with the orchard, these material symbols of loyalty are manipulated by the protagonists in accordance with their desires. In the case of the bed, Penelope grants Odysseus her recognition only when he admits that he has no idea whether the bed has been moved.

[']There is its character, as I tell you; but I do not know now,
dear lady, whether my bed is still in place, or if some man
has cut underneath the stump of the olive, and moved it elsewhere.'

(*Od.* 23.202–4)

"οὕτω τοι τόδε σῆμα πιφαύσκομαι· οὐδέ τι οἶδα,
ἤ μοι ἔτ’ ἔμπεδόν ἐστι, γύναι, λέχος, ἦέ τις ἤδη
ἀνδρῶν ἄλλοσε θῆκε, ταμὼν ὕπο πυθμέν’ ἐλαίης."

Neither Odysseus nor we know whether the bed has been moved. The bed, at first a symbol of sexual fidelity, now becomes part of the scheme designed to gain this admission of powerlessness from Odysseus, his vulnerability in the face of his wife. Odysseus must question a fidelity he had taken for granted. Her trust is cheapened if it can be guaranteed. Rather than a sign of love, the bed trick is a prequel to the possibility of love. Patriarchal obstacles must be removed for trust to have any meaning. In a paradox well known in love, in order to have his wife, he must realize he cannot have his wife: he must symbolically give her up. But in his encounter with his father, a conceptual fidelity far deeper than he ever expected appears from nowhere, and in response to a childhood request he only now remembers making.

The *Odyssey* changes the way we look at a wife, at a father. To know his wife, Odysseus must come to terms with her power. To know his father, he must see that paternal love produces a figure of impotence and degradation far from a normal paternal ideal. His illusions of both are destroyed in and through these recognitions. In the *Iliad*, by contrast, the meeting between Priam and Achilles sends them back to socially dead worlds, where their respective illusions about their love-objects are allowed to stay in place. We can end with the final words of Achilles to Patroclus.

'Be not angry with me, Patroklos, if you discover,
though you be in the house of Hades, that I gave back great Hektor
to his loved father, for the ransom he gave me was not unworthy.
I will give you your share of the spoils, as much as is fitting.'

(*Il.* 24.592–95)

This prayer, as many have realized, signals a return to the civilized values of exchange, of the acceptance of supplication, and thus away from the ritual of living death that he enacted in the attempted desecration of Hector's body. But if there is reconciliation at the end of this poem, there is no truth. Achilles's conditional "if you discover" imagines that Patroclus shares his own feelings of vengeance toward Hector. He never loses the ideal of a couple where both are "of the same mind." But even here the knowledge of his request to Thetis remains taboo and gnaws into the ideal. So too, his emphatic desire for the fair distribution of spoils returns to his fantasy of martial equality with Patroclus that his friend, in his turn, betrayed. The poem ends, for Achilles, with a restoration of social norms that have once more radically changed their meaning. He clings to a notion of equality, an idealized reciprocity that has never existed, in order to maintain his own distance from his betrayal of that ideal. If the *Odyssey* offers "recognition throughout," the *Iliad*'s truths become, for its characters, all too difficult to recognize.

Conclusion

How to Sum Up the *Iliad* in a Riddle

So who really killed Homer? If Homer's death, for Victor Davis Hanson at least, signifies the demise of Greek wisdom in all its clarity, then perhaps Homer has always been dead. For knowledge in the *Iliad*, to borrow a phrase from another Greek poet, comes through suffering, and even the most straightforward declarations of characters in this poem are beset with interpretative difficulties, if only because the words they utter are so often haunted by all they cannot bring themselves to say.

But if one were to ask an ancient Greek who killed Homer, one would receive a deceptively simple answer. A single story of his death dominated, though its details could be rearranged and their plausibility doubted. Homer, so the stories go, died because he was unable to solve the enigmatic utterance of children on the island of Ios.

As he was sitting by the sea, they say he asked some boys who were returning from fishing, "O huntsmen from Arcadia, have we caught anything?" When they replied,

"The ones we caught we left behind, the ones we missed we carry" [ὅσσ᾽ ἕλομεν λιπόμεσθα, ὅσ᾽ οὐχ ἕλομεν φερόμεσθα],

he did not understand, and asked them what they meant. They explained that they had caught nothing on their fishing expedition, but they had deloused themselves, and the lice they had caught they had left behind, but the ones they had failed to catch they were still carrying in their clothes.

(*Certamen Homeri et Hesiodi* 18)[1]

153

But how to interpret the relationship of this riddle to Homer's death?[2] How exactly does he die, what is he thinking as he dies, and why does this riddle in particular get to him? Our answers will turn out to be a way of summing up the *Iliad* and its themes. So, in my final pages, I offer four ways of making sense of this riddle, and then outline how they allude to some of the poem's crucial themes. Far more than a quaint biographical detail, the riddle can act as a mnemonic device for the story of Achilles.

It is now well known that the biographical traditions that sprang up around ancient authors are often culled from details in the works themselves.[3] But though their accuracy can be safely doubted, their broader cultural significance should not be.[4] The form of his death might help us rethink the dominance of Homer in the ancient literary and cultural landscape. At the very least the ignominy of his death betrays iconoclasm, a glee taken in the fall of a sage whose last moment of stupidity undermines a lifetime of wisdom. Call no Homer wise until he is dead. So let us look more closely at Homer's confusion before these fisher-children.

Four Readings of a Riddle

THE PROBLEM OF DESIRE

A first step is to identify with Homer and think through why he was perplexed. For, as is often the case with riddles, the challenge to our commonsense world matters as much as any solution. The children's comments force Homer to rethink what he takes for granted about ownership of objects and the process by which we acquire them. How can we gain possession of something and yet leave it behind? The concept of ownership itself is suddenly up for grabs.

The dilemma is a Socratic one, centering on the one thing that Socrates claimed to know something about: desire itself (Plato, *Symp.* 177E). For the riddle suggests that the value of objects is not independent from the desire to acquire them. To have something is to lose the desire to have it, the feelings that make you want it in the first place. We may think an object we acquire belongs to us and is added to some imaginary and ever-expanding list of our possessions. But as soon as it is safely part of our catalogue, it will be forgotten: it loses value the moment its value is properly measured. One could consider, to offer a modern example, the piles of toys that litter the rooms of spoiled children, toys they have but no longer care for. Only the toy they lack promises to solve the enigma of what they want. It is particularly poignant that Homer pauses over this problem at the end of his life. At the moment when his own personal set of objects has been acquired and left behind, and the list of past acquisitions begins to dwarf any possible future ones, desire itself, so bound up in these feelings of anticipation, is threatened by biological death. But the children, confident of the time and objects laid up in store for them, can articulate such a paradox and remain blithely indifferent to its ramifications.

LEARNING THROUGH SUFFERING

When we step outside the identification with Homer, a second reading opens up. The riddle is not just about objects, but about the difficulties of interpreting riddles themselves. The Greek word for acquiring, λαμβάνω, is a common metaphor for intellectual comprehension.[5] So, to retranslate: "What we grasp, we leave behind, but what we don't grasp, we take with us." Homer, the wisest of the Greeks, is dragged out of a world where he thinks he knows what he knows, and into a world of intellectual discomfort. He takes the words with him, they plague him, but only because he cannot understand them. So if he thinks he does not understand the riddle, in what he is doing—in the performance of his confused thinking—he understands it very well. Because he misunderstands the riddle subjectively, he understands it objectively. Since the riddle causes his death, its ultimate impact is on his body. The words go with him in the disruptions of his normal mode of physical being. The brilliance of the riddle thus lies in the way that it both explains and creates the perplexity that riddles produce. On this interpretation, even the minuteness of the lice becomes relevant. For words are even tinier and deadlier things. One thinks of the writings of the sophist Gorgias, who spoke of the nearly invisible, atom-like quality of words that creep into the body, or Socrates in Plato's *Protagoras*, who also talks of language in quasi-material terms.[6] If we buy food in the marketplace, Socrates tells the young Hippocrates, we can find someone to test it, and return it if it is bad. But when we are assailed by words, they go straight to the soul, and any damage cannot be undone. Words become a material infection for Socrates, just as the riddle's words take over Homer's body.

THE LONELINESS OF THE SAGE

Heraclitus of Ephesus, the late-sixth-century BCE philosopher known in antiquity as "the riddler," hints at a third interpretation.

Men deceive themselves in their knowledge of the obvious, even Homer, considered wisest of all Greeks. For he [died of grief over a riddle when he] was fooled by boys killing lice who said: what we see and catch we leave behind; and what we neither see nor catch we carry away.

(Frag. 56)

The philosopher adds something of his own concerns to the traditional story, making it a rather different riddle for us to step into. It now becomes about the relationship between knowledge and perception, a concern that reverberates through all his fragments. What does Heraclitus think is happening to Homer? Homer misses something that Heraclitus calls "obvious," "clear," something that should be available at first sight on the surface of things. He also offers an explanation for this misperception. Homer's mode of intellectual apprehension (γνῶσις) somehow interferes with his ability to see what is under his nose. So what is happening, and what is so obvious? What if the children, instead of answering in words alone, also show him that they are delousing, describing what they do as they go along? But should he see what they were doing, there would be no riddle at all. But what if Homer is so obsessed with the enigma he reads in their words, so attached to his own perplexity, that he misses out on the bodily referent for the message they tell him? On this reading, the wisdom of Homer, his ability to think more subtly than his interlocutors, is the very thing that makes him unable to communicate with them. Here the problem is less that he misunderstands a paradox of desire than that he understands it all too well. His desire for ambiguity, for reflection on the tragic condition of a life of unsatisfied desire, is projected onto the words of the children. In so doing he misses the simple process of delousing that they show him.

Because he does not share the children's simplicity, their unreflective confidence that their words have a clear referent in what they do, communication between them falters. Heraclitus's tale becomes one of the ultimate loneliness of the sage, isolated because of the way he cannot think beyond his theoretical sophistication. He acts out the truth of another of Heraclitus's famous sayings.

Though understanding is common, yet the many live as if they had a wisdom of their own.

(Frag. 2)

ξυνὸς γὰρ ὁ κοινός. τοῦ λόγου δ' ἐόντος ξυνοῦ, ζώουσιν οἱ πολλοὶ ὡς ἰδίαν ἔχοντες φρόνησιν.

The isolation of Homer becomes universalized. Caught in his private world, he fails to see the *logos* that could connect him to the children, but that is at least potentially available to us to see. His death is linked to an intellectual narcissism, a narcissism that will not be disrupted by external truths but swallows them up in his own worldview. Heraclitus is probably also playing with the proverbial blindness of Homer, the conventional mythic blindness which typically goes hand in hand with a greater mental insight. Homer, of course, could not see the lice if he was blind. But Heraclitus reverses this cliché, showing that Homer's wisdom, a symptom of his freedom from the deficiencies of sense perception, becomes a kind of private stupidity. This reading is the exact reverse of the second one. What stays with Homer is not something unresolved, hard to understand, but rather the reverse. For seeing riddles makes him feel comfortable.

FLEEING DEATH

A fourth and final step might follow from Homer's persistent, resourceful modes of avoidance. Homer's wisdom, on this reading, seems to be a form of avoiding any real encounter with the children and what they say. But this relates to broader strategies of avoidance that his life story in the *Certamen* suggests. Homer is now on Ios, the island where it was prophesied that he would die, though he misunderstood the ambiguous reference to the island in the utterance of the Delphic oracle that foretold his death (*Certamen* 5). The oracle told him to avoid the Nemean grove of Zeus. Homer believed the referent was a specific grove in Delphi, but, the author of the *Contest* informs us, the whole region was meant. But his apparent error, the misrecognized name of a place, is something of a red herring. What Homer does in response to the prophecy matters: he will spend the rest of his life trying to avoid death. Now, this truth returns us to the solution of the riddle. The Greek word for a louse is φθείρ, "the killer." So to solve the riddle, Homer would have to articulate a word that signifies destruction itself. The insects' name is thus the riddle's way of fleshing out the content of the thing that Homer's self-absorption is trying to avoid. His comfort-in-discomfort and his isolating wisdom turn out to be means of circling around the inevitability of death itself.[7]

Four Themes of the *Iliad*

So how does the riddle about Homer's death relate to the Homeric poems? The details, in line with what we know of other ancient biographies of literary giants, are lifted from important details in the works themselves.[8] The *Certamen* continues by telling us that Homer, in his perplexity, slipped in the mud by the seashore, and soon died. The slip in the mud is lifted directly from the slip of Ajax in Book 23 of the *Iliad*, in the funeral games for the dead Patroclus. More generally, the death that comes to Homer "from the sea" echoes the prophecy of the death that Teiresias gives to Odysseus in *Odyssey* 11, when he describes the enigmatic encounter with "a man who confuses an oar with a winnowing fan" (*Od.* 11.127–37). But while these details matter, the manner of Homer's death is also important. Not only does Homer fail to understand a riddle, but that riddle functions as a précis of the themes of his poem. There are two kinds of authorial death here: Homer dies first as a figure of wisdom and authority in general, then as a figure who can impose any authoritative meaning on his own work. Not only does he not know a correct answer; he does not know *himself*. So we can use his failures as an interpretative tool, helping us to focus on the poem's perplexities in the light of the contours of the poet's confusion.

So let us take our fourfold diagnosis of Homer and transfer it to the epic. These suggestions are offered in the spirit of the essayist, as tentative supplements to the understanding of the poem I have offered throughout.

THE *ILIAD* ON THE PROBLEMS OF DESIRE

The poem hinges on the difficult relationship between objects and desire for objects. Consider Achilles's relationship to Briseis. He begins to want her when he does not have her, and when he does have her once more, when we find him sleeping by her side in the final book (*Il.* 24.676), this tiny narrative detail is an all-too-painful reminder of the gap between her current value and the vast scale of events she set in motion. Or consider the curious detail Agamemnon adds concerning the catalogue of gifts he offers Achilles. He returns Briseis, but along with her comes his oath that he has never had sex with her, as is natural, he says, for men and women (*Il.* 9.132–34). Why not? Should we believe him, and there is no obvious reason not to, we must imagine the concubine lying around Agamemnon's tent, a living reminder of his scission from Achilles, but also a testament to his own divided desire. He does not want to enjoy her, to properly have her, because of his own peculiar relationship to the desire of Achilles. The poem throughout offers a critique of unthinking acquisition, and what it might mean. When Ajax cannot understand why Achilles rejects Agamemnon's gifts in *Iliad* 9, his is the kind of dull thinking that the riddle of the lice seeks to disrupt. Achilles is offered in Book 9 an almost unending chain of objects that are not the object that he wants, and thus turn into an impotent show of their uselessness. What Achilles gets from Agamemnon, he abandons; what he does not get from him, enigmatically voiced in his desire for fitting recompense for the disgrace he suffered, stays with him.

Another detail sheds some light on these narrative problems. In the hexameter version of the riddle given in the *Certamen*, the verb for "taking with us" is φερομαι, which is also the word typically used for winning a game. The metaphor comes from carrying off prizes for oneself after victory, making winning not an abstract notion but something closely connected to material gain, to the prizes that represent victory. So the riddle contains an even more pointed paradox: it suggests that not to gain things can nevertheless result in winning, and vice versa. The riddle unravels the metaphor for success, divorcing victory from its material sign, the prize, prodding us into reevaluating what winning and losing might be. So, too, we are offered the story of Achilles's victory over Agamemnon, but it is a victory that will prove quite meaningless to him and is experienced as a loss. As if in response to this paradox, the *Iliad* devotes an entire book, the funeral games, to the ethical difficulties involved in winning and losing a game. As we have tried to show, the games at Patroclus's funeral are designed to promote social solidarity among the competitors, but the narrative also reflects on the vagueness of the rules of the games themselves, which produce all kinds of embarrassments that threaten to disrupt the edifice of the heroic world. Achilles, as host of the games, is constantly reshuffling the winners and losers, reordering their prizes, in order to maintain the peace. If there are no clear winners, it is because there are no fixed, unchanging rules to help us understand what we want and find valuable, nor is there any ultimate guarantor of the rules themselves. This is trivially shown to be true in Achilles's challenge to Agamemnon's authority in Book 1. But this is far from the poem's last word on the matter.

HOW ACHILLES LEARNS THROUGH SUFFERING

The poem is not simply about what Achilles wants. We see him as his desires change, as he puzzles over the process of desire itself. Just as Homer puzzles over the children's riddle, phrases uttered around him puzzle Achilles. Consider the moment after Patroclus has died but before Achilles hears of the death, when he remembers a prophecy of his mother.

'Ah me, how is it that once again the flowing-haired Achaians
are driven out of the plain on their ships in fear and confusion?

May the gods not accomplish vile sorrows upon the heart in me
in the way my mother once made it clear to me, when she told me
how while I yet lived the bravest of all the Myrmidons
must leave the light of the sun beneath the hands of the Trojans.
Surely, then, the strong son of Menoitios has perished.
Unhappy! And yet I told him, once he had beaten the fierce fire
off, to come back to the ships, not fight in strength against Hector.'

(Il. 18.6–14)

The folktale motif of a fool understanding too late lurks here, ῥεχθὲν δέ
τε νήπιος ἔγνω, a motif that recurs throughout the poem and is, ironically,
uttered by Achilles himself (*Il.* 20.198). But without interpreting the
prophecy, we can pay attention to the process of interpretation Achilles
models for us. His perplexity suggests that these words, far from being
transparent, mean different things depending on the time and place
from which he reads them, and in his understandings and retroactive
misunderstandings of these words, he traces out his own story.

Since Achilles is one of many of the poem's exegetes, it is worth trying to place him within traditional schools of Homeric criticism. Within
antiquity, there was a conflict between an allegorical tradition, which
treats Homer's words as enigmatic, signifying some deeper truth, and
a tradition based on the assumption of Homer's clarity. This school,
stretching from Aristotle and Aristarchus to its modern epigones in
figures as diverse as Matthew Arnold, Milman Parry, and Victor Davis Hanson, leans on the transparency of Homer's language, the swift
succession of ideas that make up the poem.[9] At first blush Achilles's
difficulty in understanding these words suggests an allegiance with
the allegorical school. For surely there is nothing transparent about the
prophecy, and if it becomes transparent, it is only with hindsight: the
"best" of the Achaeans will turn out to be Patroclus, not Achilles. But
there are further problems. The words of the prophecy, we find out,
have clearly stayed with Achilles, influencing his behavior in all sorts
of ways.

how while I yet lived the bravest of all the Myrmidons
must leave the light of the sun beneath the hands of the Trojans.

(Il. 18.10–11)

Μυρμιδόνων τὸν ἄριστον ἔτι ζώοντος ἐμεῖο
χερσὶν ὕπο Τρώων λείψειν φάος ἠελίοιο.

All of the key terms of the prophecy—"light," "sun," *aristos*, "hands"—
are words that have momentous importance for the narrative, and

Achilles's role in it. The openness and extent of the process is the crucial critical question.[10] The prophecy does not simply predict the future;
it brings about a series of reactions to its own ciphered message that
prompt Achilles into difficult self-questioning. There is no single sub-
text. Instead, we have a process wherein words provoke desires and
denials, actions and failures to act. If clarity is available, this occurs retroactively, and only contingently so. So rather than expecting allegory
or clear meaning, I suggest we turn again to Heraclitus, but this time to
his remarks concerning the Delphic oracle; Homeric language "neither
hides nor reveals but signifies."

"ὁ ἄναξ, οὗ τὸ μαντεῖόν ἐστι τὸ ἐν Δελφοῖς, οὔτε λέγει οὔτε κρύπτει ἀλλὰ
σημαίνει."

(Fragment 93)

The prophecy was not an attempt to fool him with a hidden meaning.
Nor was its meaning always available and clear. Rather, it is part of a
complex array of words that slowly reveal to Achilles, and to us, who
he is, the constraining parameters within which he makes his choices.

Let us look in greater detail at the complexity of the poem's constraining network of words. Consider the following episode from Book 1.
Achilles, insulted by Agamemnon, asks his mother to ask Zeus to help
the Trojans in order to bring him honor, and he reminds her of her boasts
that she alone of the gods helped Zeus when the rest sought to bind him
in chains. The speech culminates in a pun, linking the Greek word for
binding, δέω, with the word for fear, δέίδω.

Since it is many times in my father's halls I have heard you
making claims, when you said you only among the immortals
beat aside shameful destruction from Kronos' son the dark-misted,
that time when all the other Olympians sought to bind him,
Hera and Poseidon and Pallas Athene. Then you,
goddess, went and set him free from his shackles, summoning
in speed the creature of the hundred hands to tall Olympos,
that creature the gods name Briareus, but all men
Aigaios' son, but he is far greater in strength than his father.
He rejoicing in the glory of it sat down by Kronion,
and the rest of the blessed gods were frightened and gave up binding him.

(*Il.* 1.396–406)

πολλάκι γάρ σεο πατρὸς ἐνὶ μεγάροισιν ἄκουσα
εὐχομένης, ὅτ᾽ ἔφησθα κελαινεφέϊ Κρονίωνι
οἴη ἐν ἀθανάτοισιν ἀεικέα λοιγὸν ἀμῦναι,

ὁππότε μιν <u>ξυνδῆσαι</u> Ὀλύμπιοι ἤθελον ἄλλοι,
Ἥρη τ' ἠδὲ Ποσειδάων καὶ Παλλὰς Ἀθήνη·
ἀλλὰ σὺ τόν γ' ἐλθοῦσα, θεά, ὑπελύσαο <u>δεσμῶν</u>,
ὧχ' ἑκατόγχειρον καλέσασ' ἐς μακρὸν Ὄλυμπον,
ὃν Βριάρεων καλέουσι θεοί, ἄνδρες δέ τε πάντες
Αἰγαίων'—ὁ γὰρ αὖτε βίην οὗ πατρὸς ἀμείνων—
ὅς ῥα παρὰ Κρονίωνι καθέζετο κύδεϊ γαίων·
τὸν καὶ <u>ὑπέδεισαν</u> μάκαρες θεοὶ <u>οὐδ' ἔτ' ἔδησαν</u>.

But Achilles's emphasis on the tale of binding sets up a narrative puzzle.
For when Thetis makes her request to Zeus, she does not mention this
rescue story. She simply asks for help, and when she gets no reaction,
she asks again.

'Bend your head and promise me to accomplish this thing,
or else refuse it, you have nothing to fear, that I may know
by how much I am the most dishonoured of all gods.'

                                                    (*Il.* 1.514–16)

"νημερτὲς μὲν δή μοι ὑπόσχεο καὶ κατάνευσον
ἢ ἀπόειπ', <u>ἐπεὶ οὔ τοι ἔπι δέος</u>, ὄφρ' ἐῢ εἰδέω
ὅσσον ἐγὼ μετὰ πᾶσιν ἀτιμοτάτη θεός εἰμι."

But if she chooses not to mention the past even here, the words she
uses seem to remember it for her. For the wordplay between "fear"
and "binding," set up in Achilles's former speech, is now replaced with
only the word for fear (δέος). But we can pick up the other half of the
pun, and thus can link this curtailed speech to Achilles's story of Zeus's
binding.

Now this half-pun could be understood as intentional on the part of
Thetis, a hint that Zeus picks up on, a tactful request that does not stoop
to the level of threat. It could just as easily be unintentional on the part
of the producer of the sign, yet understood as a sign by the receiver:
Thetis might just mean "you have nothing to fear" in total innocence,
while Zeus might nevertheless hear (whether consciously or not) the
echo of "binding." This, of course, as upholders of the epistemologi-
cal problems of the intentional fallacy could point out, remains quite
unknowable. But the aptness of this metaphor of binding via the pun
on "fear" is of interest. Obligations, ties to others, go hand in hand with
the workings of language, the links between near homonyms, δέω and
δέος. Regardless of the intentions of either character in the poem, we can
see the reminder of the past objectively, in this link between signifiers.
And this has far-reaching significance: the most powerful figure in the

poem, Zeus, is himself constrained, painted into a corner by previous debts and fears.

The physical chains suffered by Zeus turn into the poem's signifying chain. They resonate and proliferate, making themselves heard every time we hear Zeus claiming that he is not afraid, when he makes his own threats of binding, or boasts of his own absolute power. This is true not just of Zeus's words, his own false beliefs about himself, but of Zeus's image in the eyes of others. In Book 14 Agamemnon claims to know very well that Zeus has betrayed him, changing his mind about the sack of Troy. Agamemnon realizes that Zeus now gives glory to the Trojans, while he has "bound the Greeks hand and foot" (*Il.* 14.73). But what Agamemnon's words reveal, in ways he may not know, is that the apparent whim of the god is itself constrained. Agamemnon, at the very moment of understanding his betrayal by Zeus, misunderstands both Zeus himself and the source of that betrayal. This tale of the binding, a simple aside from Achilles in the opening book, has the effect of a trauma that will resonate throughout the poem.

THE LONELINESS OF HOMER, THE LONELINESS OF ACHILLES

There is a long history of seeing Achilles as a brilliant child, petulant in his failure to compromise and his hatred of authority, but also singularly equipped to dissect the hypocrisies of the social world around him. This set of associations traces well the contours of his literary character.[11] But the short phrase of Heraclitus, "we are deceived by our understanding of what is obvious," offers a theoretical explanation for them. Because of his intellectual powers, he is unable to perceive what is "obvious": the depth of concern for those around him, and most importantly the depth of his feelings for Patroclus.

This self-absorbed cleverness is a danger for the critic too. Perhaps criticism of the *Iliad* and *Odyssey*, more than any other poetry, has been beset by Parry's warning that we should not find "falsely subtle meanings" in Homer's formulaic language—that is, project our own cleverness onto material that will not allow it.[12] Parry's warning is in part a defensive gesture; he tries to protect preemptively his own critical achievements in demonstrating the oral and formulaic nature of the Homeric poems from a critical ingenuity that would undermine them. Others have voiced similar warnings, though with quite different things at stake. Consider the following remarks by the great Unitarian critic J. T. Sheppard from his book *The Pattern of the "Iliad,"* first published in 1922. He has noticed a link between a moment in Book 24, where

Achilles tells the suppliant Priam not to provoke him, and one in the first book, when Achilles is on the point of killing Agamemnon. But it is Sheppard's reflection on this process of textual remembering that is of interest here.

> But of course we shall not suggest that Homer meant his hearers to be thinking about Agamemnon while he was telling them about Priam and Achilles. He did not want his audience, like a company of Roman poetasters, to applaud his *callida junctura*, to cry "Sophos! Oh, brilliant, novel, tragic application!" He simply wanted them to be absorbed in his story. But he knew that they, like us, were touched by reminiscences and repetitions, even when they were least conscious of the cause.[13]

One can read in this an almost desperate attempt to keep Homer free from the taint of literary pedantry, from the inner circle of knowing poet-experts whose appreciation of the sophistication of the text is a mirror of their own belief in sophistication.[14] It is perhaps one of the benefits of the tradition of Homer's clarity that it has shielded the *Iliad* from this kind of criticism. But such critical sophistication also shields critics from the truths about language's power over us that the poem demonstrates over and over. The words of Sheppard's imaginary critic signal the exact opposite of what they seem to say: there is nothing "novel" about the reading; rather, it is a clichéd mirror image of the critic's belief in what is novel. If there is tragedy, it lies in the way the shared critical vocabulary of sophistication is a form of self-distancing from the dangers of the world outside. And at this point such critics fall into the same situation as the Homer of the riddle of the lice, and as Achilles. For his brilliance is not simply a symptom of his isolation but something that actively brings it about, dissociating him from his desires even as he remains far more attached to the world than he realizes.

So we can accept readily these critical warnings and the danger of narcissism. But we should register something amiss here. Parry's concern that critics find "false subtlety" in Homer runs the risk of confirming its hidden presupposition: that the meaning of words is self-evident, that no critical engagement is required in order to unpack them. But this conflicts with the narrative of the poem. Achilles may begin by taking the meaning of words for granted, but his lack of care over language will cost him. That he understands too late is perhaps simple, gnomic wisdom, perhaps a structural and elegiac truth of the human condition. But Achilles's failure to understand his mother's riddles is also an injunction to pay closer attention to the words of others, a retroactively released hope that such care might have produced a narrative of less suffering. The *Iliad* seems to demand a reading of engagement that tries to work through the significance of Homer's "reminiscences and repetitions" even when we are "least conscious of the cause."

ACHILLES FLEEING DEATH

Patroclus, when he asks Achilles to return to battle, allows him a loophole.

> But if you are drawing back from some prophecy known in your own heart
> and by Zeus' will your honoured mother has told you of something,
> then send me out at least . . .
>
> (*Il.* 16.36–38)

There is something strange about the statement. Achilles tells the embassy in Book 9 that his mother told him he has two fates leading him to his death. Patroclus clearly heard him. So the innocence of the question strikes us as disingenuous. Patroclus suggests that Achilles's failure to fight comes from the fear of a short life, but perhaps his mode of avoidance is deeper: less his fear of biological death than his fear of making any choice at all. His indecision has the effect of keeping both options open, as if he could live in a world where such choices need not be made. In short, he acts as if he was not mortal, avoiding the choice that outlines two different kinds of death: social death in Phthia, removed from any possibility of fame, and biological death at Troy.

This nexus of themes, the spiraling connections of Homer's language, which challenges any reduction to an obvious meaning, and the poem's obsession with death are with us from the very start, though tracing them will involve some critical work. We could begin by unpacking another enigmatic utterance, one that can offer a window into the sophistication of Homer's language. In the middle of the quarrel with Agamemnon, as Achilles utters his first threat to depart from Troy and thus leave Agamemnon's command, he does so in dense, metaphorical language.

> ['']and I am minded no longer
> to stay here dishonoured and pile up your wealth and your luxury.'
>
> (*Il.* 1.170–71)

> "οὐδέ σ' ὀΐω
> ἐνθάδ' ἄτιμος ἐὼν ἄφενος καὶ πλοῦτον ἀφύξειν."

We have already considered the metaphor of ἀφύξειν, the word commonly used for drawing water from a well, or wine from a crater for drinking. It has clear servile connotations and thus conveys what Achilles believes his real relationship to Agamemnon to be. But there is a further puzzle in line 171, signaled by the word ἄτιμος, lacking in honor. Now, this adjective is formed by joining the normal word for "honored" with an alpha privative, producing the meaning "lacking in honor," ἄ-τιμος. But here is the problem. John Keaney once elegantly demonstrated two patterns concerning the use of alpha-privative adjectives in Homer.[15] First, when we are given an adjective with an alpha privative linked to a substantive, and there is a second adjective beginning with alpha in the phrase, the second adjective is almost always another alpha-privative adjective. Second, the use of at least one of these adjectives is directly motivated by the context. He gives the useful example of Thetis's reply to Achilles's lament, later in *Iliad* 1.

If only you could sit by your ships untroubled, not weeping,
since indeed your lifetime is to be short, of no length.

(Il. 1.415–16)

αἴθ' ὄφελες παρὰ νηυσὶν ἀδάκρυτος καὶ ἀπήμων
ἦσθαι, ἐπεί νύ τοι αἶσα μίνυνθά περ, οὔ τι μάλα δήν . . .

The first adjective, "lacking in tears," ἀ-δάκρυτος, directly sets up an expectation for a second such adjective, "lacking in trouble," ἀ-πήμων, which is duly fulfilled, and the first adjective is also directly motivated, since it responds to the tears that Achilles is shedding. The problem in 1.171 is that ἄτιμος does not have a second adjective to match it. But what is more interesting is that, at the level of form, there are two more words that begin with alphas: ἄφενος and then ἀφύξειν. But neither of them has an alpha privative meaning "lacking in" something. The first is a word for wealth, and the second, as we have seen, is a verb for "drawing" water or wine.

But the expectation set up for the alpha-privative meanings invites us to probe further, to see sets of possible meanings lying behind what Achilles means to say. That is, were these words to be examples of alpha-private adjectives, what could they mean? If we are attuned to the patterns of Homeric verse, the line seems to have set up an expectation only, at least on the surface, to deny it. But this should encourage a second look. Let us look first to the second word, ἀφύξειν. What would *it* mean as an alpha-privative word? Here, one answer is provided by Agamemnon's reply to it. Achilles ends with ἀφύξειν, and Agamemnon replies with an order: "flee!" (*Il.* 1.170–74).

"οὐδέ σ' ὀΐω
ἐνθάδ' ἄτιμος ἐὼν ἄφενος καὶ πλοῦτον <u>ἀφύξειν</u>."

Τὸν δ' ἠμείβετ' ἔπειτα ἄναξ ἀνδρῶν Ἀγαμέμνων·
"φεῦγε μάλ', εἴ τοι θυμὸς ἐπέσσυται, οὐδέ σ' ἔγωγε
λίσσομαι εἵνεκ' ἐμεῖο μένειν ..."

The text seems to hint at the possibility that the verb does not only mean
"draw" but is also the future of a nonattested verb, from an alpha privative attached to φεῦγε, meaning something like "fail to flee."

But what can it mean that Achilles simultaneously says that he will
go home and says that he will *not* flee? There is a foreshadowing of the
later discrepancy between what he says he will do and what he will actually do: he says he will go home in Book 1, but this is never fulfilled.
He seems to say, and mean, "I will go," but his inaction matches a possibility opened up by the double negative: he does not *not* flee. Achilles
speaks in two voices here, and their conflict traces out the contours of
the plot, as Achilles hovers between fleeing and not fleeing. The nonsense of the words that mean contradictory things simultaneously is a
key to what Achilles wants. For is not his entire existence a testament
to his desire for the impossible, his desire to resist the kind of choice
where he must give something up? Achilles lives in the logical space
opened up by this double negative: he will not *not* flee, though he will
not flee either.

Agamemnon's wordplay, whether he realizes its significance or not,
should encourage us to pay attention to our second word that begins
with an alpha, ἄφενος. If we were to make it into an alpha-privative
adjective, it would have to mean something like "lacking in slaughter,"
as if it came from the verb for slaughter, φένω, with its noun derivative,
φόνος. Achilles would then be saying, "I don't think I'll stay here without honor, not participating in slaughter." But we have now stumbled
on the very thing that he will do for the next eighteen books of the narrative. Before Book 1, we know, he stayed in Troy as the most efficient
and direct proponent of Trojan slaughter, but only received a pittance
of honor. After the quarrel, he will stay dishonored, but will not indulge personally in slaughter, though he will be implicated in it: that is,
though physically *a-phonos*, he will nevertheless be the absent architect
of the slaughter of the Greeks.

But there is a more tragic way of reading these lines. Achilles's entire
speech is replete with a vocabulary of death. Slaughter lurks in ἄφενος,
but so does the word for wealth. For the god of wealth, Πλοῦτος, will
later be confused with an alternative name for the god of the dead,
Πλούτων, or Pluto. It is impossible to be sure how early this confusion

of wealth and death began in Greek culture; Plutus as god is first at-
tested in the fifth century, as is his bracketing with the god of the underworld.[16] But I would suggest that the context here makes a good case
for deliberate ambiguity.[17] Achilles's speech picks up an association of
wealth and death within archaic poetry, where Hades is conventionally
rich. For the pun would suggest that Achilles not only refuses to draw
wealth for Agamemnon, but also refuses to draw death for him, as if
he knows all too well that this is his true job. Underlying the pretense
of gaining material goods for Agamemnon is the grimmer truth that
he kills for Agamemnon. Achilles's attempt to distinguish between the
value of goods and the value of life, so central to his great speech in *Iliad*
9, would begin here in the confusion of the two discourses suggested by
the phrase's double meaning. Achilles's quest to find the meaning of his
own life runs hand in hand with his quest to come to terms with himself
as the dispenser of others' lives, ultimately on the orders of another. But
if we make use of the meaning "fail to flee," Achilles will once more be
articulating a denial of his own future: for he will indeed stay in Troy
and fail to flee death. This time, of course, the death he fails to flee will
not only be that of other Greeks, but his own, and mediated by a death
that joins the two together, the death of Patroclus.

Now if this seems to force the meaning of these verbal plays, I would
suggest that later parts of the poem, as well as later Greek literary culture, pick up on them. First, consider the word ἀφύξειν. There is no verb
"not to flee" in Greek, but there will be a later adjective ἀφύκτος, which
means "that which cannot be fled" and is often associated with death.
A typical example would be arrows that cannot be fled.[18] But with this
in mind, we might be tempted to interpret Achilles's lines as a displacement of something that is almost a cliché of the poem—the inability
of mortals to flee fate. We could, for example, read them alongside the
parting words of Hector to Andromache in *Iliad* 6.

[']No man is going to hurl me to Hades, unless it is fated,
but as for fate, I think that no man yet has escaped it
once it has taken its first form, neither brave man nor coward.[']

(*Il.* 6.487–89)

"οὐ γάρ τίς μ' ὑπὲρ αἶσαν ἀνὴρ Ἄϊδι προϊάψει·
μοῖραν δ' οὔ τινά φημι πεφυγμένον ἔμμεναι ἀνδρῶν,
οὐ κακὸν, οὐδὲ μὲν ἐσθλόν, ἐπὴν τὰ πρῶτα γένηται."

These lines are a teasing out of Achilles's cryptic phrase—πλοῦτον
ἀφύξειν—though they bring further riddling problems of their own.

What, for example, does the vague phrase ἐπὴν τὰ πρῶτα γένηται, "when first things come into being," mean? But compare also a later speech made by Poseidon to Agamemnon, where the phrase returns. After the wounding of a series of Greek heroes culminates in Patroclus's mission to find out the identity of the wounded healer Machaon, Poseidon tries to rouse Agamemnon back to war, and as he does so, he reminds him of the absent Achilles.

> 'Son of Atreus,
> I think that now that baleful heart in the breast of Achilleus
> must be happy as he stares at the slaughter of the Achaians
> and their defeat. There is no heart in him, not even a little.
> Even so may the god strike him down, let him go to destruction.
> But with you the blessed gods are not utterly angry.
> There will still be a time when the lords of Troy and their counsellors
> shall send dust wide on the plain, and you yourself shall look on them
> as they take flight for their city away from the ships and the shelters.'
> (*Il.* 14.138–46)

> "Ἀτρεΐδη, νῦν δή που Ἀχιλλῆος ὀλοὸν κῆρ
> γηθεῖ ἐνὶ στήθεσσι, φόνον καὶ φύζαν Ἀχαιῶν
> δερκομένῳ, ἐπεὶ οὔ οἱ ἔνι φρένες, οὐδ' ἡβαιαί.
> ἀλλ' ὃ μὲν ὣς ἀπόλοιτο, θεὸς δέ ἑ σιφλώσειε·
> σοὶ δ' οὔ πω μάλα πάγχυ θεοὶ μάκαρες κοτέουσιν,
> ἀλλ' ἔτι που Τρώων ἡγήτορες ἡδὲ μέδοντες
> εὐρὺ κονίσουσιν πεδίον, σὺ δ' ἐπόψεαι αὐτὸς
> φεύγοντας προτὶ ἄστυ νεῶν ἄπο καὶ κλισιάων."

The crucial phrase here is φόνον καὶ φύζαν, which echoes the phrase of Achilles in Book 1, ἄφενος καὶ πλοῦτον ἀφύξειν, almost perfectly, but without the alpha privatives. "Lack of slaughter" and "failure to flee" are replaced by slaughter and flight.[19] Poseidon's reversal of Achilles's language once more allows us to see the complexity of the narrative situation. Achilles's failure to flee Troy allows him to rejoice in the Greek flight, just as he now slaughters the Greeks by his failure to become physically involved in the slaughter. In a similar vein, Poseidon's promise that Agamemnon will one day look upon the flight of Trojans ("and you yourself shall look on them / as they take flight for their city") verbally recalls Achilles's failed promise that the Greeks will be able to look on his ships in the morning, as he flees home after the failure of the embassy ("you will see, if you have a mind to it and if it concerns you, my ships in the dawn at sea on the Hellespont," *Il.* 9.359–60).

Is it not hopelessly speculative psychologizing to say that Achilles fears death? We do not need to project desires onto Achilles in order to see that death is everywhere in his words. At first glance we have a hero who is the greatest at mastering death, whose bravery and martial worth are unquestioned. For this kind of hero, the choice between two fates, a long life or a short, glorious one, is not corrupted by his possible cowardice. But we can turn this upside down. Precisely because of his knowledge of the prophecies from his mother, far from his being in any way a master of death, the problem of death masters him, creating the parameters for his actions. And in this sense his attitude to death is indeed inside him, in both his language and the way he orchestrates the entire epic universe as an experiment for his inquiry into the value of life and death. Just as Homer sought to avoid death and thus carried the concept of death with him, his life lived in that denial, so too Achilles's story is conditioned by the problem of what his mortality means.

Finally, in the story of Homer's avoidance of death, we also have a poignant comment on what it means to write a catalogue of everyone else's death, the careful chronicling of that vast expenditure of life that somehow passes the quasi-immortal narrator by. At the end of the *Odyssey*, when Odysseus meets his father, Laertes, in his garden, he points out that Laertes pays careful attention to everything in the garden around him, but his ragged appearance suggests that he fails to care for himself. An exception to his rule of universal care, this could stand as a double for the poet of the *Iliad*, whose discourse of death is itself already a way of avoiding his own. The riddle dramatizes the moment when his own story catches up with him.[20]

Time and Homeric Language: Arguments for Slow Reading

Homer's narrative, then, is sensitive to the process whereby signs change their meaning, but also to the creative power of language to set up the parameters of any future activity. As such, it seems to argue against the fashionable thesis that Homeric language is swift and easy to understand, a thesis that has two major components: first, the formulaic nature of Homeric verse, and, second, the "fundamental rule" of linear, progressive composition, which argues that the poetry moves forward without ever doubling back on itself. But using the riddling language of Homer as our base, we can at least make a partial dent in this edifice of Homeric criticism.[21]

Let us deal with formulae first. Parry famously argued that the repetition of fixed phrases within Homeric poetry was a symptom of the oral conditions of production, and thus responsible for its swiftness. Because, say, ships are always referred to as "black" in the dative and "well-balanced" in the accusative to fill the metrical requirements of Homer's hexameter, the adjective "black" in the phrase "black ship" can have no meaning; the whole phrase functions as a simple shorthand for the essential idea "ship." A rule describing the constraints on poetic production (bards using language as a tool) transforms itself into a rule for how listeners are to understand the poem: we can skip over descriptive details and register only the "essential meaning" of the phrases, since a ship is (always) just a ship. Now, it is easy enough to show that this is an untenable theory of language, for all that it does register an important aspect of Homeric poetry. For it focuses on language at the point of production, the making of verse, and ignores the process of meaning, language's provisional realization in the way it is understood or misunderstood by the hearer.[22] Jesper Svenbro has pointed out that the extraordinary emphasis on the disjunction between writing and speaking/singing in studies of archaic and classical Greek culture has resulted in an almost total disregard for the process of reading.[23] But this is equally true for the process of listening, and for all the efforts of the oral theorists to show us how an active, listening audience can influence poetic production, this has too rarely resulted in any major challenge to the interpretative assumptions of Homer's simplicity. But I do not wish to mount another attack on Parry from the outside; instead, I want to show the way in which the notion of formulaic phrases as reflecting an essential meaning is a compelling, if illusory, one for the characters within Homeric epic themselves. That is, the poem deals in advance with Parry's theory by showing us the effect of the reception of its language as offering "essential meanings"—and then it explores the consequences.

Of course, the point here is not that Parry's theory is simply wrong. To be sure, the formulaic nature of the verse is deeply embedded in the conditions of oral performance. But one of the attractive lures, as well as one of the hazards of formulaic verse is that it encourages us to "understand" too quickly, skipping over the details of the language. And in riddling language we have a counterpoint to this, a resistance to this "swiftness." Consider the words of Priam to Achilles in *Iliad* 24.

Fifty were my sons, when the sons of the Achaians came here.
Nineteen were born to me from the womb of a single mother,

and other women bore the rest in my palace; and of these
violent Ares broke the strength in the knees of most of them,
but one was left me who guarded my city and people, that one
you killed a few days since as he fought in defence of his country . . .

                                                              (*Il.* 24.495–500)

The meaning of these lines will soon be transferred to Achilles, the only
son of Peleus, who has failed to protect his aging father. Achilles's own
critique of the war in Book 1, where he suggested that he had no quarrel
with the Trojans, perhaps also makes itself felt. But what is most poignant
here is the heartbreaking inappropriateness of the phrase ἀμυνόμενον
περὶ πάτρης, "defending his country." For this is the very thing that Hector failed to do: he abandoned his parents and country to fight Achilles
outside the walls of Troy in Book 22, and he explicitly rejected the possibility of a defensive fight within the walls, even when that was suggested, for the third time, by Priam himself (*Il.* 22.56–59, where Priam
echoes the earlier appeals of Andromache and Poulydamas).

Meaning is clearly being essentialized here. Priam, one could say,
treats Hector as if he is always, essentially, someone who defends his
country, as if he had experienced the swiftness and verity of Homeric
language from within the poem itself, and was prey to the lures of "understanding too quickly." The statement, coming so soon after Hector's
death, also has the flavor of an anticipatory funerary epigram. The final
image of Hector is frozen forever, a way of remembering an idealized
version of him. We can contrast Priam's words here with another imagined epitaph, but this time composed by Hector, as he imagines his success in the duel with his prospective victim in Book 7.

And some day one of the men to come will say, as he sees it,
one who in his benched ship sails on the wine-blue water:
"This is the mound of a man who died long ago in battle,
who was one of the bravest, and glorious Hektor killed him."

                                                              (*Il.* 7.87–90)

καί ποτέ τις εἴπῃσι καὶ ὀψιγόνων ἀνθρώπων,
νηῒ πολυκληῒδι πλέων ἐπὶ οἴνοπα πόντον·
"ἀνδρὸς μὲν τόδε σῆμα πάλαι κατατεθνηῶτος,
ὅν ποτ' ἀριστεύοντα κατέκτανε φαίδιμος Ἕκτωρ."

Here, the glory of the victim, projected into the future, is located in the
present participle ἀριστεύοντα. He dies at the moment he is "being the
best," and the flotsam and jetsam of the contingent, mundane details of
this imaginary hero's life are filtered away, leaving only this essential
detail for future generations to read: he fought well, as the best of war-

riors. But there is also something very strange in this *sema*. The victim is not named, and pragmatically this is because the identity of Hector's opponent has not become clear. But Hector has now created a beautifully paradoxical version of an epitaph, one that can tell us little about the imagined dead warrior, but much more about himself. The identity of the victim is entirely eclipsed by the identity of the man who killed him, and the "falseness" of the present participle, ἀριστεύοντα, used of a man who is now dead and so no longer fighting, is transferred into the person of his killer, where the image of a man continually killing does still apply. Soon Hector, at the acme of his martial power, will wish that this state of "being the best," of enjoying the moment of victory, could last forever (*Il.* 8.538–41), translating himself into a paradoxical living *sema*, frozen in the moment of his greatest power.

But what matters most, for the contrast with Priam's words, is that these words function as Hector's own epitaph for himself. In talking of the glory of his victim, he is telling us what he imagines a "beautiful death" to be. But this is not the kind of death that Priam offers him after he has really been killed. An ethics of fighting in the front lines for glory comes up against the defensive philosophy of Priam, a tension that is at work throughout the "tragedy of Hector." The meaning of Hector's death, is contested and fought over in advance, not least by Hector himself, as are the future words that will sum up his life. The terrain of this conflict is made up of the partial, essentializing worldviews of the participants, who are, as it were, a victim of the allures produced by one aspect of Homeric language itself: that Hector is *always* the hero who fights on behalf of his city, always fighting as an *aristos* in the front lines.

We might compare Priam's words with another, much later, funerary epigram of Callimachus.

Twelve years old, his male child, the father Philip put
Here, his great hope, Nikoteles.

(Epigr. 19; my translation)

Δωδεκέτη τὸν παῖδα πατὴρ ἀπέθηκε Φίλιππος
ἐνθάδε, τὴν πολλὴν ἐλπίδα, Νικοτέλην.

The power of the poem lies in the way the single identifying description of the boy, "great hope," no longer applies. The child's qualities are empty, nothing but the hopes of the father that are now perpetually lost. He has died twice over: first in his biological life, second as a social being, in his failure to become anything more than a cipher for the desires of others. More, the meanings of the protagonists' names—Philip the "horse-lover" and the son "Victor"—also suggest the way in which the desires of the father are projected onto the son. Instead of memorializing forever a quality of the son, the father's desires and his hopes for athletic victory (perhaps passed on to him by his own father, the one who called him "Philip") eclipse his son's identity. This adds to the poignancy of referring to the qualities of someone as if the person were still alive. It is one thing to freeze someone's actions forever, but another to freeze hopes and expectations. This involves a projection into the future of an empty fame, a version of Freud's joke about the man "with a great future behind him."[24] One might even see some Oedipal tension between Nikoteles and Philip. The boy's death is perhaps not just the termination of the father's dreams for him, but a melancholy final victory for the child, who escapes his father's desires for him by his death, as if death is a final refuge from these ancestral pressures.

If we now turn back to the phrase "defending his country," we might note how Priam's fantasy eclipses the dreams of the son and reduces him to the role of defender of his country, and the way in which reality has made a mockery of Priam's hopes for the future of his city: Hector's death signals the end of Troy. Priam utters a cliché of Hector, but one that now, with the passage of time, can only function as a pathetic denial. The poem deftly exploits the gap between what seem to be repeated truths in the form of identical words, and the changing events that make a mockery of the inflexibility of human beliefs. In generic terms, might we not also say that Parry's idealizing faith in the clarity of formula is the idealizing and impossible faith behind the genre of funerary epigram?

But we should also pause over what this means for our understanding of Hector in the poem. Priam's description of Hector can help us see what, in hindsight, was Hector's own protracted and confused resistance to the way others viewed him. He rejects a series of attempts to make him defend Troy, coming from Andromache, Poulydamas, Hecabe, and Priam. And this resistance, in turn, relates to how he treats his own son.

Hektor's son, the admired, beautiful as a star shining,
whom Hektor called Skamandrios, but all of the others
Astyanax—lord of the city; since Hektor alone saved Ilion.

(Il. 6.401–3)

Ἑκτορίδην ἀγαπητὸν, ἀλίγκιον ἀστέρι καλῷ,
τόν ῥ᾽ Ἕκτωρ καλέεσκε Σκαμάνδριον, αὐτὰρ οἱ ἄλλοι
Ἀστυάνακτ᾽· οἶος γὰρ ἐρύετο Ἴλιον Ἕκτωρ.

It remains a puzzle why Hector should resist the name that all of Troy uses for his son, Astyanax, the "lord of the city." But it is partly solved when we consider how Hector, at all the crucial times, chooses to leave the suffocation of Troy: his departure from Andromache in Book 6, his rejection of Poulydamas's advice to return within the city walls in Book 18, his decision to face Achilles in Book 22. Rather than someone who accepts his identification with his own city, Hector lingers on the fringes of the city, his personal choices geographically traced out in the distance he maintains from the gates of Troy. In the naming of his son, Hector is caught between his own embedded social role as defender of the city and the flow of the city's major river, the Skamander, which offers a promise of escape. Homer's geography figures a more fundamental split between a desire for fixity and the flux of a malleable identity, the burden of social responsibility and freedom from it. And this is true even as Hector himself at times identifies with his own civic myth, the social pressure of the ideals thrust upon him by those who call his child Astyanax.

With this in mind, as we return to the final encounter between Priam and Achilles, what is being shared, along with the bread they eat, is not simply hitherto undiscovered truths about the other, their shared vulnerability, the depth of the failures they perceive in their status as father and son, but also the space where their own illusions of themselves can be maintained.

Now let us turn to a second reason given for Homer' swiftness: the linearity of his narrative technique. Let me borrow the excellent and influential summary of this position from G. S. Kirk: "The development of the sentence is controlled by a fundamental rule of Homeric style, which is that thought together with expression is always or for the most part *linear* and *progressive*; it does not turn back on itself or delay, or artificially rearrange, important elements of meaning."[25] The trouble with this kind of critical statement is that although it takes the form of description, it exercises a performative power. That is, if we believe it to be true, we will then read linearly and progressively, rejecting any need to retrace our steps. The only way to counter it is to perform ongoing sets of critical experiments and see what happens if we do double back. In other words, this kind of statement has to be transgressed before it can be argued against. In many ways this entire book has been a violation of Kirk's suggestion. But we can return to the *Contest of Homer and Hesiod*, a critical text that suggests that in antiquity it was already possible to play with the presumed linearity of Homeric narrative.

The central contest between the poets involves Hesiod offering Homer a hexameter line, but one that seems to say something embarrassing, sacrilegious, or entirely at odds with what we know of the Homeric poems. Homer then adds a line, and retroactively changes the meaning to something acceptable. It is a well-known critical cliché about Homeric hexameter that single lines tend to produce discrete units of sense, and that the following line often expands on this, the process known as enjambment. A typical example comes from the first two lines of the poem.

Sing, goddess, the anger of Peleus' son Achilleus
and its devastation . . .

Μῆνιν ἄειδε, θεὰ, Πηληϊάδεω Ἀχιλῆος
οὐλομένην . . .

Μῆνιν gets picked up on and expanded by an adjective, οὐλομένην, and a phrase is added to that. It has been argued further that this kind of narrative technique is bound up with the "oral" aspect of poetry. On this view, oral communication demands the kind of repetition and clear organizing that enjambment embodies. Now the game between Hesiod and Homer certainly subverts this Homeric technique. But this does not necessarily mean that it takes the clarity of Homeric discourse for granted. We are invited to read Homer differently, even as we are offered counter-readings of an iconic Homer. Consider one of the lines Hesiod offers up to Homer, and Homer's response.

Agamemnon prayed earnestly that they would all die—
never on the sea. This was the word he spoke.

(Certamen 133–34)

τοῖσιν δ' Ἀτρεΐδης μεγάλ' εὔχετο πᾶσιν ὀλέσθαι
μηδέ ποτ' ἐν πόντῳ, καὶ φωνήσας ἔπος ηὔδα.

The first line of the hexameter, cut off from what follows, shocks. It affronts the nobility of the leader of the expedition to Troy, but also the epic nobility of Homer's poetry itself. Because of this, the next line is required to readjust the sense, to halt the politically incorrect suggestion of a leader's hatred of his troops. But for all its apparent silliness, this hexameter line is not so easily divorced from much of what goes on at the start of the *Iliad*. Book 1 charts the complexity of the leader's attitude toward his troops, and Achilles accuses Agamemnon of willful disregard for their well-being. What escapes in Hesiod's nonsensical first line is a comic deflation that links itself to the tragic deflation of Agamemnon's pretenses. It comes to the brink of bringing a secret of the poem all too crudely out into the open: Agamemnon's ambivalence toward his people.[26] One way of plotting the narrative of the poem is through the transfer of this aggression toward the Achaeans away from Agamemnon and onto Achilles himself, who will campaign physically to destroy them. But there is a purely formal point to be made. We need to pay attention to the temporal process by which we hear words, the information that is continually escaping, rather than having any easy recourse to the obviousness of what is said. Adding words, apparently to clarify meaning, might also be a coverup.

The *Certamen* offers us an ancient version of the process of "close reading" that in our own times has been encouraged by reader-response criticism. And we should entertain the possibility that this is not just a game played by Hesiod and Homer, but a nod toward the kind of subversion going on within Homer's poetry. The literary game also provides a fitting preliminary to the *Certamen*'s story of Homer's death. At first we see Homer as sage, the guarantor of meaning. He tries to reject any misreading of his clear message in order to ensure the clarity of Homeric discourse. But his failure to solve the riddle retroactively suggests that his effort to guarantee the meaning of his own poems is a losing battle.

Let me give one simple example from *Iliad* 1, which will itself generate a myriad of narrative problems. In Book 1 Agamemnon orders the heralds to get Briseis from Achilles's tent, and threatens to take Briseis himself if he refuses.

> 'Go now
> to the shelter of Peleus' son Achilleus, to bring back
> Briseis of the fair cheeks leading her by the hand. And if he
> will not give her, I must come in person to take her
> with many men behind me, and it will be the worse for him.'
>
> (*Il.* 1.321–25)

> "ἔρχεσθον κλισίην Πηληϊάδεω Ἀχιλῆος·
> χειρὸς ἑλόντ' ἀγέμεν Βρισηΐδα καλλιπάρῃον·
> εἰ δέ κε μὴ δώῃσιν, ἐγὼ δέ κεν αὐτὸς ἕλωμαι
> ἐλθὼν σὺν πλεόνεσσι· τό οἱ καὶ ῥίγιον ἔσται."

What escapes here at the end of line 324, before the following line clarifies it, is the image of Agamemnon meeting Achilles face to face. It returns us to the failed hand-to-hand combat that was forestalled earlier in the book, when Athena stopped Achilles from drawing his sword against Agamemnon. It is as if, in what he says, Agamemnon forgets himself and identifies with the position of the man who is best equipped to fight duels. His bravado outruns him. But the next line returns us to the major narrative conflict, between the fighter and the man who "rules more people," even as it cannot quite forget the fear that is hinted at in the former line. It is a verbal backing down. The timing of the phrase ἐλθὼν σὺν πλεόνεσσι, immediately after the previous line threatens to leave the two alone, is crucial. "I'll come with more people" is a show of power, but also a sign of pathetic weakness, a veiled admission of his own physical inadequacy, his need for "more men" to inflict defeat on Achilles. In the case of the *Certamen*, Homer corrects the "impossible" line produced by Hesiod. Here, Agamemnon corrects himself.

The return to the usual conflict showcases how a king can act without being physically present, as his henchmen become appendages of him. The heralds themselves have no power, but are signs of Agamemnon's power, a human synecdoche for the power of the whole army. But as if to underline the discrepancy between these men as a sign of power and Agamemnon's own physical inadequacy, the poem lingers over their terror at confronting Achilles. The fear that is hinted at (but glossed over) in the retraction of bravado in Agamemnon's speech is displaced onto the heralds themselves: "These two terrified and in awe of the king" (*Il.* 1.331). It is not simply that the heralds themselves are afraid, caught between the orders of one king and their physical terror before another: they exhibit the very fear that Agamemnon manages to avoid directly showing. They fear his fear for him.

This shift away from bravado is prepared for by Agamemnon's earlier series of near challenges using the same language of face-to-face combat.

Either the great-hearted Achaians shall give me a new prize
chosen according to my desire to atone for the girl lost,
or else if they will not give me one I myself shall take her,
your own prize, or that of Aias, or that of Odysseus,
going myself in person . . .

(Il. 1.135–39)

but I shall take the fair-cheeked Briseis,
your prize, I myself going to your shelter . . .

(Il. 1.184–85)

But Agamemnon's boasts bring more problems. If we treat their meaning as clear, we will be forced to admit that all of these claims are manifestly untrue. Agamemnon will not come himself with more people to visit Achilles, but will at first send only his heralds. But this incongruence should point us toward a narrative logic. Agamemnon's threat looks forward not just to the mini-embassy to take Briseis in Book 1, but to the later embassy in Book 9. Then, too, Agamemnon will send forth "more" people (though precisely how many is a notorious critical crux, one that is itself being signposted as a crux in advance), though he himself will again not go, and the result of that embassy will indeed be worse for Achilles.

Not only is the general form of this embassy foreshadowed (more people), but even the cast of characters. For, with pleasing economy, the narrative red herrings of Ajax and Odysseus, the two men whose prize Agamemnon will not take, will be the very peers of Achilles that Agamemnon chooses to send to him in Book 9. And can we not say that the problematic status of Phoenix, the embassy's "odd man out," is also being anticipated here by his very absence? At any rate, when Achilles, during his great speech in Book 9, talks of Agamemnon's cowardice, claiming that Agamemnon would not dare to look him in the face, the significance stretches beyond his absence in Book 9 to his delegation of power in Book 1. The heralds become symptoms both of Agamemnon's fear and of his power, just as the heroes Agamemnon does not alienate from his rule, Ajax and Odysseus, who are allowed to keep their spear-prizes, are the first on the list to play the role of men subservient to his interests. Their trip to Achilles's tent signifies the leader's ability to project his own desires beyond himself, but without personal risk. It is the political equivalent of the battle technique of the archer, who shoots from a distance and thus remains invulnerable, and precisely because of this is constantly derided for his cowardice, his failure to stand up in battle face to face with the enemy.

But we also have a window into the haphazard way in which Agamemnon's power operates, running parallel to the poet's own narrative economy: the embryonic plan behind the embassy in Book 9 is thought up here, on the spot, as it were, mixed together from the individual ingredients in the random threats he makes. Agamemnon's own language forms the parameters of how he will later act, even if he has no idea what he is doing. With hindsight we can see that Book 1 operates as a preliminary outline of the parameters of the embassy scene, which therefore drags the politics of the failed encounter between Achilles and Agamemnon along with it: the arrival with "more men" is still linked to Agamemnon's display of power; his presence also designates his fear. Indeed, this overlap gives us insight into why the embassy fails. It cannot rid itself of the structural problem of the abuse of Agamemnon's power through others on show in the first book, which is repeated by the presence of "more people." Yet the text also highlights the ways in which this use of his own words by Agamemnon hints at far broader meanings that he has no sense of: the embassy will "be worse" for Achilles in ways no one in Book 1 could quite imagine.

The Death of an Author

When Roland Barthes pronounced the death of the author, the provocative catchphrase often obscured the consequence Barthes tried to draw from this death: the liberation of the critic.[27] Rather than mourning for lost intentionality, Barthes's essay offers instead the possibility of a democratic critical experiment, a project of collective involvement in contesting the meaning of literary and cultural documents. In many ways the objects of Barthes's wrath, in particular the capitalism-inspired fascination with the cult of the author, the celebrity-driven culture that promoted it, and the consequent violence done to the critical spirit itself, seem very distant from biographical stories of Homer's death. And yet, are they so different? We can read the story of Homer's death as a *peripeteia*: a poet who at first desperately tries to maintain the clarity of his own words against the playful sabotage of a perverse reader, ends by demonstrating his acute failure to read. The clarity of Homeric poetry seems twinned with the icon of a wise Homer to guarantee that clarity; but the tale of his death undermines this link.

Of course, decades of research on the oral background to the Homeric poems have bracketed, if not ignored, the status of any "monumental composer" of the poems. But clichés about Homer's clarity and simplicity have stayed in place, as if transferred from the poet-icon to the process of the oral tradition itself. What I have tried to show is that there are benefits to be derived from identifying with the puzzled Homer, the figure who cannot understand apparently simple language, and yet whose puzzlement begins his engagement with that language. And I offer this empty Homer as an alternative to the assorted full versions of Homer that are often turned to in order to buttress certain interpretations and foreclose others, whether he is viewed as a poet of clarity, an upholder of an aristocratic tradition, or an "instructor of princes." We should try to make Homer's language and poems opaque again, because tarrying with this opacity has interpretative rewards. Because Homer is dead, a victim of the narcissistic wound inflicted by riddling children who did not know that they were speaking in riddles, Homer's poetry has a chance of staying alive. Someone killed Homer? Perhaps just as well.

Notes

Preface

1. *Bryn Mawr Classical Review* 98.5.20.
2. Marx 1973, 111.
3. Perhaps the most important of these are Cedric Whitman, Jamie Redfield, Greg Nagy, and Michael Lynn-George. Their names crop up throughout this book, but I owe far more to the breadth of their approaches than the endnotes can suggest.

Introduction

1. Most brilliantly evoked in Whitman 1958, chap. 8.
2. On this open aspect of riddles, see Zupankic, 200–201.
3. On the opening riddle of the *Odyssey*, see Goldhill 1991, chap. 1, with bibliography.
4. As Nagy 1979 argues.

Chapter 1. The Tragedy of Achilles

1. Whitman 1958, passim, but especially chap. 9 on Achilles.
2. Parry 1956; Whitman 1958.
3. For this general approach, see Gill 1996; Martin 1989; Wilson 2002.
4. The quotation comes from Nancy Felson and Laura Slatkin, in Fowler 2004, 101.
5. An irony noted in Muellner's discussion (1996) of the possible association of the poem's first word, *menis*, with *menos*, strength. Achilles, the hero of force, will be most forceful when he does nothing.
6. For example, Lateiner's summary of the plot in the *Cambridge Companion to Homer* (Fowler 2004, 24–25) elides this crucial moment.

7. On this motif, see Wathelet 1989.

8. See for example Blundell 1989.

9. A powerful elaboration of this idea is offered in the opening chapter of Snell 1953. See also the elegant critique by Williams 1993.

10. Among the translators of the poem, the notable exception to the rule is Stanley Lombardo, who, with typical bluntness, translates: "I loved him, and I killed him."

11. Lacan 2004, 8, at the end of "The Mirror Stage." The first epigraph to this chapter comes from "The Subversion of the Subject" (ibid., 293).

Chapter 2. Comedy and Class Struggle

1. Freud 1990, 293.

2. Struck 2004, 21.

3. For pioneering work on the "class struggle" involved in the Thersites episode, see Thalmann 1988.

4. Freud 1990, 255.

5. Part of the "modern triumvirate" of theories of laughter, in Halliwell's phrase (2008, 11): superiority, incongruity, release.

6. Vernant 1991, chap. 2.

7. Leaf and Bayfield 1971, *ad loc.*

Chapter 3. The Politics of Poetry

1. Noticed by Hubbard 1992, among others.

2. Noted by both Nagy (1979, 185) and Lynn-George (1988, 115).

Chapter 4. The Poetry of Politics

1. In particular Lynn-George 1988, 265–67.

2. Schmitt 2007, 35.

3. "The Contest of Homer," in Kaufmann 1976, 33–34.

4. On the social significance of equids in antiquity, see Griffith 2006b.

Chapter 5. Couples

1. Chantraine 1984–90, s.v.

2. Scarry 1985, where the critique of war in the opening chapter resonates throughout the book.

3. Scholia *ad Il.* 6.433–39: ἀντιστρατηγεῖ γὰρ τῷ Ἕκτορι. See the discussion in Kirk 1985–94, *ad loc.*

4. Kirk 1985–94, ad loc.

5. Davidson 2007, chap. 10.

6. Text and translation from the Loeb edition of H. G. Evelyn-White.

7. Nagy 1996, 72; emphasis in original.

8. As Cunliffe's Homeric dictionary (1977) states, ἀνώγει can take both an accusative and infinitive construction and a dative and infinitive.

Chapter 7. The Afterlife of Homer

1. The text is from J. M. Edmonds; the translation is my own.

2. Discussed provocatively by Whitman 1958, and in greater depth in the final chapter of Lynn-George 1988.

3. Lynn-George 1988, 245.

4. Ibid., 242.

5. Pucci 1996, 5.

6. Henderson 1997, esp. 100–102.

7. Pucci 1996, 7.

Conclusion

1. Though the text of the *Contest of Homer and Hesiod* that we have dates to the Antonine period, it is generally agreed now that is based on a fifth-century BCE version, possibly written by Alcidamas. The riddle of the lice itself is even older and was already known to Heraclitus.

2. Hanson's 1998 polemic can at least can be credited with provoking sustained reflection by professional classicists on the importance of the literary and cultural legacy of antiquity. He has nothing to say about the story of Homer's death in antiquity. This might be, in part, because it undermines the simplified view of Homer, and antiquity, that Hanson promotes.

3. Lefkowitz 1981.

4. For recent approaches to this question, see Graziosi 2002; Kahane 2005.

5. A solution hinted at in Porter 2000, 319. See also Rethy 1987.

6. Gorgias, *Encomium of Helen*, 8: "Logos is a great dynast, who accomplishes the most divine acts with the smallest and most invisible body." Plato, *Prot.* 313a–314b.

7. This interpretation has recently been teased out at some length by Ahuvia Kahane (2005, chap. 1).

8. Levine 2002/3.

9. There has been renewed interest in the allegorical school in recent years. See Lamberton and Keaney 1992; Struck 2004.

10. Critical questions too often ignored. The pioneering efforts of Cedric Whitman here, esp. Whitman 1958, chaps. 6–7, have largely been left to dangle.

11. Most brilliantly in Whitman 1958, but see also MacCary 1982.

12. Milman Parry review quoted by Whitman (1958, 249).

13. Sheppard 1966, 13.

14. Cf. Kennedy 1984 on this ingrained habit in contemporary critical circles.

15. Keaney 1981.

16. See *LSJ* s.v. on Πλούτων, offering Sophocles's Frag. 259 as evidence.

17. Compare also the conflation of wealth and death in the *Homeric Hymn to Demeter*, 486–87.

18. Used, for example, of Eros's arrows by Euripides in *Medea* 530.

19. Thanks to Josh Katz for pointing out this parallel to me.

20. Thanks to Alex Purves for this suggestion.

21. I realize I am in excellent company. For a theoretical defense of Homer's sensitive use of language, see Lynn-George 1988; Pucci 1995 and 1996.

22. This deconstructive, reader-response-influenced critique of Homeric criticism by Lynn-George (1988) is still largely ignored by Homerists.

23. Svenbro 1993, esp. the introduction.

24. Freud 1990, 27.

25. Kirk 1985, vol. 1, xxx.

26. For the epic obsession with the relationship between ruler and ruled, see Haubold 2000.

27. Barthes 1986.

References

Barthes, Roland. 1986. *The Rustle of Language*. New York.

Blundell, Mary Whitlock. 1989. *Helping Friends and Harming Enemies: A Study in Sophocles and Ethics*. Cambridge.

Chantraine, Pierre. 1984–90. *Dictionnaire etymologique de la langue Grecque*. 2 vols. Paris.

Cunliffe, Richard John. 1977. *A Lexicon of the Homeric Dialect*. Oklahoma.

Davidson, James. 2007. *The Greeks and Greek Love*. New York.

Felson, Nancy, and Laura Slatkin. 2004. "Gender and Homeric Epic." In *The Cambridge Companion to Homer*, edited by Robert Fowler, 91–114. Cambridge.

Ford, Andrew. 1992. *Homer: The Poetry of the Past*. Ithaca.

Fowler, Robert, ed. 2004. *The Cambridge Companion to Homer*. Cambridge.

Freud, Sigmund. 1990. *Jokes and Their Relation to the Unconscious*. Trans. J. Strachey. New York.

Gill, Christopher. 1996. *Personality in Greek Epic, Tragedy and Philosophy: The Self in Dialogue*. Oxford.

Goldhill, Simon. 1991. *The Poet's Voice*. Cambridge.

Graziosi, Barbara. 2002. *Inventing Homer: The Early Reception of Epic*. Cambridge.

Griffith, Mark. 2006a. "Horsepower and Donkeywork: Equids and the Ancient Greek Imagination." *CP* 101:185–246.

———. 2006b. "Horsepower and Donkeywork: Equids and the Ancient Greek Imagination—Part 2." *CP* 101:307–58.

Halliwell, Stephen. 2008. *Greek Laughter: A Study of Cultural Psychology from Homer to Early Christianity*. Cambridge.

Hanson, Victor Davis, and John Heath. 1998. *Who Killed Homer?: The Demise of Classical Education and the Recovery of Greek Wisdom*. New York.

Haubold, Johannes. 2000. *Homer's People: Epic Poetry and Social Formation*. Cambridge.

Henderson, John. 1997. "The Name of the Tree: Recounting Odyssey 24.340–42." *JHS* 97:87–116.

Hubbard, Thomas K. 1992. "Nature and Art in the Shield of Achilles." *Arion* n.s. 3:16–41.

Kahane, Ahuvia. 2005. *Diachronic Dialogues: Authority and Continuity in Homer and the Homeric Tradition.* Lanham.

Kaufmann, Walter, ed. 1976. *The Portable Nietzsche.* New York.

Keaney, John J. 1981. "ALITHMVN: *Iliad* 24.157." *Glotta* 59:67–69.

Kennedy, Duncan. 1984. "Review of Woodman and West: Poetry and Politics in the Age of Augustus." *LCM* 9:157–60.

Kirk, G. S. 1985–94. *The Iliad, a Commentary.* 4 vols. General editor, G. S. Kirk. Cambridge.

Lacan, Jacques. 2004. *Ecrits: A Selection.* Trans. Bruce Fink. New York.

Lamberton, Robert, and John Keaney, eds. 1992. *Homer's Ancient Readers: The Hermeneutics of Greek Epic's Earliest Exegetes.* Princeton.

Lattimore, Richard, trans. 1961. *The Iliad of Homer.* Chicago.

Leaf, Walter, and M. A. Bayfield. 1971. *The* Iliad *of Homer.* London.

Lefkowitz, Mary R. 1981. *The Lives of the Greek Poets.* Baltimore.

Levine, Daniel B. 2002/3. "Poetic Justice: Homer's Death in the Ancient Biographical Tradition." *ClJ* 98:141–60.

Lynn-George, Michael. 1988. *Epos: Word, Narrative and the Iliad.* Atlantic Highlands, NJ.

MacCary, W. Thomas 1982. *Childlike Achilles: Ontogeny and Phylogeny in the Iliad.* New York.

Martin, Richard P. 1989. *The Language of Heroes.* Ithaca.

Marx, Karl. 1973.*Grundrisse.* London.

Monro, David B., and Thomas W. Allen, eds. 1920. *The Iliad.* 2 vols. 3rd ed. Oxford.

Muellner, Leonard. 1996. *The Anger of Achilles.* Ithaca.

Nagy, Gregory. 1979. *The Best of the Achaeans.* Baltimore.

———.1996. *Poetry as Performance: Homer and Beyond.* Cambridge.

Parry, Adam. 1956. "The Language of Achilles." *TAPA* 87:1–7.

Porter, J. I. 2000. *Nietzsche and the Philology of the Future.* Stanford.

Pucci, Pietro. 1995. *Odysseus Polutropos: Intertextual Readings in the "Odyssey" and the "Iliad."* Ithaca.

———. 1996. "Between Narrative and Catalogue: Life and Death of the Poem." *Metis* 11:5–24.

Rethy, Robert. 1987. "Heraclitus, Fragment 56: The Deceptiveness of the Apparent." *Ancient Philosophy* 7:1–7.

Richardson, N. J., ed. 1974. *The Homeric Hymn to Demeter.* Oxford.

Scarry, Elaine. 1985. *The Body in Pain: The Making and Unmaking of the World.* Oxford.

Schmitt, Carl. 2007. *The Concept of the Political.* Trans. George Schwab. Chicago.

Sheppard, J. T. 1966. *The Pattern of the "Iliad."* New York.

Snell, Bruno. 1953. *The Discovery of the Mind.* Oxford.

Struck, Peter. 2004. *The Birth of the Symbol: Ancient Readers at the Limits of Their Texts*. Princeton.

Svenbro, Jesper. 1993. *Phrasikleia: An Anthropology of Reading in Ancient Greece*. Trans. Janet Lloyd. Ithaca.

Thalmann, W. G. 1988. "Thersites: Comedy, Scapegoats, and Heroic Ideology in the *Iliad*." *TAPA* 118:1–28.

Vernant, Jean-Pierre. 1991. *Mortals and Immortals*. Princeton.

Wathelet, Paul. 1989. "Rhésos, ou la quête de l'immortalité." *Kernos* 2:213–31.

Whitman, Cedric Hubbell. 1958. *Homer and the Heroic Tradition*. Cambridge, Mass.

Williams, Bernard. 1993. *Shame and Necessity*. Berkeley.

Wilson, Donna F. 2002. *Ransom and Heroic Revenge in the "Iliad."* New York.

Zupancic, Alenka. 2000. *The Ethics of the Real*. New York.

Index

Achilles: Agamemnon in context of desire to know identities compared with, 19–22; Athena and, 177; beauty of body of, 65–66; Calchas's identity riddle and, 5–6, 21, 22–23, 33, 47; comedy and, 65–66, 69, 72; conflict management in context of gift exchange and, 108–13, 158–59; death of, 73–74; descents to Hades in context of love and, 147–48, 152; desire to know identities and, 19; fear/binding pun in request to Thetis by, 161–63; flight/not flight from death and, 165–70; on Greeks' and Trojans' desires as intermingled, 14; Greeks' death as caused by, 12, 22, 32, 38, 49–52, 97; healer/sufferer pun and, 26; Hector in context of desire to know identities compared with, 22–23; identity riddles and, 4, 6–7, 7–8; language in cultural world of characters and, xii, 31–36, 181n5; learning through betrayal for, 159–63; loneliness of, 163–65; love for and loss of Patroclus in context of desire to know identities and, 23–28; lying remarks made by, 29–31; Patroclus's conceptual relationship with, 125–29; Patroclus's

death as caused by, 49–52, 97–99, 128–29, 183n8; peace versus war and, 93; Peleus and, 19, 121–22, 172; Priam and, 152, 171–72, 175; Priam's sons' death and, 97–98; pun in flight/not flight from death and, 166–68; self quest of, 39, 44–51, 161; zero-sum game of power, friendship, and enmity between Agamemnon and, 41, 51, 53, 55–56, 60, 61–63, 69–70, 72. *See also* Hector's imagined romantic scenario with Achilles

afterlife: descents to Hades and, 146–51; family truths in context of reconciliations and, 151–52; households as materially ruined and, 142–46; Mimnermus on impermanence of life and, 142

Agamemnon: Achilles in context of desire to know identities and, 19–22; Athena and, 62; betrayal of Achilles and, 32–36, 37, 39–40, 42; Briseis and, 42, 57, 87; Chryseis and, 11, 13, 57, 109, 111; Clytemnestra and, 2, 13, 29, 57; conflict management in context of gift exchange and, 158–59; desires as intermingles and, 10–13; desire to know identities and, 8–9, 19–22; Diomedes's tension with, 37;

WISCONSIN STUDIES IN CLASSICS

General Editors
William Aylward and Patricia A. Rosenmeyer

E. A. THOMPSON
Romans and Barbarians: The Decline of the Western Empire

H. I. MARROU
A History of Education in Antiquity
Histoire de l'Education dans l'Antiquité, translated by George Lamb

JENNIFER TOLBERT ROBERTS
Accountability in Athenian Government

ERIKA SIMON
Festivals of Attica: An Archaeological Commentary

WARREN G. MOON, editor
Ancient Greek Art and Iconography

G. MICHAEL WOLOCH
Roman Cities: Les villes romaines by Pierre Grimal, translated and edited
by G. Michael Woloch, together with A Descriptive Catalogue of
Roman Cities by G. Michael Woloch

KATHERINE DOHAN MORROW
Greek Footwear and the Dating of Sculpture

JOHN KEVIN NEWMAN
The Classical Epic Tradition

JEANNY VORYS CANBY, EDITH PORADA, BRUNILDE
SISMONDO RIDGWAY, and TAMARA STECH, editors
Ancient Anatolia: Aspects of Change and Cultural Development

ANN NORRIS MICHELINI
Euripides and the Tragic Tradition

WENDY J. RASCHKE, editor
The Archaeology of the Olympics: The Olympics and Other Festivals in Antiquity

PAUL PLASS
Wit and the Writing of History: The Rhetoric of Historiography in Imperial Rome

BARBARA HUGHES FOWLER
The Hellenistic Aesthetic

F. M. CLOVER and R. S. HUMPHREYS, editors
Tradition and Innovation in Late Antiquity

BRUNILDE SISMONDO RIDGWAY
Hellenistic Sculpture I: The Styles of ca. 331–200 B.C.

BARBARA HUGHES FOWLER, editor and translator
Hellenistic Poetry: An Anthology

KATHRYN J. GUTZWILLER
Theocritus' Pastoral Analogies: The Formation of a Genre

VIMALA BEGLEY and RICHARD DANIEL DE PUMA, editors
Rome and India: The Ancient Sea Trade

RUDOLF BLUM
HANS H. WELLISCH, translator
Kallimachos: The Alexandrian Library and the Origins of Bibliography

DAVID CASTRIOTA
Myth, Ethos, and Actuality: Official Art in Fifth Century B.C. Athens

BARBARA HUGHES FOWLER, editor and translator
Archaic Greek Poetry: An Anthology

JOHN H. OAKLEY and REBECCA H. SINOS
The Wedding in Ancient Athens

RICHARD DANIEL DE PUMA and JOCELYN PENNY SMALL, editors
Murlo and the Etruscans: Art and Society in Ancient Etruria

BRUNILDE SISMONDO RIDGWAY
Hellenistic Sculpture III: The Styles of ca. 100–31 B.C.

ANGELIKI KOSMOPOULOU
The Iconography of Sculptured Statue Bases in the Archaic and Classical Periods

SARA H. LINDHEIM
Mail and Female: Epistolary Narrative and Desire in Ovid's "Heroides"

GRAHAM ZANKER
Modes of Viewing in Hellenistic Poetry and Art

ALEXANDRA ANN CARPINO
Discs of Splendor: The Relief Mirrors of the Etruscans

TIMOTHY S. JOHNSON
A Symposion of Praise: Horace Returns to Lyric in "Odes" IV

JEAN-RENÉ JANNOT
Religion in Ancient Etruria
Devins, Dieux et Démons: Regards sur la religion de l'Etrurie antique,
translated by Jane K. Whitehead

CATHERINE SCHLEGEL
Satire and the Threat of Speech: Horace's "Satires," Book 1

CHRISTOPHER A. FARAONE and LAURA K. MCCLURE,
editors
Prostitutes and Courtesans in the Ancient World

PLAUTUS
JOHN HENDERSON, translator and commentator
Asinaria: The One about the Asses

PATRICE D. RANKINE
Ulysses in Black: Ralph Ellison, Classicism, and African American Literature

PAUL REHAK
JOHN G. YOUNGER, editor
Imperium and Cosmos: Augustus and the Northern Campus Martius

PATRICIA J. JOHNSON
Ovid before Exile: Art and Punishment in the "Metamorphoses"